AF608246

RACE, ETHNICITY, AND THE PARTICIPATION GAP

Understanding Australia's Political Complexion

JULIET PIETSCH

Race, Ethnicity, and the Participation Gap

Understanding Australia's Political Complexion

UNIVERSITY OF TORONTO PRESS
Toronto Buffalo London

Toronto Buffalo London
utorontopress.com

ISBN 978-1-4875-0415-1

Library and Archives Canada Cataloguing in Publication

Pietsch, Juliet, author
Race, ethnicity, and the participation gap : understanding Australia's political complexion / Juliet Pietsch.

Includes bibliographical references and index.
ISBN 978-1-4875-0415-1 (cloth)

1. Minorities – Political activity – Australia. 2. Immigrants – Political activity – Australia. 3. Race – Political aspects – Australia. 4. Ethnicity – Political aspects – Australia. 5. Cultural pluralism – Australia. 6. Australia – Ethnic relations. 7. Australia – Race relations. 8. Australia – Politics and government. I. Title.

DU120.P54 2018 305.800994 C2018-903121-2

University of Toronto Press acknowledges the financial assistance to its publishing program of the Canada Council for the Arts and the Ontario Arts Council, an agency of the Government of Ontario.

Canada Council for the Arts Conseil des Arts du Canada

Funded by the Government of Canada Financé par le gouvernement du Canada Canada

Contents

Figures and Tables

Figures

Tables

Acknowledgments

In the very early stages of writing this book in late 2011, I was invited to speak at a workshop on the Political Immigrant at Concordia University in Montreal. Workshop participants from around the world talked openly about the diversity of their national parliaments and the different levels of immigrant and ethnic minority representation. Meanwhile, I thought to myself how different Australia was from other immigrant countries. As I saw it, Australia, unlike many other countries, had historically very low rates of immigrant and ethnic minority political representation at the federal level. Australia's House of Representatives was essentially an all-white institution. I had become accustomed to thinking it was normal to have our parliament led by representatives of predominantly British or European heritage. How could such a parliament possibly be considered truly representative? This book is an effort to explore the numerous dimensions that help to answer this question.

I have many people to thank who both challenged my ways of seeing the world and encouraged me to write a book on race and ethnicity in Australian politics. I am especially grateful to Fiona Barker, Karthick Ramakrishnan, and Shamit Saggar, who acted as intellectual sounding boards, helping to refine many of my ideas, both at the Australian National University and in New Zealand, the United States, and England, respectively. I also thank colleagues at a variety of universities, including Antoine Bilodeau, Karen Bird, Anna Boucher, Michael Jones-Correa, James Jupp, Jen Kwok, Kate McMillan, Laura Morales, and Steve White for their enthusiasm, collegiality, and intellectual creativity. I was delighted to have the opportunity for a Visiting Fellowship at Oxford University from late 2015 to early 2016, and for the lively and critical conversations with Anthony Heath in the Nuffield College dining room that formed an important turning point in the completion of this book.

I am especially thankful to all the various ethnic community members and leaders who gave me their precious time and insights into the needs of their communities and the barriers to politics in Australia. I would also like to thank the Members of Parliament who openly and honestly shared their insights into some of the party and political barriers they face in trying to recruit minority candidates and connect with their local communities. I was grateful for each and every conversation, whether it was in a local club, coffee shop, office, or at the Australian Parliament House. I particularly thank Tim Soutphommasane, Australia's Race Discrimination Commissioner, for sharing with me his own story of growing up in Western Sydney. These conversations provided me with the personal inspiration needed to write this book.

I also wish to thank my electoral studies colleagues Clive Bean, Hilde Coffé, Russell Dalton, David Farrell, Mark Franklin, Rachel Gibson, Simon Jackman, Richard Johnston, Jeffrey Karp, Aaron Martin, Ian McAllister, Pippa Norris, Bruce Tranter, and Stephen White for their support for my never-ending attempts to find small numbers of immigrant and ethnic groups in surveys; finding those from particular backgrounds was like trying to find a needle in a haystack. I also wish to thank Paul Myers and Natasha Vickers from the Centre for Social Research in Melbourne for assisting me with finding new and innovative ways to uncover under-researched groups hiding away in increasingly large haystacks.

I am also grateful to my academic colleagues in Australia and abroad for their lively personal and critical support for this research project. I thank April Biccum, Sarah Cameron, Ann Evans, Anika Gauja, Benjamin Goldsmith, Kim Huynh, Renee Jeffery, Kate Lee-Khoo, Maria Maley, Vicky Mason, James Raymer, and Ariadne Vromen.

I am indebted to my book editors Rachel Salmond and Barry Norris, and interview transcriber Karen Clark. Their attention to detail was impressive. I also thank Daniel Quinlan at the University of Toronto Press for his editorial advice and intellectual support. Together with the anonymous referees, his input was crucial as I fine-tuned my ideas, thoughts, and academic ponderings towards publication for a broader international audience.

Finally, I thank especially my husband Marshall and children Peter, Tristan, and Alina. They have accompanied me on fieldwork trips around the world, and have been a constant source of pride, love, and joy.

RACE, ETHNICITY, AND THE PARTICIPATION GAP

Understanding Australia's Political Complexion

Introduction

The way I phrase it is they will be quite happy for you to be the chief engineer of the ship but not the captain of the ship.

— ethnic minority political candidate (Australian Labor Party)

Like many who came before or around the time when I came, I regarded Australia as a land of opportunity. However, that opportunity seemed to exist only for Australians and people from other countries of the British Commonwealth and not the likes of me. Even though I had sworn my allegiance, Australians saw in me an un-Australian.

— Ouyang Yu (2002, 25)

This book is an interdisciplinary study of political participation and representation in comparative perspective, drawing on three settler countries: Australia, Canada, and the United States. In its appropriation of migration theories and various empirical tools, the book examines why these three settler and multicultural countries differ in the political participation and representation of their immigrants and ethnic minorities. The book begins with the normative argument that institutions in settler and culturally diverse societies ought to mirror their multicultural populations. Compared with Canada and the United States, however, Australia has very low rates of political representation at the federal level, the Commonwealth Parliament – particularly in the House of Representatives, which is essentially an "all-white" assembly. One has to ask how such an assembly can be truly representative when those it represents are so much more ethnically diverse than the assembly itself (Phillips 1995, 6). Low or non-existent immigrant and ethnic minority representation is a symbolic indicator of social structures of inequality. In a political context, it also calls into question the quality of representative democracy.

The research underpinning the arguments presented in this book draws on existing findings from Canada and the United States, both of which are considered successful immigrant settler countries, on the political representation of immigrants and ethnic minorities. Added here for the first time is a detailed empirical study of Australia, comparative scholarship on which has been lacking in this field. Historically, as a member of the Commonwealth with similar multicultural policies to those of Canada, Australia should be on par with Canada in the numbers of immigrants and ethnic minorities regularly elected to Parliament, but this is not the case. Indeed, Australia lags behind other settler countries, in terms not only of the actual numbers of immigrants and ethnic minority representatives in national-level politics, but also in terms of their opportunities for political integration. As a country with an immigrant history that is similar to that of both Canada and the United States – particularly in terms of migration by Asians, the fastest-growing pan-ethnic group in all three settler countries – Australia nevertheless has taken a different path. This book seeks to discover the reasons for that alternative path and its effects on the political representation of immigrants and ethnic minorities in Australia.

This research calls for a multilevel exploratory approach, which recognizes the importance of historical and institutional context, individual and group characteristics, and behavioural and attitudinal factors in explaining political participation and representation. The book is divided into two main parts. Part One begins with an overview, in Chapter 1, of the important developments in the cross-national comparative theoretical literature that have contributed to studies on the representation of immigrants and ethnic minorities in national legislatures. The chapter aims to identify and highlight potential gaps in our understanding, most obviously because of Australia's absence as a comparative case study of a major settler country with a significant migration history. A weakness of migration research, according to Koopmans and Statham (2000), is the lack of systematic cross-national references in explaining specific national cases, a void this book aims to fill by addressing the Australian case while systematically drawing on important comparisons with Canada and the United States. Chapter 1 provides the conceptual and theoretical framework for the book, which seeks to explore why the ethnic composition of Australia's national legislature is still predominantly of European origin despite decades of "non-white" non-European immigration to Australia. The chapter ends with an outline of the research design of the book and methodological limitations.

Chapter 2 provides empirical evidence of the significant political representation gap in Australia, and compares these findings with those for Canada and the United States. The puzzle of political underrepresentation in multicultural Australia is then explored through various avenues by drawing on comparisons with the other two settler countries, a pattern that, in effect, characterizes the whole book.

Chapter 3 presents the Australian historical, demographic, and legal-institutional context for the research. The chapter begins with a look at European and Asian migration settlement patterns in Australia – until the 1930s at least, Australia was considered a leader in immigration reforms among labour movements and nativist organizations around the Pacific Rim – and the major laws and policies that had an effect on settlement experiences, particularly the implementation of racial discrimination laws and restrictions on immigration. The chapter also compares the political opportunity structures – such as citizenship regulations, electoral systems, and party-political barriers – that facilitate or hinder the participation and representation of immigrants and ethnic minorities in formal political institutions in settler countries.

Part Two shifts to a behavioural approach that explores political attitudes and behaviour from the perspective of both elite and everyday Australian citizens. Chapter 4 presents interviews with over thirty Members of Parliament (MPs), who offer their reasons for the political underrepresentation of immigrants and ethnic minorities in Australia. Selections of these explanations, which can be characterized as "elite perceptions," are then examined using empirical research methods, which enable cross-national comparisons with Canada and the United States.

One elite perception is that immigrants to Australia do not share a politicized identity. I explore this perception in Chapter 5, which considers whether the shared experiences of immigrants and ethnic minorities in Australia have led to a pan-ethnic group consciousness, as is demonstrated in Canada and the United States. The findings reveal that, in fact, Australia's largest "non-white" pan-ethnic group has a distinctive voting behaviour, although this group has been less likely than groups in other settler countries to mobilize pan-ethnic-group-based collective action for better policy outcomes. I offer several explanations for such collective action in Australia, including the lack of a civil rights infrastructure that fosters bottom-up mobilization and the absence of a national dialogue on race and persistent inequalities.

Another explanation for low representation raised in the academic literature is ties to homeland. It is suggested that one reason immigrants and ethnic minorities might not choose to become fully incorporated into their host societies is because of ongoing attachment to and greater interest in the politics of their birthplace, particularly on the part of those who come from countries that are less democratic. I analyse this possibility in Chapter 6, which explores whether home country politics has an effect on the participation of immigrants and ethnic minorities in Australian politics and on their overall satisfaction with the country's democratic system.

Underpinning all mainstream explanations is the possibility that discrimination and racism are significant factors blocking the participation and full incorporation of immigrants and ethnic minorities in national politics. Chapter 7 thus addresses perceptions of discrimination among immigrants and ethnic minorities and in Australian society more generally. The findings reveal that inequalities based on not having European heritage are reproduced through a variety of discriminatory practices. Although such practices are difficult to prove, non-European immigrants and ethnic minorities are more than twice as likely to experience discrimination in high-income professional occupations than are their European counterparts. This finding is particularly relevant in a strong party-political system that is highly professionalized and dependent on candidates from high-income professional backgrounds.

The book concludes, through a process of elimination, with a summary discussion of the salient social and institutional factors underpinning the differences in the political representation of immigrants and ethnic minority groups in Australia, Canada, and the United States.

PART ONE

Chapter One

Political Representation in Comparative Perspective

The political participation and representation of immigrants and ethnic minorities in national-level politics carries important symbolic and normative implications for political parties and for the entire democratic political system (Bloemraad and Schönwälder 2013). As nations become more culturally diverse, political institutions are under increasing pressure to better reflect the populations they serve (Scarrow and Gezgor 2010). A lack of diversity within national-level politics sends a signal of systemic exclusion and the existence of a democratic deficit (Phillips 1995). Research to date has focused largely on candidate selection processes and discrimination. In practice, however, there are often formidable barriers to immigrant and ethnic minority representation in national-level politics. These barriers consist of a broad array of societal and institutional constraints, which often vary according to ethnic, religious and socio-economic background, and migration status, and are often magnified by racial and ethnic discrimination. Such discrimination is both direct and indirect, the latter increasingly so as individuals, organizations, and institutions find more innovative ways to hide prejudices.

Much of the research on the political participation and representation of immigrants and ethnic minority groups in national politics has been conducted in the United States, Canada, the United Kingdom, and the rest of Europe (Banducci, Donovan, and Karp 2004; Bilodeau 2016; Bird 2005; Black 2013; Bloemraad 2013; Heath et al. 2013; Jones-Correa 2005; Lien 1997; Ramakrishnan and Bloemraad 2008; Saggar 2007, 2013, 2016). Australia, however, has been a very different case: in this country, only limited studies of migration and representation have been undertaken, and most appeared in the late 1990s and early 2000s

(Jupp 1997, 2003; Zappala and Castles 2000). Since then, scant research has been conducted on this important topic in Australia, even though first- and second-generation immigrants now account for 44 per cent of the population, making Australia one of the most diverse immigrant democracies in the world (Kwok and Pietsch 2017; Pietsch 2017).

Comparative research in Canada and the United States has illustrated the growing "politicization" of race and ethnicity, involving the emergence of minorities as political actors and elected representatives in national government (Alba and Foner 2009; Bird 2005; Bird, Saalfeld, and Wüst 2011; Black and Hicks 2006; Saggar 2000, 2016). There is a general consensus in the academic literature that the political mobilization and participation of immigrants and ethnic minorities in politics has been facilitated by legal-institutional frameworks that encourage naturalization, and by symbolic and material support for cultural diversity (Bird, Saalfeld, and Wüst 2011; Bloemraad 2006a). In this context, a multicultural country such as Australia should, in theory, be encouraging the participation of immigrant and ethnic minority political actors in the Commonwealth Parliament. In practice, however, less than 1 per cent of members of the House of Representatives could be categorized as either "visible minority" or "non-white" minority – two classifications officially used in Canada and the United States. The reasons for the participation gap between "non-white" and "white" in Australian politics are complex and multifaceted. To launch this discussion, the next section provides a comparative theoretical and conceptual framework that will also establish a foundation for the empirical analysis of subsequent chapters.

Theories of Political Representation

A great deal of research has been undertaken on the meaning and normative foundations of political representation in liberal democracies (Andeweg and Thomassen 2005; Hibbing and Theiss-Morse 2002; Mansbridge 1999, 2011; Rehfeld 2006, 2009, 2011). These theoretical concerns have become increasingly important, especially in the context of the debate over the existence of a "democratic deficit" and declining public confidence in representative institutions (Norris 2011; Pharr, Putnam, and Dalton 2000). Pivotal to normative studies of representation is the distinction between descriptive and substantive representation in national parliaments (Mansbridge 1999, 2011; Phillips 1995; Pitkin 1967; Williams 1998). The distinction is based on the actual numbers counted (descriptive) and the effects of minorities in parliament (substantive). The normative argument for descriptive representation comes from the idea that political institutions should reflect the social composition of the populations they serve. In other words, legislatures in Western democracies should aim to mirror as close as possible the social characteristics of their electorates. Substantive representation, however, demands that the policy preferences of electorates be translated into legislative behaviour.

The two concepts of descriptive and substantive representation are often intertwined. For example, Phillips (1995) has argued for the importance of a "politics of presence," where the parliamentary presence of minority groups enhances the quality of democracy. She suggests that there is a link between descriptive and substantive representation, since elected minorities are often best equipped to deal with the issues affecting minority groups. Other researchers have similarly demonstrated the importance for democracy of minority group presence in national parliaments. For example, a significant amount of research has shown how the election of members from traditionally underrepresented groups has a positive effect on policy making and on overall feelings of trust in the political system (Banducci, Donovan, and Karp 2004; Bratton 2006; Crisp et al. 2016; Juenke and Preuhs 2012; King and Marian 2012; Minta 2009; Pande 2003; Saalfeld and Bischof 2013; Saalfeld, Wüst, and Bird 2011), while the lack of representation has been shown to increase feelings of alienation among minority groups (Jones-Correa 1998; Pantoja and Segura 2003).

The importance attached to the descriptive characteristics of representatives and their level of responsiveness might depend on the type of electoral system (Duverger 1995; Farrell and McAllister 2006). There is general scholarly consensus that electoral systems with proportional representation (PR) increase ethnic minority representation, while those with single-member districts (SMDs) tend to exclude ethnic minorities, in part because of the lower electoral threshold necessary to gain representation. The relative success of PR systems might be conditional, however, on several other factors, such as whether the voting system is party centred or candidate centred or whether a closed-list system is used (or a combination of both factors). In closed-list PR systems, the popularity of the candidate might depend either on the popularity of the party or on where the candidate's name appears on the list (Mitchell 2000), but particularly when districts increase in size, party reputation becomes more important than the characteristics of candidates.

In contrast, in an open-list system with smaller districts, the personal reputation and characteristics of candidates will be more important to voters, and the legislature is more likely to include representation from different ethnic and social groups, and parties might have a greater incentive to put forward candidates from a variety of backgrounds (Mitchell 2000; Strömbäck 2009). Within SMD systems, the legislative representation of immigrants and minority groups might depend on group size, pan-ethnic mobilization, geographical concentration, and the ability of groups to constitute a critical mass in a given electoral district (Moser 2008).

In recent decades, scholarly debate has paid increasing attention to the representation of "visible minority" or "non-white" immigrant and ethnic minority groups in politics (Bilodeau 2016; Bird 2016; Bird, Saalfeld, and Wüst 2011; Black 2016; Van Heelsum, Michon, and Tillie 2016; Jones-Correa 2016; Morales 2009; Morales and Pilati 2011; Saggar 2016). Much of the literature stems from the observation that "non-white" immigrants are underrepresented in formal political institutions despite their having a long presence in the country of destination. In ethnically diverse settler societies such as Australia, Canada, and the United States, integration is unlikely to succeed without adequate representation of "non-white" immigrants and their diverse interests. As Jones-Correa (1998, 35) observes, immigrants' political marginalization undermines the process of democratic representation and accountability and perpetuates the view of immigrants and their descendants as outsiders. Such feelings of exclusion then might affect their successful social and economic integration, and their lack of presence in the political system might result in the failure of the policy process to address their needs. The adequate political representation of "non-white" immigrants and ethnic minority groups thus has important implications for the overall quality of democracy – indeed, it is an expected outcome of pluralist models of democracy.

Scholars have expanded the concept of political representation to include a deeper concept of "political incorporation." This has been done by showing that the inclusion of immigrants and ethnic minority groups in democratic institutions requires them to have full access to participation, to be represented in important decision-making processes and institutions, or to be able to influence government decisions and the adoption of public processes that address minority concerns and socio-economic equality across groups (Bloemraad 2006a, 2006b; Hochschild and Mollenkopf 2009; Wolbrecht and Hero 2005). Figure 1.1 illustrates a

Figure 1.1. A Model of Political Incorporation

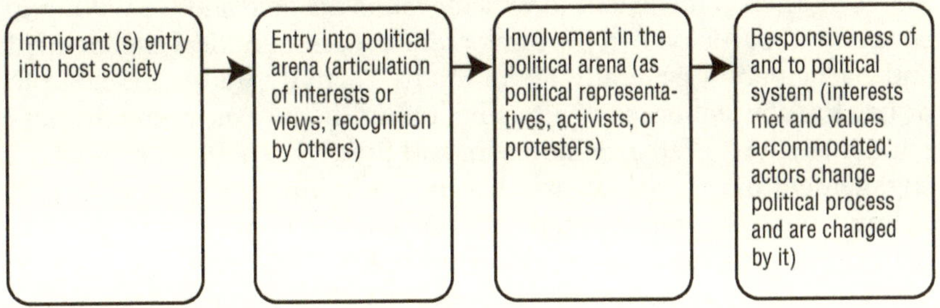

Source: Hochschild and Mollenkopf (2009, 17).

model proposed by Hochschild and Mollenkopf (2009) of the successful political incorporation of such groups. The first step involves entry into the political arena through the articulation of interests, and recognition of those views by others in the system. The second step involves entry as political representatives or activists. The final stage of political incorporation occurs when the political system is responsive to the interests of immigrants and ethnic minorities, and can be measured by assessing the extent to which self-identified group interests are represented at the national level. The traditional behavioural literature on assimilation and integration places much of the onus on individual or group agency, with unsuccessful incorporation usually perceived as some sort of failure on the part of the individual or group. Recent studies, however, also emphasize the role of political practices, laws, regulations, and institutions in facilitating or hindering political incorporation (Bloemraad 2006b; Vickers and Isaac 2012).

Since the 1990s, comparative scholarship in the United States and Europe on political representation has provided several explanations as to why immigrants and ethnic minority groups are under-represented in politics. That scholarship, however, relies on vastly different perspectives. Research in the United States traditionally focused predominantly on the economic and social incorporation of immigrants and their descendants; more recent US research, however, has reversed this trend (Bloemraad 2006a, 2006b; Hochschild and Mollenkopf 2009; Jones-Correa 2001, 2005; Lien 2001, 2004; Ramakrishnan and Bloemraad 2008). In contrast, scholarship in Europe has concentrated mainly on issues of social and political integration (Fieldhouse and Cutts 2008a; Heath et al. 2013; Ireland 2000; Koopmans et al. 2005; Morales and Giugni 2011; Saggar 2016; Togeby 2008). A key factor in political representation is the extent to which groups are able and/or willing to engage and participate in the democratic process. Political engagement and participation generally refers to any "activity that is intended to or has the consequences of affecting, either directly or indirectly, government action" (Verba, Schlozman, and Brady 1995, 9). Thus, political engagement may include a whole range of political activities, such as voting, contacting representatives, contributing financially to political parties and interest groups, following political issues in the news or on the Internet, attending protests and marches, running for political office, and variations of civic engagement that describe a broad array of activities ranging from church and sporting involvement and associational membership to more formal modes of political participation (Mutz 2002; Stolle, Hooghe, and Micheletti 2005; Zukin et al. 2006).

Adding to the extensive literature on participation is a more focused understanding of the political behaviours, attitudes, and participation of immigrants and ethnic minorities in politics. Research has shown that those with a positive attitude and orientation towards political institutions and elites are generally more likely to be politically active (Jones-Correa 1998; Morales and Giugni 2011). For instance, high levels of trust, political efficacy, and confidence in the democratic process among immigrants and ethnic minorities are often used as indicators of successful political representation and incorporation (Fieldhouse and Cutts 2008a; Morales 2009; Morales and Giugni 2011; Tillie 2004).

Generational patterns are also viewed as a significant predictor of the political attitudes and behaviour of immigrants and ethnic minorities. Ramakrishnan and Espenshade (2001) find that such patterns in political participation vary across racial and ethnic groups. For example, in the United States, the highest participation rate is among long-term Latino immigrants, with a straight-line pattern among African Americans, and a tapering off in the participation of Asian Americans; among white immigrants, participation increases with each generation. These findings indicate that racial and ethnic characteristics might trump socio-economic status and other traditional indicators of participation and, ultimately, political incorporation, as some groups face greater barriers than others. Other studies in the United States and Europe have confirmed that race often might overwhelm the influence of socio-economic background or language (Koopmans and Statham 2000; Portes and Rumbaut 2001). Indeed, according to Portes and Rumbaut (2006, 162), in the United States, race regularly trumps class as a motive for collective mobilization. In other words, racial and ethnic minorities do not always become assimilated into the political system over time, as hypothesized in resource mobilization models (see also DeSipio 2002; Gimpel and Tam Cho 2004; Lien 2004; Lien and Harvie 2012; Samson 2014).

Among other reasons put forward for why particular groups of immigrants and ethnic minorities might be less likely to achieve political representation are socio-economic status (Portes and Rumbaut 2006; Verba and Nie 1972; Verba, Schlozman, and Brady 1995), English competence, and duration of stay in the country of destination (Ramakrishnan and Espenshade 2001). Studies show the importance of socio-economic group resources and mobilization in generating political awareness of democratic politics and in encouraging engagement and participation. For instance, in the context of Europe, the literature reveals the importance of social capital and involvement in religious and voluntary associations for political participation and representation (Eggert and Giugni 2011; Jacobs, Phalet, and Swyngedouw 2004; Koopmans 2004; Morales and Pilati 2011; Myrberg 2011; Tillie 2004).

In the United States, research has focused more on the idea of pan-ethnicity and group mobilization, particularly as it relates to African Americans, Latinos, and Asian Americans (Austin, Middleton, and Yon 2012; DeSipio 2002; Lien 2001; Lien, Conway, and Wong 2004; Wong et al. 2011). This research finds pan-ethnic categories useful in mobilizing political activity across heterogeneous groups that might share common experiences of discrimination. For example, Portes and Rumbaut (2006) show that, although immigrants in the United States might vote according to their own particular interests, they often cooperate pan-ethnically on common issues such as support for bilingualism and opposition to restrictive and anti-immigration policies. A common consciousness based on a pan-ethnic identity has been found to have a greater effect on political participation and representation than other social and political factors. Such approaches have been found to replace the socio-economic determinism of class by the cultural characteristics of the group itself – such as homeland ties or a common language or cultural heritage – as the determinant of political behaviour (Koopmans and Statham 2000, 15).

The level of democratization in their country of origin is also a significant factor in the political participation and engagement of immigrants and ethnic minorities, two factors that are central to their achieving political representation (Bilodeau 2008; Bilodeau, McAllister, and Kanji 2010; Helbling et al. 2016; Pietsch and McAllister 2016). Studies have found that immigrants whose formative years were spent in a country with an authoritarian regime might know less about democratic politics and be less likely to engage in the democratic process (Peterson, Duncan, and Pang 2002). Another factor contributing to lower rates of participation among immigrants from authoritarian countries is that many have simply formed the habit of disengaging from politics, as they continue to repeat the political behaviour they developed under the constraints on political practice imposed in their country of origin. The theory of habit and voting anticipates that the disruption of social and physical contexts, which is brought about by mobility, can alter habits of political participation (Aldrich, Montgomery, and Wood 2011). Thus, upon arriving in a democratic country, immigrants with the habit of not participating in politics might take a while to learn a new system; on the other hand, immigrants can become relatively quickly engaged in the new system, especially if the desire for political freedom was one reason for migrating.

Studies have also shown the beneficial effect of country of origin on immigrants' political engagement in the receiving country (Escobar 2004; Morales and Morariu 2011; Morawska 2003; Portes and Rumbaut 2006; Vertovec 2009). For instance, political activism in home-country politics frequently generates political skills and capital that immigrants can use to mobilize others who share the same origins (Morales and Morariu 2011, 141), with such practices varying according to existing levels of individual and group-based socio-economic resources among immigrants. The legal-institutional context of the receiving country also might make a difference as to whether or not skills and capital acquired in the immigrants' home country are valued in the receiving country (Koopmans and Statham 2003), with transnational ties devalued, particularly if they are viewed as representing a threat to social cohesion and national identity.

The legal-institutional context has attracted a great deal of scholarly interest as a determinant of the political representation of immigrants and ethnic minority groups (Bloemraad 2006a, 2006b). Differences in their political representation can be explained by contemporary laws, policies, and practices that include or exclude on the basis of citizenship rules and regulations (Bloemraad 2015). For instance, host citizenship laws determine the conditions for citizenship acquisition through *ius sanguinis* (the award of citizenship based on birthplace or descent) or *ius soli* (the award of citizenship based on residence). Following the acquisition of citizenship, the overall type of citizenship model a country adopts can either facilitate or hinder the political participation and representation of immigrants (Koopmans et al. 2005). González-Ferrer and Morales (2013) find that citizenship models have long-lasting effects on the political participation and representation of immigrants and ethnic minority groups. This is because the rules underpinning the models are likely to influence immigrants' and ethnic minorities' perception of the extent to which the receiving society welcomes them as members of the social and political community. For instance, the lack of inclusive citizenship policies has been shown to increase the political alienation felt by immigrants and ethnic minorities (Pantoja and Segura 2003; Saalfeld and Bischof 2013). Bloemraad (2015, 593) presents empirical evidence that countries with multicultural citizenship frameworks and policies are places where immigrants and ethnic minority groups are more likely to become citizens, more trusting of political institutions, and more attached to a national identity.

Multicultural citizenship frameworks and policies are normatively underpinned by a vast body of philosophical literature on modern liberalism and multiculturalism (Faulks 1998; Favell 1998; Isin 2008; Kymlicka 1995; Kymlicka and Banting 2006; Levey and Modood 2009). In culturally pluralist societies, multiculturalism is frequently associated with a "politics of difference" or a "politics of recognition," a discourse which challenges dominant patterns of representation of minority groups (Appiah 1994; Gutmann 2003; Taylor 1994; Young 1990). Kymlicka (1989, 1995) has examined "differentiated citizenship rights" as a way of responding to religious and ethnic diversity and providing equal citizenship across culturally diverse societies such as Canada. These collective rights could be held by individuals or groups, such as minority nationals or Indigenous peoples who might want to claim the right to self-determination. Kymlicka argues that differentiated citizenship rights, on the one hand, must protect a cultural community (such as African Americans or black South Africans) from forced segregation and, on the other, must be flexible enough to protect other communities (such as Indigenous peoples) from forced integration. The main political challenge is to allow constitutional mechanisms – such as special seats for underrepresented groups in national legislatures – to be flexible enough to allow legitimate claims for specific group rights, but not so flexible as to allow racism and oppression (Kymlicka 1989, 255). These issues of the recognition of the rights of ethnic and cultural minorities are among the most salient on the political agenda of many democratic societies (Gutmann 1993; Joppke 1996).

One political challenge for governments in culturally pluralist societies is to ensure that minority groups have social agency and the resources to maintain cultural independence, while recognizing the rights of women and taking active steps to protect vulnerable people from illiberal practices (Barry 2001; Gatens 2004, 2012; Kukathas 2002). Although there are genuine concerns that "differentiated citizenship rights" could violate egalitarian practices, liberal multiculturalists challenge these concerns by showing that a commitment to group rights is compatible with equality (Barry 2001; Shapiro 2001), especially as they relate to being treated with equal respect and the extent to which people feel alienated from society and its institutions. According to Ivison (2012, 137), "citizens come to value their membership in the general community when they feel that their identity-related differences, among other things no longer block or distort their access to the opportunities and resources of a liberal political order." Hence, immigrants and ethnic minorities need to be recognized and valued by the majority culture. Kymlicka (1995) makes an important distinction between, on the one hand, "internal restrictions" that inhibit individuals' freedom in the interests of group cohesion and, on the other, rights associated with "external protections" that secure minority rights against the majority community. From here on in, this book's understanding of multiculturalism is based on the latter rights, which primarily relate to minority language rights, land claims, and the need for minority group political representation.

The institutional framework that adopts laws, policies, and practices that include or exclude based on citizenship rules can also constrain the extent to which political representatives engage with and encourage their ethnic constituents to participate in the political process. The institutional context, for example, might discourage political representatives from lobbying on behalf of ethnic interests. Representatives are often forced to "toggle" between meeting the demands of their ethnic constituents while appealing to the mainstream. According to Collet (2008, 172), "toggling" is a strategy used to build an electoral coalition in a potentially polarized, multicultural environment through the balanced communication of broad – that is, "mainstream" – and narrowcast messages, symbols, issue positions, personal characteristics, and socio-cultural cues to specific racial and ethnic groups.

Moving beyond historical, individual, and institutional constraints, representation might be impeded by social barriers posed by political parties, discriminatory practices, and racial prejudice. Even though the representation of immigrants and ethnic minorities is likely to carry important symbolic and normative implications related to the legitimacy of political parties and the political system, parties are still reluctant to put forward candidates from particular backgrounds unless, from a strategic perspective, doing so might increase the party's attraction in the eyes of immigrant and ethnic minority voters. Public attitudes of the majority group towards immigrants and ethnic minorities in certain constituencies might become an important factor in these decisions, as will the size and geographical concentration of these groups (Bloemraad and Schönwälder 2013; Fieldhouse and Cutts 2008b).

In party-oriented systems, the recruitment of a candidate for election to political office also depends upon service to the party and, as previously mentioned, on the candidate's having the characteristics that party selection committees perceive as likely to be popular with voters (Fennema and Tillie 2001; Inglis and Model 2007; McAllister 2003). Candidates will often need to work for a party for a long time, often at the subnational level, before they can win a nomination or move up into a more winnable slot on the party list. During this process, parties measure their potential candidates' suitability for public office in terms of their professional background, knowledge of the political process, and whether they can deliver a speech and argue persuasively on a particular topic (Müller 2000, 328).

A range of other factors – including gender, age, and appearance – also might limit or enhance a candidate's suitability for electoral success. For example, studies have shown that a candidate's photo on the ballot paper can predict his or her likelihood of electoral success to national parliaments, with more "attractive" or "competent-looking" candidates doing better (Berggren, Jordahl, and Poutvaara 2006; King and Leigh 2009; Klein and Rosar 2005). The combination of these factors makes it difficult for potential immigrant and ethnic minority candidates, who not only have to face discrimination in the broader electorate, but, in many cases, have not lived in the country long enough to acquire the necessary social and political capital to be preselected. Over time, as immigrants become more integrated and mobilized politically, it is expected that political representation will become more achievable, though still not without significant barriers (Black and Erickson 2006; Bloemraad and Schönwälder 2013).

Finally, the persistence of racial prejudice and discrimination remains a significant barrier to the political representation of immigrants and ethnic minorities. Inequalities based on skin colour are reproduced through a variety of practices stemming from new forms of racism.

Bonilla-Silva (2003, 92) refers to the emergence of a form of "color-blind" racism, which helps to sustain the prevailing racial order. For example, surveys conducted across Western immigrant societies show that "race" continues to play a significant role in structuring life chances and the experiences of "visible" and "non-visible" minorities (Heath and Cheung 2007; Song 2004). While acknowledging great diversity in the experiences of different racial and ethnic groups, research shows that citizens, institutions, and cultures are shaped by racial views, norms, and beliefs that are so deeply entrenched that they are invisible (Tolley 2016). Although some racial and ethnic minorities have managed to achieve "white" status through generations of assimilation and socio-economic mobility, others continue to experience the symbolic and often invisible effects of racialization and discrimination. In Australia, for instance, people of non-European backgrounds are more than twice as likely to experience discrimination and/or racial prejudice than those of European origin (Markus 2013).

The Conceptual Framework

The theoretical approaches discussed above provide an interesting puzzle that this book seeks to explore. If we reflect on similar historical and institutional factors, then the extent of cultural diversity represented in Australia's Commonwealth Parliament should look like Canada's House of Commons and, perhaps, should be more culturally diverse than the US House of Representatives given that the United States has never officially embraced multiculturalism. As I demonstrate empirically in Chapter 2, however, this is not the case: the gaps in political representation in Australia are significant compared to those in Canada and the United States, altogether revealing a democratic deficit in Australia. This gap is even more puzzling given the comparatively large proportion of Australia's population – approximately 17 per cent – that comes from a "non-white" immigrant or ethnic minority background.[1]

Through detailed empirical observation, I argue that, although many factors contribute to lower levels of representation in Australia, the main cause appears to be the persistence of low-level and sometimes invisible forms of discrimination and racial prejudice that permeate

1 This estimate is based only on reported ancestries; the Australian census does not ask about race or skin colour.

Australian society and, in general, the country's national institutions. Historically, this has barred new immigrants and ethnic minorities from a measure of social inclusion, a necessary precondition to political participation and representation. Furthermore, unlike Canada and the United States, Australia does not have, other than through legislation against racial discrimination, a strong counternarrative – in the form of a strong civil society movement and/or affirmative action legislation, policies, and programs – to combat racial prejudice.

Through a careful analysis, with a focus on "visible minority" or "non-white" immigrants and ethnic minorities, I demonstrate how Australia has managed to diverge, sometimes quite strikingly, from Canada and the United States on these issues. Drawing on quantitative and qualitative research evidence, I show that the main theoretical explanations for the political underrepresentation of "non-white" immigrants and ethnic minorities in otherwise similar societies simply do not apply to Australia. For instance, the representation gap in Australia is not due to a lack of political engagement or interest on the part of immigrants and ethnic minorities insofar as these groups have similar levels of political engagement with those from European backgrounds. The gap is also not due to an adverse citizenship or "legal-institutional" context insofar as Australia has embraced a multicultural framework and encourages immigrants to take up citizenship. Instead the causes of underrepresentation need to be explained by discriminatory practices and the lack of incentive by the main political parties to recruit "non-white" immigrants and ethnic minority candidates. Figure 1.2 depicts the conceptual framework for the analysis throughout the remainder of the book.

The working model to examine the factors that shape the political representation of immigrants and ethnic minorities in Australia, Canada, and the United States is based on the comparative theoretical literature on such representation. The model includes five main dimensions, which influence political engagement, participation in politics, and, ultimately, the representation and participation of immigrants and ethnic minorities in national-level politics. The first dimension on the top left-hand side includes historical and institutional factors. This dimension is especially important in the Australian context, given that racialized exclusion meant that Australia did not officially end its "White Australia" policy until 1973, when it became clear that the policy had to be rejected in the interests of Australia's foreign policy interests. Historical comparative research has found that the White

Figure 1.2. A Theoretical Model to Explain Political Representation and Participation in Australia

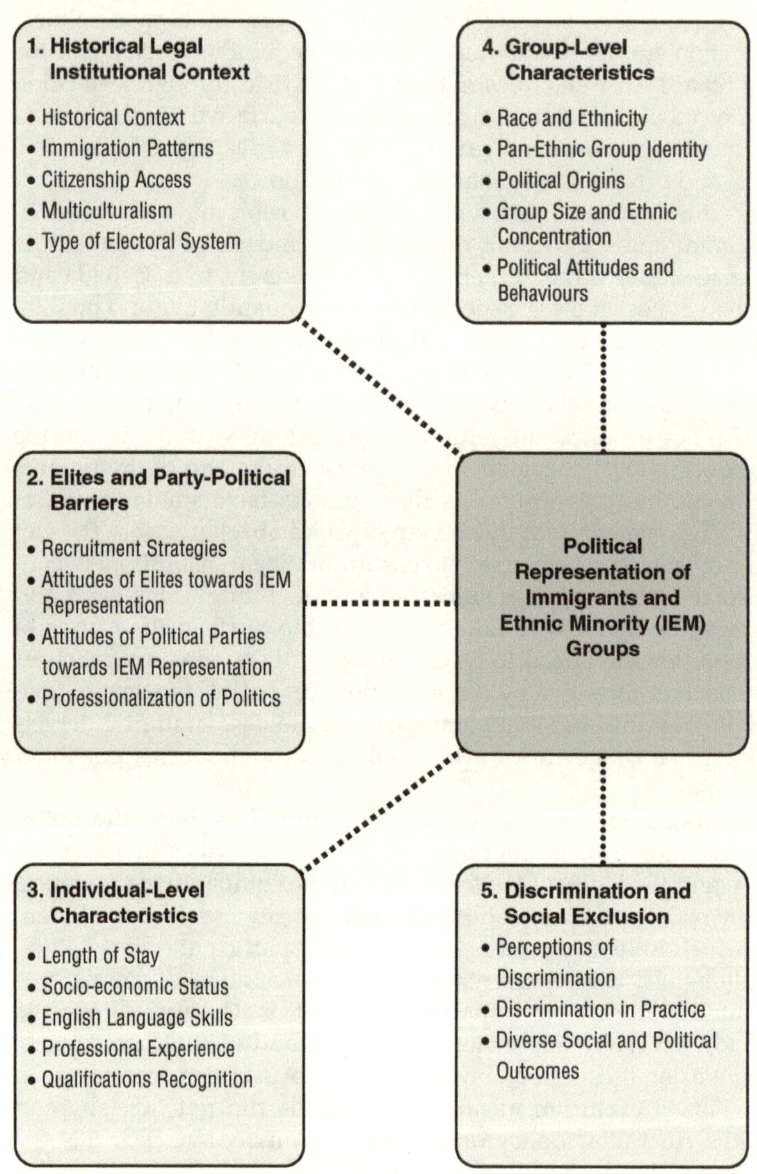

Australia policy was much harsher and lasted for much longer than similar policies in other settler societies (FitzGerald and Cook-Martin 2014), and had a profound effect on Australia's cultural and political identity for over three-quarters of a century. Since that policy ended, immigration, multicultural, and citizenship policies have played an important role in determining the ebb and flow of migration to Australia. For example, the shift from family migration to skilled selection processes has meant that Asian immigrants from low socio-economic and non-English-speaking backgrounds have done comparatively worse than other immigrants under the skilled migration program. This is due to the emphasis placed on English-language skills. Institutional variables such as citizenship access, multicultural policies, and the type of electoral system are also theorized to play an important role in the likelihood of "non-white" immigrant and ethnic minority descriptive and substantive representation.

The second dimension shows the role of elites and political parties in facilitating or creating barriers to the descriptive and substantive representation of immigrants and ethnic minorities. Clearly, elites and political parties often adopt underlying social values and prejudices to be re-elected. Without institutional forms of leadership in party recruitment processes that recognize the significance of immigrant and ethnic minority participation in national-level politics, particular groups will struggle to gain a foothold in political parties because of existing individual and social constraints, as well as the need to have the active support of a large ethnic constituency.

The third and fourth dimensions include individual and group-level characteristics. Apart from traditional individual-level indicators of political participation such as socio-economic status and length of stay, group-level factors such as race, ethnicity, political origins, pan-ethnicity, and voting behaviour are considered important factors underpinning the likelihood of successful political participation in terms of descriptive and substantive representation. For example, theories of the political participation of immigrants and ethnic minorities point to the importance of political behaviour and attitudes such as party identification, strength of partisanship, political trust, political efficacy, and political knowledge. It is expected in the comparative literature that these factors will play a significant role in whether "non-white" immigrants and ethnic minorities are likely to get involved in politics.

In the fifth and final dimension, discrimination and social exclusion throughout society can affect all areas of political participation and representation. The presence of discrimination, either direct or indirect, can block important opportunities and pathways for immigrants and ethnic minorities to move into the higher echelons of national institutions and political parties. It is in the higher echelons, of course, where important decision making takes place. With discriminatory practices and processes remaining entrenched, immigrants and ethnic minorities – particularly those from "visible minority" or "non-white" backgrounds – frequently find themselves locked out of leadership roles that might use their skills, qualifications, and experience for the benefit of the country's future direction.

In its entirety the model delineates supply-and-demand dimensions that affect immigrant and ethnic minority legislative representation (Norris and Lovenduski 1995). I argue that it is on the demand side, rather than the supply side, where Australia diverges from Canada and the United States in its capacity to build an inclusive political culture. To substantiate this argument, I draw on the conceptual framework to address the following broad three research questions:

1. To what extent does Australia differ from Canada and the United States in terms of the historical and legal-institutional context that underpins immigrant and ethnic minority representation?
2. To what extent does Australia differ from Canada and the United States in terms of the political attitudes and behaviour of immigrants and ethnic minorities?
3. To what extent does Australia differ from Canada and the United States in terms of the social context that underpins immigrant and ethnic minority representation?

Methodology

The research methodology I adopted is an exploratory, mixed-methods approach (Creswell 2008; Greene 2007; Maxey 2003), which mixes quantitative methods of data collection and analysis with a qualitative research paradigm. Such an approach arguably provides an opportunity for much deeper insights about the main barriers to political representation of immigrants and ethnic minorities. Moreover the inclusion of a case study of Australia, which until now has not been covered in the comparative literature, will give future studies, especially those conducted in Canada and the United States, a meaningful comparison as a major settler immigrant country.

Definitions

Central to the study of immigrant and ethnic minority representation is an understanding of ethnicity as a socially constructed identity based on racial, linguistic, or cultural backgrounds (Horowitz 1985). In different national contexts, ethnic groups can encompass both singular and plural identities (Chandra 2011, 152). For instance, in its broadest sense, "white" and "non-white" can be classified as ethnic-based identities. In this sense, everyone can be considered "ethnic" or belonging to an "ethnic" group. The use of the terms "immigrants" and "ethnic minorities" also reflects national conventions. For instance, comparable terms such as "visible minorities" in Canada and "non-white" immigrants in the United States reflect categories of disadvantage based on physical differences that are real or assumed (Bloemraad and Schönwälder 2013). Subcategories under the broader "visible minority" and "non-white" classifications are also categorized and reported differently in national government statistics.

This research acknowledges the process of "racialization" – most dominant in the United States – by which new immigrant groups are fitted into the "white" and "non-white" race and power hierarchy (Vickers and Isaac 2012, 226). According to Smedley and Smedley (2011, 26), during the period of greatest European expansion, "all colonial peoples were seen as distinct races, all had to be ranked somewhere below whites, and even some Europeans had to be divided into racial groups and ranked." In this context the racialized groups are immigrants from "non-white" backgrounds, while "whites" are considered the host group. It was not until the nineteenth and early twentieth centuries, when the cultural construction of race reached its full development, that the idea of racial differences was seized upon to divide, separate, and rank European populations (Smedley and Smedley 2011, 27). The research in this book draws on these hierarchies to both document empirically and critique the contemporary existence of a racial hierarchy within the formal political institutions of the three settler societies of Australia, Canada, and the United States. The existence of racial hierarchies in formal political institutions represents an inconsistency with the democratic ideals of representation and accountability in pluralist societies. Even though these binary categories and definitions are not widely used in Australia or throughout Europe, it does not mean that racial hierarchies do not exist there. Until these hierarchies are broken down, such categories are useful in explaining the existence and maintenance of social and political inequalities that prevent minorities from being elected.

Adding to the complexity is the different interpretations of "immigrant" and "migrant" in different countries. In Australia "migrant" is the preferred term to refer to people born overseas who reside in Australia, whereas in the United States and Canada "immigrant" is more commonly used. The development of an ethnic self-identification question has also presented researchers and government administrative organizations with major challenges in terms of the wording of such a question and the multiple ways to capture perceptions of ethnic identity. Response categories need to be consistent over time and recognizable among the various subgroups of the population. For example, the use of the term "black" is almost unknown among Australia's broader population and would generate a great deal of confusion if used in the census; instead the term is occasionally – and unofficially – used to refer to Indigenous and Torres Strait Islander peoples, and is not widely understood to refer to those with African or Caribbean origins. In contrast "black" is frequently used in Canada, the United States, and parts of Europe to refer to those with African and Caribbean origins.

There is also the added complication that many people now hold multiple ethnicities and, as such, any measurement needs to factor in the multiplicity and complexity of people's perceptions of their own ethnic identity. Overall there is a lack of consensus across countries about how best to articulate ethnic identity because differences in the use of immigrant and ethnic categories are embedded in the social, political, and historical experiences of groups in each country. In the context of the United States, for example, this includes the legacy of slavery and the continued experience of racial discrimination.

Despite these limitations, this book brings together primary and secondary data sources on immigrant and ethnic minority political representation in Australia, Canada, and the United States using overlapping criteria for racial and ethnic identity. It is the first systematic comparison of the descriptive representation of "visible minority" or "non-white" immigrants and ethnic minorities in national-level politics. The research considers the fact that, in each of the three countries, there are long-held traditions and ways of measuring immigrant and ethnic minority representation in politics that reflect demographics, policies, and conventions. In Canada, for instance, as mentioned, research on descriptive representation is discussed in terms of "visible minority," as opposed to "non-visible minority," representation (Black 2008, 2011,

2013; Black and Erickson 2006; Black and Hicks 2006). In the United States "non-white" racial and ethnic minority representation is usually reported in much broader racial terms, such as "black," "Asian," and "Latino" (Manning 2014).

In Australia, most non-British and non-Irish ethnic minorities other than Indigenous and Torres Strait Islanders fall under the broad umbrella of immigrants from a "non-English-speaking background" or from a "cultural and linguistically diverse background." Overall, ethnic minorities are understood in Australia as referring to those not of British or Irish origin. Race is also understood very differently in Australia than in Canada and the United States. A racial minority in Australia is usually taken to mean someone from an Aboriginal or Torres Strait Islander background. Therefore any examination of minority representation in Australian politics would normally include Indigenous and/or non-British/Irish European immigrants because there is no official collection and reporting of "visible minority" or "non-white" categories. Although this research acknowledges that non-English-speaking European immigrants historically have faced discrimination due to language barriers and cultural differences, their assimilation over time has meant that in general they are indistinguishable in external appearance and socially invisible. The gap between non-English-speaking European immigrants and other Australians is smaller than between "white" and "non-white" Australians and, as has been the case in North America, has narrowed over time (Tolley 2016, 7). Therefore, for comparative purposes, although not the convention in Australia, the term "immigrants and ethnic minorities" in this book refers only to those of a "visible minority" or "non-white" origin unless stated otherwise.

These terms and official categories are contested domains and the subject of considerable social and academic critique because of the ways they are used by government and the media not only to include and exclude, but also to manage and contain groups within the existing power structure; they are also often associated with historical and political struggles over their meaning. Unfortunately, to contest these power structures scholars rely on government statistics, surveys, reports, and a wide variety of other sources that use these same socially constructed categories to compare and contrast experiences of disadvantage both within and across groups. This categorization is particularly relevant for my research, first, because it relies on broad categories of race and ethnicity as political resources to examine patterns of political marginalization and social discrimination and bring to the fore political structures that frequently exclude based on race and ethnicity; and, second, because categories of race and ethnicity are an effective mobilizing tool for groups who have faced similar experiences of racism and discrimination and/or share similar policy preferences or homeland ties.

Inevitably, in such a broad cross-national research project, important internal cultural, ideological, and social differences sometimes can be overlooked when providing an overarching story of social and political marginalization. There are also many individuals of mixed heritage whose identities are fragmented and segmented by the use of official definitions and categories in government statistics and the media. For this reason, I approach the findings I present here with caution and with an "up-front" acknowledgment that there will always be individuals who do not share the experiences of the broader ethnic or racial grouping or who, for one reason or another, have overcome the constraints and barriers that many experience. For example, not all "non-white," "visible minority," or non-English-speaking background immigrants have experienced racial or ethnic discrimination; indeed, many hold positive attitudes towards their migration experience. Therefore, from this point onwards, I draw on broader racial and ethnic categories while recognizing the importance of documenting internal variation within and across groups wherever possible.

The Data

Data are drawn from a wide array of quantitative and qualitative surveys and interviews, government reports and statistics, historical records, and the websites of political parties. In order to measure cross-national comparisons in the political outcomes of immigrants and ethnic minorities, I use a mixture of statistical data from the Australian Bureau of Statistics, Statistics Canada, the US Department of Homeland Security, the Congressional Research Service, the Australian Public Service Commission, and the Public Service Commission of Canada.

A major task of this book was to find out about the party-political barriers that limit opportunities for immigrants and ethnic minorities to enter mainstream politics. This was achieved through qualitative interviews conducted with thirty-four members of the House of Representatives and four senators in the Commonwealth Parliament of Australia. The questions were modelled on a comparative survey of members of Parliament (MPs) in the United Kingdom conducted by Norris and Lovenduski (1995) that aimed to provide a full account of legislative recruitment in that country over a twenty-five-year period. To that survey I then added questions specific to the Australian context and the major theoretical questions outlined in this book. The aim of the qualitative interviews was to find out from Australian MPs what they felt were some of the main party-political barriers to political representation of immigrants and ethnic minorities. The approach, particularly in the program of interviews with MPs, gave primacy to the subjective consciousness of the interviewees and focused on their direct experiences. This enabled a rich description of the reasons parties are reluctant to recruit "non-white" immigrants and ethnic minorities.

To complement the qualitative interviews, I used survey research to investigate the political attitudes and behaviour of the Australian population more broadly and of subgroups of immigrants and ethnic minorities. The questions analysed were modelled on similar questions used in the Canadian Election Study, the American National Election Study, and the National Survey of Asian Americans to draw meaningful cross-national comparisons. The surveys used include the Australian Election Study (AES) and the National Survey of Asian Australians (NSAA). The 2013 AES was the tenth in a series of surveys beginning in 1987 timed to coincide with Australian federal elections. The series builds on the 1967, 1969, and 1979 Australian Political Attitudes Surveys, and aims to provide a long-term perspective on the political attitudes and behaviour of the Australian electorate and to investigate the changing social bases of Australian politics. Data collection for the 2013 AES was primarily conducted via a hard-copy survey booklet mailed to the selected sample. Voters were also given the option of completing the survey online. To maximize the response rate, voters were offered an incentive, in the form of a prize draw, to complete and return the survey. A random sample of 12,200 adults was selected from the Australian electoral roll provided by the Australian Electoral Commission and the total sample size for analysis in this book was 3,955, which includes a significant sample of immigrants and ethnic minorities.

The 2013 NSAA was part of a collaborative project with the National Asian American Survey conducted by social scientists in the United States (Ramakrishnan et al., 2008). The Asian Australian survey aimed to build on the US survey and explore the opinions and experiences of adults aged eighteen years and older who had migrated to Australia from Asia – or whose parents did – as well as an in-depth perspective on political attitudes and behaviour. As with the 2013 AES, data collection for the NSAA was conducted via a hard-copy questionnaire booklet mailed to the selected sample, with included instructions on how to complete the questionnaire online, and an incentive – again in the form of a prize draw – to complete and return the survey. As part of a surname sampling process, the first step was to develop a list of common Asian surnames from various online sources. Using this list, an in-scope sample frame was developed, from which an equal proportion of sample records (n = 950) from each of the major source countries was randomly selected. The total sample size for analysis was 540 Asian respondents.

Methodological Limitations

Surveys are highly beneficial for comparative research, but they are not without their limitations. It is rare for one data source to provide a complete picture of the political experience of immigrants and ethnic minorities in Western democracies. One significant limitation with analyses of the AES and the NSAA, for example, is that they cannot explain some of the contextual and institutional factors that shape the political participation and representation of immigrants and ethnic minorities – thus my use of a mixed methodology that, as mentioned, draws on material from a variety of sources.

A second limitation is the difficulty of measuring race and ethnic identity in the Australian context, where race as an official category is rarely used and "ethnic" applies only to those from non-English-speaking backgrounds. In national surveys, ancestry data are often used to gain a better understanding of race or ethnic background, but Australians, particularly those with multiple European ancestries, are often confused when asked to identify their "race," resulting in an imperfect measure of ancestry as a marker of identity. This is because of the high level of subjectivity and confusion about what the question on ancestry means. For these reasons, I focus primarily on the country of origin of the respondent and of the respondent's parents, rather than on racial or ethnic identification. As mentioned, this study defines as immigrants and ethnic minorities in Australia those who would be classified as "visible minorities" in Canada or as "non-white" immigrants in the United States. In Australia the largest group falling into this category are first- and second-generation immigrants and ethnic minorities from Asia; the country does not have a large population with black/African or Hispanic, Spanish, or Latino origins. As such the primary focus of the book is on Asian immigrants and ethnic minorities, as there is a large constituency of these groups with a similar migration trajectory in all three settler countries.

A final limitation is my focus on national-level, rather than state and locally based, politics. This approach is necessary, however, to draw cross-national comparisons, since theories of political participation and representation based on cross-national evidence draw primarily on representation at the national level, where key decisions on issues of national importance typically are made.

Chapter Two

Representation: Comparisons with Canada and the United States

Fair and adequate political representation of immigrants and ethnic minorities in political institutions is often undermined by the notion that there is no real need for descriptive representation. This is particularly the case in Australia, with its absence of legislation, policies, or a national discourse aimed at redressing the empirical fact of low immigrant and ethnic minority political representation. This lack of representation is of concern, especially given that the democratic quality of a political system can be assessed in terms of whether the representation of distinctive social groups in formal political institutions reflects the social composition of society (Vickers and Isaac 2012, 107). Moreover, as Jones-Correa (1998) asserts, if immigrants and ethnic minorities do not have a political voice, democratic processes of representation and accountability are undermined.

In Canada and the United States, there has been considerable research on the recruitment of immigrants and ethnic minorities to national-level politics, in part because of the much greater numbers of such candidates and representatives in politics. In Canada, for instance, Tolley (2016) has researched extensively the racialized media framing of "non-white" candidates and representatives during election campaigns. Such racialized media coverage focuses on the candidates' skin colour, ethnicity, linguistic background, and level of interest in minority issues such as multiculturalism and immigration. Although this Canadian media coverage is both positive and negative, in Australia no such media coverage exists. This is because minorities are rarely selected for competitive electoral districts, even those with high rates of ethno-cultural diversity. The general perception is that, first, minority interests are subsumed by traditional left-right political economic cleavages, thus negating the need for specific representation of immigrants and ethnic minorities. Second, immigrant and ethnic minority candidates are simply perceived as not able to represent "all" Australians and might even generate disharmony within racial and ethnic communities, as I demonstrate in later chapters. Third, racial and ethnic politics is often relegated to state or local politics, where strategically political representatives need to pay closer attention to their ethnic constituents due to their greater size and concentration in local and state electoral districts.

This chapter systematically compares the descriptive representation of immigrants and ethnic minorities in national-level politics in Canada, the United States, and Australia. Comparatively speaking, the findings reveal that Australia is behind in making progress towards establishing an inclusive national legislature that represents the country's multicultural society. There are broad implications for the role of government and the quality of representative democracy if large sections of the Australian community appear to be locked out of significant positions of national political leadership. According to Andrew et al. (2008b, 8), the racial and ethnic composition of political institutions "makes a statement about role models and about legitimacy, about who is included in our institutions and has access to public space, who is excluded, and who represents what and who we are." Before looking at these issues in greater detail, it is important first to establish empirically the differences in the representation of immigrants and ethnic minorities in the national legislatures of Canada, the United States, and Australia, and to consider the proportion of particular demographic groups both in elected office and in the general population.

Measuring Descriptive Representation

Of the three settler countries, Canada has taken more seriously the political incorporation of "non-white" immigrants and ethnic minorities in national-level politics as part of its commitment to multiculturalism and the need to ensure equal access and participation for all Canadians in political life. For this reason, the following sections compare Canada's levels of descriptive representation of visible minorities to those in the United States and Australia. Although the optimal approach would be to rely on self-reported statistics, this information is not always reported voluntarily by MPs in either Canada or Australia. Accordingly, their visible minority origins are usually found using a multi-method methodology that relies on a combination of surname analysis and biographical information that MPs have provided voluntarily on parliamentary and party websites. Previous research in Canada has proven this method to be reliable and effective in determining the background of parliamentarians (Black 2011; Black and Erickson 2006; Tolley 2016). In the United States the racial and ethnic minority origins of political representatives in the House of Representatives are usually found using secondary sources from the Congressional Research Service. In tandem with identifying immigrants and ethnic minority members as a proportion of the total membership in the House, the United States traditionally reports the share of minorities in the total population.

To begin, it is important to look closely at how racial and ethnic minorities are officially classified and counted in each of the three countries. As mentioned, in Canada, "non-white" ethnic minorities are commonly referred to as "visible minorities" who, in the language of the 1995 Employment Equity Act, are "persons, other than Aboriginal peoples, who are non-Caucasian in race or 'non-white' in skin colour." The main groups in this category are those with Chinese, South Asian, black, Filipino, Latin American, Southeast Asian, Arab, West Asian, Korean, and Japanese ethnic origins. Visible minorities are counted using Statistics Canada's National Household Survey, which is conducted every five years and, among other things, asks respondents: "Is this person …," with the main visible minority origins mentioned as response options. Canadians can tick more than one box to indicate that they have mixed ethnic origins.

In the United States the main source of data for information on racial and ethnic minorities is the Census Bureau, which conducts a census of the population every ten years and the monthly Current Population Survey. Americans are asked to classify their race as: white; black, African American, or Negro; American Indian or Alaska Native; Asian; or Native. Information on Hispanic persons is also gathered by using a self-identification question. Respondents are first asked if they are of Hispanic, Spanish, or Latino origin; based on their response, they are further classified as Mexican, Mexican American, or Chicano; Puerto Rican; Cuban; Central or South American; or other Hispanic, Spanish, or Latino.

In Australia immigrants and ethnic minorities are, as noted earlier, categorized according to non-English-speaking backgrounds or culturally and linguistically diverse backgrounds. Europeans from non-English-speaking backgrounds who are neither British nor Irish are generally regarded as ethnic minorities. The self-perceived ethnic identity question in the census – held every five years – measures whether Australians identify with a particular ancestry. Respondents are asked: "What is your ancestry?" and can provide only two ancestries as a measurement of mixed ethnic identity.

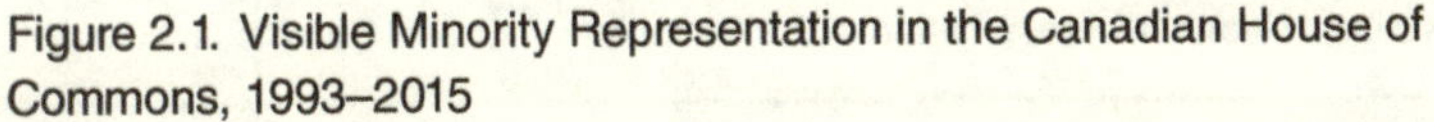

Figure 2.1. Visible Minority Representation in the Canadian House of Commons, 1993–2015

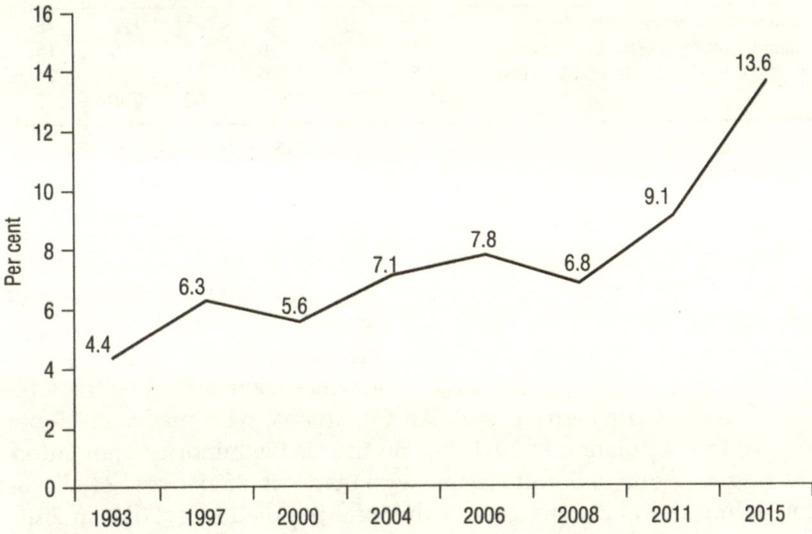

Source: Author's compilation from Parliament of Canada website, http://www.ourcommons.ca/Parliamentarians/en/members.

Although classification of racial and ethnic minority groups is not always directly comparable in each of the three settler societies, it is possible to observe the share of "non-white" or "visible minority" groups in each country's national legislature and the corresponding share of each group in the total population. Although not perfect, given the different demographics of each country, these data allow us to explore general patterns of descriptive representation and the relative importance attached to the political representation of immigrants and ethnic minorities in each country.

Ethnic Representation in Comparative Context

Canada

Beginning with Canada, Figure 2.1 shows a pattern of steady growth in visible minority representation in the House of Commons from 4 per cent of MPs in 1993 to 9 per cent in 2011, and a noticeable spike to 14 per cent by 2015.

Table 2.1. Visible Minority Representation in the Canadian House of Commons, 2000–15

	2000	2004	2006	2008	2011	2015
Visible minority MPs	17	22	24	21	28	46
Visible minority MPs *(%)*	6	7	8	7	9	14
Visible minorities in population *(%)*	13	15	16	17	19	23
Total MPs	301	308	308	308	308	338

Note: Figures for visible minorities in the population in 2015 are projected.
Sources: Black 2008, 2011, 2013, 2016, 2017.

This increase in the political representation of visible minorities has been attributed in part to the increase in these groups in the broader population through expansive immigration programs, which have resulted in an increasing number of electoral districts with majority-minority populations. According to Statistics Canada (2011), the largest visible minority group is Asian Canadians, who made up 15 per cent of the population in 2011. Within the visible minority population, the largest group is South Asians, who made up 25 per cent of all visible minorities and 5 per cent of the total population in 2011. In 2015, twenty-one out of forty-six visible minority MPs were either born in India or were of Indian descent. There were also two MPs from Pakistan, one from Afghanistan, one from Sri Lanka, and one from Iran. Proportionally speaking, South and West Asian ethnic minorities are well represented at the national level in Canada, making up 8 per cent of the total membership of the House of Commons. The second-largest group of Asians is the Chinese, who comprise more than 21 per cent of the visible minority population and 4 per cent of the total population. In the 2015 federal election, five Chinese were elected to the House of Commons, representing 1.5 per cent of MPs. Canadians with black, African, or Caribbean origins made up 15 per cent of the country's visible minorities and 3 per cent of the total population in 2011. In the 2015 federal election, five Canadians of black, African, or Caribbean descent were elected, accounting for 1.5 per cent of the total House membership.

In looking at the overall results over time (Table 2.1), it is clear that Canada achieved a significant increase in visible minority MPs, particularly between 2011 and 2015, which might be explained in part by the increase in the total visible minority population from 19 per cent to 23 per cent over the same period. This observation, however, is a simplistic one, as there are many other explanations of Canada's progress in closing the visible minority political representation gap. Importantly, although minority representation has increased, not all ethnic groups have fared well. For example, according to the 2011 census there were 157,450 Vietnamese Canadians, making up 0.4 per cent of the total population, yet only one Vietnamese-born candidate was elected to the House of Commons in 2015. Chinese are also underrepresented, despite their large numbers throughout Canada, and there is no representation of those with Korean and Japanese origins, even though large numbers of immigrants from these countries arrived in Canada during and after the Korean War and the Vietnam War.

The United States

In the United States, the share of members of the House of Representatives from "non-white" ethnic minority backgrounds has shown a similarly upward trajectory over time, from 15 per cent in 2001 to 20 per cent in 2015 (Figure 2.2). Compared with their share of the US population, however, the representation gap of such groups has increased. According to the decennial census, between 2000 and 2010 the "non-white" population in the United States showed little change, from 24.9 per cent to 25.2 per cent,[2] while by 2014 that population had increased significantly from 25 per cent to 37 per cent due to the increase in Hispanic or Latino migration; people with those ethnic origins accounted for 17 per cent of the total US population in 2014. During the same period, however, "non-white" representation in the House of Representatives increased only marginally, from 17 per cent to 20 per cent.

Looking closely at which groups have made gains in political representation, Table 2.2 shows that between 2000 and 2015 there was an increase in the numbers of Hispanic and Latino candidates elected to the House of Representatives. Relatively speaking the numbers are still very small. For example, in 2015 there were thirty-two Latino or Hispanic representatives, accounting for 7 per cent of the total membership of the House. This share, however, fell well below the 17 per cent of Latinos and Hispanics in the total US population that would be needed to achieve descriptive representation. The representation deficit is somewhat smaller for Asian and black Americans. In the 2010 census the Asian American population accounted for 5 per cent

2 Respondents to the decennial census were given the option to identify with one or more racial categories. The "non-white" population refers to all of those who did not identify as white alone.

Figure 2.2. "Non-white" Ethnic Minority Representation in the US House of Representatives, 2001–15

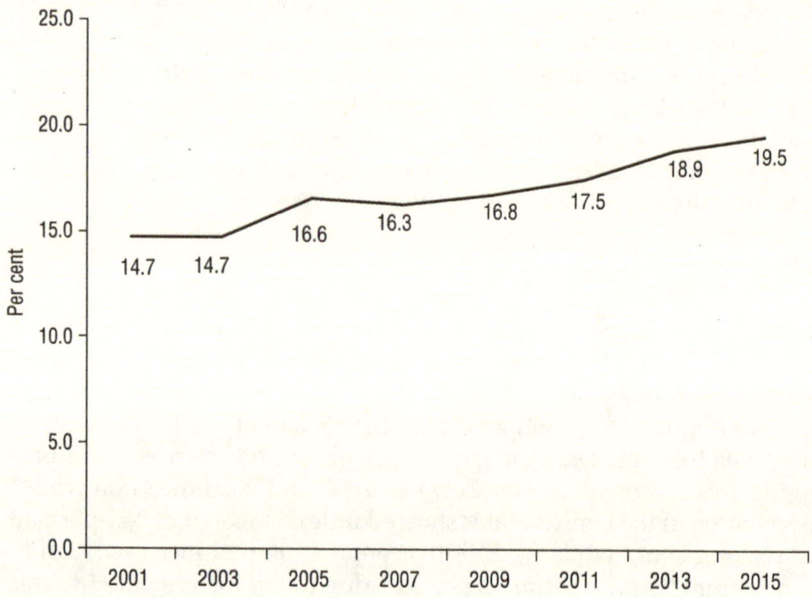

Source: Author's compilation from Congressional Research Service Reports for Congress.

Table 2.2. "Non-white" Ethnic Minority Representation in the US House of Representatives, 2001–15

	2001	2003	2005	2007	2009	2011	2013	2015
Native Americans	3	2	1	1	1	1	2	2
Hispanics or Latinos	19	24	26	26	26	27	31	32
African Americans	37	36	40	40	39	41	41	44
Asian Americans	8	4	6	5	8	8	10	9
Total in House	64	64	72	71	73	76	82	85
Share in House *(%)*	15	15	17	16	17	18	19	20
Share of total population *(%)*	32	34	35	36	38	38	38	39

Note: Figures do not include delegates or resident commissioners.
Sources: Author's compilation from Congressional Research Service Reports for Congress.

of the population, yet for only 2 per cent of the members of the House in 2011.

Black Americans accounted for 12 per cent of the population in the 2010 census and for 9 per cent of House members. This relatively small gap is partially explained by the drawing of majority-minority districts under the Voting Rights Act of 1965 to compensate for a long history of systematic disenfranchisement and the need for substantive representation of black American interests. The act has provided a way to protect the numbers of black Americans in national office so that their numbers are roughly proportional to the black American population as a whole. Some conditions must be applied, however, to ensure that the creation of majority-minority districts is in the interest of protecting racial minorities, not to provide partisan advantage. These conditions – often referred to as *Gingles* conditions, after the US Supreme Court's *Thornburg v. Gingles* case – include (i) the extent of concentration or coherence of the minority group; (ii) the political cohesion of the minority group; and (iii) the likelihood that, if in the majority, white voters will tend to vote against that group's preferred candidate (Newkirk 2017). Sadly, redistricting in the United States has been abused in congressional elections to dilute the voice of racial and ethnic minorities at the polls. For example, there has been a process of *packing* more black voters into certain districts and diluting their voting strength in others. Another tactic is *cracking*, which involves the splintering of minority populations into small pieces across several districts (Levitt 2018).

Australia

Turning now to Australia, we can see that Canada and the United States perform better when it comes to descriptive representation at the national level (Figure 2.3). Looking at the ethnic composition of the Commonwealth House of Representatives, we find very few "non-white" or "non-European" ethnic minority members. Between 2001 and 2010 there was only one Euro-Asian representative, in 2013 there were two Euro-Asian representatives, and in 2016 another two representatives with Middle Eastern heritage were elected, increasing the representation of "non-white" minorities to four, or 2.7 per cent of the total membership of the House of Representatives. These figures are proportionally low given that, according to the 2016 census, more than 17 per cent of the Australian population potentially could

Figure 2.3. "Non-white" Ethnic Minority Representation in the Australian House of Representatives, 2001–16

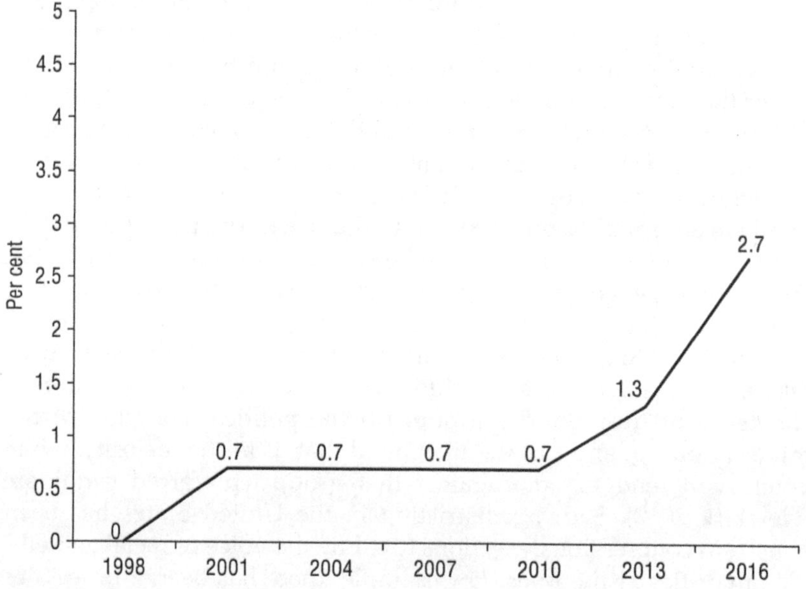

Source: Author's compilation from Parliament of the Commonwealth of Australia website.

be classified as "non-white"[3] – that is, who identified as having North African, Middle Eastern, Asian, Pacific Islander, or African ancestry as their first response; another 4 per cent reported having at least one of these ancestries as their second response. The "non-white" population has steadily increased since the 2006 census, when 11 per cent of the population identified as having North African, Middle Eastern, Asian, Pacific Islander, or African ancestry as their first response and 2 per cent as their second response; in the 2011 census, these responses increased to 14 per cent and 3 per cent, respectively.

If the analysis is broadened to include European ethnic minorities, Australia's record on descriptive representation shows some improvement. As previously mentioned, unlike in Canada and the United States, in Australia non-British/Irish immigrants are considered in official statistics as having ethnic minority status because of their

3 This figure does not include Indigenous representation, as Indigenous peoples are not officially classified as ethnic minorities in Australia.

Table 2.3. "Non-white" Ethnic Minority Representation in the Australian House of Representatives, 1998–2016

	1998	2001	2004	2007	2010	2013	2016
Non-European ethnic minorities	0	1	1	1	1	2	4
European ethnic minorities	10	12	13	13	14	13	13
Non-European ethnic minorities *(%)*	0	0.7	0.7	0.7	0.7	1.3	2.7
European ethnic minorities *(%)*	6.7	8.0	8.7	8.7	9.3	8.7	8.7

Source: Author's compilation from Parliament of the Commonwealth of Australia website.

non-English-speaking background. Table 2.3 shows that the numbers of representatives who reported that they were born or whose parents were born in a non-English-speaking European country accounted for between 6 and 9 per cent of the total membership of the House of Representatives between 2001 and 2013. In the 2016 census, up to 11 per cent of the population identified as having a non-British/Irish European ancestry as their first response and 8 per cent as their second response – a decline from the 2006 and 2011 censuses when the proportions were 13 per cent and 6 per cent, respectively. As for birthplace, in 2016 only 4 per cent of Australians were born in a European country outside the British Isles, while up to 8 per cent had a mother and 9 per cent a father born in Europe outside the British Isles. With respect to descriptive representation, then, non-British/Irish Europeans appear to be well represented in the House of Representatives.

In comparing the three settler countries, the most underrepresented group is Asian Australians, the largest "non-white" immigrant and ethnic minority group in Australia, accounting for 13 per cent of first ancestry responders and 2 per cent of second ancestry responders in the 2016 census. However, in 2016 only two Euro-Asian ethnic minorities were elected to the 150-member House of Representatives.[4] By comparison, in 2015 in the United States there were nine Asian Americans in the 435-member House of Representatives. It should be noted here that the accomplishments of the United States in the representation of ethnic minorities, especially with its history of slavery, gerrymandering, and ongoing racial challenges, are only marginally better than those of Australia. In Canada, in contrast, up to 31 Asian Canadians were elected to the 338-member House of Commons in 2015 (Rana 2016).

4 This is an estimate only, based on reported ancestries; as noted, the Australian census does not ask questions based on race or skin colour.

Figure 2.4. "Non-white" Ethnic Minority Representation in the Civil Service, Australia and the United States, 1999–2013

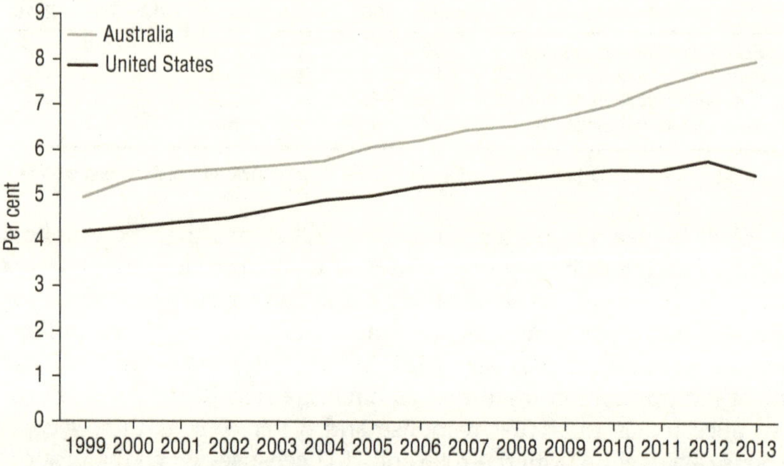

Source: Author's compilation from Australian Public Service Commission, State of the Service Series; and United States, Office of Personnel Management, *Affirmative Employment Statistics*.

Representation in the Civil Service

Another way to measure political representation is by looking at the share of immigrants and ethnic minorities in the civil service, where greater diversity is expected to lead to greater bureaucratic responsiveness. According to Kim (2005, 451), "a diverse workforce with regards to race, ethnicity, national origin, or gender leads a bureaucracy to be not only internally democratic but also responsive to citizen needs." Here I focus only on Asian immigrants in the three settler countries, as Australia does not have a large black, African, or Caribbean population with which to make comparisons. As Figure 2.4 shows, in terms of ethnic minority representation in the civil service, Australia has done somewhat better than has the United States, with the share of Asian Australians increasing from 5 per cent in 1999 to 8 per cent in 2013, while the share of Asian Americans in the civil service rose only slightly, from just over 4 per cent to about 5 per cent over the same period. Australia's better record could be explained in part by section 18 of the Public Service Act of 1999, which requires public service departments and agencies to implement cultural diversity programs.

In the United States, the relatively modest improvement in minority representation in the civil service can be attributed to the 1960s civil rights movement and the implementation of affirmative action programs aimed specifically at providing equal opportunities for minority groups in employment. For example, under section 717 of the Civil Rights Act of 1964, the Equal Employment Opportunity Commission was made responsible for the overall maintenance and evaluation of affirmative action programs aimed at reducing and eliminating under-representation in the federal civil service. Such affirmative action programs have ensured that various quotas are reached. More progress is needed, however, to ensure that quotas are also reached within the Senior Executive Service, which has influence over major policy areas and public programs – indeed, it is frequently in the senior levels of federal employment that the underrepresentation of Asian Americans is more evident, revealing the possibility of a glass ceiling (Kim 2005). Similarly, in Australia, the underrepresentation of Asian Australians is evident in senior manager and senior executive levels of the civil service, where important decision making with government representatives on major policies and programs takes place (Australian Public Service Commission 2013).

In Canada, ethnic representation in the civil service is enhanced by the country's deep commitment to racial equality and the political representation of visible minorities. Each census since 1901 has categorized respondents by their "visible minority" status. Originally these categories were used to control "non-white" visible minorities through a range of discriminatory immigration policies (Vickers and Isaac 2012); more recently, however, they have been used to identify underrepresentation in organizations in both the public and private sectors. For instance, at the federal level, the political representation of visible minorities is facilitated by the Employment Equity Act of 1995, which ensures that federal government organizations and private sector employers with one hundred or more employees report annually on the representation of women, Indigenous peoples, persons with disabilities, and members of visible minorities. In 2014 visible minorities accounted for up to 20 per cent of all permanent full-time employees in the federally regulated private sector (Government of Canada 2015). A report by the Standing Senate Committee on Human Rights (Senate of Canada 2010), while not having specific information on Asian representation in the federal civil service, shows that objectives for the representation of women, Indigenous people, and persons with disabilities in federal civil service were being met, but that those for visible minorities were not, despite the coming into force in 1995 of the Employment Equity Act, which requires federal government departments and agencies to implement policies and practices aimed at closing the representation gap.

Conclusion

Australia lags both Canada and the United States in the political participation and representation of "non-white" immigrants and ethnic minorities in its political institutions. Without quotas in place to address the obvious representation gaps, Australia's immigrants and ethnic minorities struggle to gain such representation, which is most evident when we look at the numbers of Asian Australians in the House of Representatives compared with Asian representation in Canada's House of Commons and the United States' House of Representatives.

The representation gap in Australia suggests a broader social problem – namely, that Australia's goal of achieving racial and ethnic equality within a multicultural framework has yet to be realized. For example, it appears that multiculturalism in Australia is broadly supported only so long as minorities do not place demands on national political institutions to ensure greater political equality and, ultimately, their presence in national decision-making processes. Even though Asian Australians make up more than 13 per cent of the population, there are sharp differences in the political representation of those with British/Irish and European descent and those without. In Canada and the United States, in contrast, the presence of "non-white" racial and ethnic minorities in national-level politics and in the civil service has increased due to the existence of legislative instruments and policies specifically aimed at closing representation gaps.

Since, as noted earlier, Australia does not have a large black, African, or Caribbean population, for comparative purposes the focus of the remainder of this book is on Asian immigrants and ethnic minorities, which represent a significant group in all three settler countries. The next chapter explores some of the background historical and institutional factors underpinning the low representation of immigrants and ethnic minorities in the Australian political system compared with Canada and the United States.

Chapter Three

The Historical and Legal-Institutional Context

Understanding the historical context of "whiteness" as associated with people of northwestern European origin and the categories of "in-betweenness" or "non-whiteness" as a basis for exclusion is of key importance to contemporary studies of race, ethnicity, and political participation. Although differences in the political representation of "non-white" immigrants and ethnic minorities are generally attributed to local context and the kinds of immigrants who move to Western countries, the historical context of colonialism reveals a pattern of shared immigration policies among the settler countries that systematically excluded people on the grounds of their race and skin colour. Historically, subjects of Britain's North American and Australian colonies enjoyed the privileges of naturalization and special rights throughout the British Empire, while non-British and Irish immigrants faced various forms of racialized discrimination. Over time, Europeans who were neither British nor Irish were gradually accepted as "white," and racialized immigration policies once considered the norm in settler societies were gradually replaced with the passage of antidiscrimination legislation. Despite these significant changes, the maintenance of British hegemony and white domination in the colonial period profoundly influenced the nature and composition of contemporary political institutions. Although racial discrimination became a defining characteristic of attempts to control the flows of "non-white" immigration into settler societies, each responded differently to the social, economic, and political challenges of such immigration, with some imposing harsher legislative and policy measures for longer periods. Some of the early measures taken to restrict the flow of Asian immigrants had a significant influence on the racial and ethnic composition of settler countries, and prevented the long-term settlement of such immigrants, particularly those of lower-working-class origins.

In recent decades, there has been a significant transformational shift away from the British Isles and the rest of Europe as sources of immigration to North America and Australia. Yet studies have shown that immigrants and ethnic minorities from "non-white" backgrounds continue to face various forms of social and political exclusion because of the colour of their skin or perceived cultural and religious differences. As we will see in this chapter, examining the historical patterns of racialized exclusion in Australia, Canada, and the United States provides us a background for understanding why immigrants and ethnic minorities frequently struggle to gain political representation and influence.

The Historical and Demographic Context

In mid-nineteenth-century China, population pressures in the south, widespread poverty, bitter civil wars, and rebellions encouraged emigration to neighbouring countries in Asia and to Western countries where there were labour shortages in mining, railroad construction, and agriculture. The movement of Chinese labourers from East to West was pivotal for rapid population growth, urbanization, industrialization, and agricultural development in settler countries. The large pool of Asian labour in these countries, however, faced harsh penalties, discrimination, riots, and, finally, outright exclusion because of their race.

The underrepresentation of immigrants and ethnic minorities in Australian politics can be partly explained by the country's history of restrictive immigration laws, policies, and political practices from the late nineteenth century to the mid-1970s, which involved the systematic exclusion of racial and ethnic minorities. Australia's assertiveness in the latter half of the nineteenth century in restricting such flows was largely a result of anxieties, which persisted well into the 1940s and beyond (Walker 1999), relating to the sparsely populated country's proximity to unstable Asia. Concerns about cheap labour and the threat to working conditions by labour movements were also prominent. It is possible that the introduction of prohibitive legislation before and after the formation of the Australian Commonwealth in 1901 had a lasting impact on Australia's national identity and political institutions. In the first half of the twentieth century, Australia was considered, among labour movements and nativist organizations across the Pacific Rim, a leader in legislative "reforms" to restrict Asian immigration. It would not be for another several decades that Australia would abandon its White Australia policy, begin to embrace the principle of racial equality, and renounce exclusionist policies based on race – indeed, Australia was the last of the three settler countries under review here to do so.

The first piece of Australian national legislation to restrict immigration, the Immigration Restriction Act, was passed in 1901, the year in which the various colonies federated to become the Commonwealth of Australia. The act effectively ended all Asian immigration for nearly three-quarters of a century by requiring immigrants to pass an English-language dictation test, causing great offence to its Asian neighbours, especially Japan.[5] Elsewhere, supporters of a "white" national identity in British Columbia and California applauded the new act because it made no direct reference to any particular race, thereby avoiding judicial challenge.[6] The passage of the act capped several decades of discussion among community and political leaders on how to deal with what was seen at the time as the problem of other races, and was partly influenced by developments in the United States and Canada, which had previously implemented restrictive immigration policies – namely, the Chinese Exclusion Act of 1882 in the United States and the Immigration Restriction Act of 1885 in Canada.

Agitation against Chinese immigrants in Australia was inspired in part by reports of a worsening situation in Canada and the United States (Chang 2009; Kee and Reynolds 2008). Canada's Immigration Restriction Act specifically imposed a head poll tax of $50 on immigrants from China, many of whom were labourers on the Canadian Pacific Railway and could not afford the tax. The full banning of Chinese immigrants

---

5 The Japanese government, drawing attention to the discriminatory nature of the dictation test, requested, through the British Foreign Office, the withdrawal of the bill on 16 December 1901, just one week before it was passed. In Australia itself, the government of Queensland, which had been encouraging migrants from Germany and Scandinavia to settle there since the 1870s, was initially concerned that the dictation test would exclude a large group of desirable migrants from Europe.

6 After the passage of the act, there followed a period of hostility during which Asian British subjects who were already residing in Australia were targeted. For example, in 1910, a Labor member in the Western Australian Legislative Assembly asked the minister for railways "whether in view of the strong objections of the white population travelling by train in the same compartments as Asiatics," he would have separate compartments designated for Asian travellers ("Cars for Asiatics," *Bendigo Independent*, 16 September 1910, available online at http://nla.gov.au/nla.news-article227156566).

to Canada, however, did not come into effect until the implementation in 1923 of the Chinese Exclusion Act, which was repealed only in 1947.[7] Canada also imposed a number of entry restrictions on black immigrants from the Caribbean, who, while viewed by employers as important for the cheap labour necessary for unskilled and domestic work, were stigmatized as morally and socially inferior (Calliste 1993–94). Overall, characteristics such as race and sex were used as major principles to guide Canada's immigration policies until the 1960s, when race and national origin were eliminated as criteria for entry and replaced with a points system (Arat-Koc 1999; Li 1992; Whitaker 1991).

As in Australia and Canada, in the United States a range of administrative measures was similarly introduced to restrict the flow of Chinese and other Asian immigrants to California in the 1850s. American historian Kornel Chang (2008, 672) has showed that it was their mutual opposition to Asian migration that brought Canada and the United States together as settler countries dedicated to the preservation of Anglo-American civilization. Not only was there cooperation between governments, but also among labour organizations and protectionist movements in British Columbia and California that shared information that helped them pressure their respective governments to restrict the flow of Chinese, Japanese, and South Asian immigrants across the United States–Canada border.

In 1852 the governor of California introduced a law that imposed a $55 tax on Chinese immigrants, and in 1858 Californian authorities tried to forbid Chinese immigration altogether. These attempts to control Asian immigration were strongly resisted, however, by federal government authorities in Washington; indeed, the US Supreme Court ruled as unconstitutional one of the first attempts to restrict Chinese immigration to California (McKenzie 1928). In the 1860s and 1870s, Californians became increasingly frustrated by the power of the federal government and by the 14th Amendment to the US Constitution, adopted in 1868, which required all states to guarantee to all persons equal protection under their laws (Kee and Reynolds 2008). Eventually the US Congress caved to mounting pressure from California and initiated an inquiry in 1877–8 into Chinese immigration. In their testimony to the congressional inquiry, the local Californian authorities pushed for tighter restrictions and the prohibition of Chinese immigration. The

7 The ban did not include diplomats or foreign students.

result was the Chinese Exclusion Act of 1882, which created a labour shortage and opened up new opportunities for Japanese immigrants to work on the railroads throughout the Pacific Northwest; between 1905 and 1907, Japanese comprised up to 40 per cent of the railroad labour force in Oregon (Azuma 1993, 316). Since they received much higher wages in the United States than they could in Japan, Japanese workers were often prepared to tolerate exploitation and poor working conditions. Even though Japanese immigrants worked extremely hard, many Americans considered them unable to assimilate because of their presumed racial and cultural devotion to the Japanese homeland. White labourers also feared that Japanese willingness to accept poorer working conditions would adversely affect their own working conditions and pay standards. It was initially thought that the Japanese would be sojourners who would go home when their job contracts ended, but many found work in other industries, including agriculture, and became US citizens with the right to acquire land (Johnson 1996, 177–8).

Despite calls by white Americans to restrict Japanese immigration throughout the Pacific Northwest, the US government had to take into account its 1894 treaty with Japan and the Gentlemen's Agreement of 1907, which constrained any efforts to impose harsh measures that would end all Asian immigration. In the Gentlemen's Agreement, the Japanese government agreed not to issue passports to Japanese citizens trying to enter the United States as labourers through Hawaii, and the US government agreed to accept the presence of Japanese who were in America already and to the immigration of their wives, children, and parents. This resulted in the growth of a sizable Japanese American community of about 111,000 by 1920 (Daniels 2001, 10). During this time, the US government did its best to diffuse anti-Asian agitation in California and throughout the Pacific Northwest to protect US trade links with Japan.

The Gentleman's Agreement was soon challenged, however, by mounting social pressure from the American Federation of Labor and other organizations, which demanded a dictation test similar to that imposed in Australia. In response to this pressure, Congress passed the Immigration Act of 1924, which was intended to regulate the racial composition of the United States by applying quotas for immigrants from each country. Under the act, there was a quota for Chinese immigrants, which, though small, was a step towards reducing racial inequality in the United States, which was particularly prevalent in California. Further legislative changes gradually allowed Chinese to enter the United

States in larger numbers, and in December 1943 Congress repealed the Chinese Exclusion Act of 1882. It was not until the passage of the Immigration and Nationality Act of 1965 that the quota system ended, substantially opening the United States to potential immigrants from around the world.

The repeal of exclusion acts in the United States and Canada during the 1940s were reported in Australian newspapers, but the prime minister at the time, John Curtin, remained committed to the White Australia policy, and Chinese and other Asian immigrants continued to be barred from entering Australia unless they had a certificate of exemption to work on a year-by-year basis. After the Second World War, Australia embarked on a vigorous immigration program, but Asians continued to be excluded. Indeed, in September 1944, the Commonwealth Parliament had passed a resolution stating that a "necessary requisite for the adequate defence of Australia was a vigorous immigration policy of selected immigrants of the *white races*."[8]

The timing of the repeal of immigration restriction laws in the three settler countries must overshadow any investigation as to why Canada and the United States are ahead of Australia in the political inclusion of "non-white" immigrants and ethnic minorities. After all, it was not until 1975 that the Australian government finally buried the White Australia policy with the introduction of the Racial Discrimination Act, by which time Australia lagged the other two settler countries by three decades in its embrace of immigrants from Asia. For example, the Asian American population increased substantially from 900,000 in 1960 to 3.5 million by 1980, mainly due to the increased emphasis on family reunification and the removal of national-origin quotas (Daniels 2001, 43). Canada similarly witnessed a rapid increase in its Asian population after the removal of national-origin quotas in 1962 and the introduction of the points system in 1967. In the decade between 1971 and 1981, Asian immigrants in Canada constituted up to 14.3 per cent of the foreign-born population (Basavarajappa and Verma 1985).

Australia, in contrast, accepted its first wave of Asian migrants – refugees from Vietnam, Cambodia, and Laos only in 1976 (Martin 1978, 33). In April that year, a fishing boat carrying Vietnamese asylum seekers arrived in Darwin, followed by fifty-six additional boats over the next

8 "Migrants after home needs met," *Courier-Mail* (Brisbane), 11 November 1944, available online at http://nla.gov.au/nla.news-article48960040, emphasis added.

Table 3.1. Top Five Source Countries of Immigrants to Australia, Canada, and the United States

	Australia		Canada		United States	
	Per cent of all immigrants					
1	UK/Ireland	24	UK/Ireland	9	Mexico	29
2	New Zealand	9	China	8	India	4
3	China	5	India	7	Philippines	4
4	Italy	5	Philippines	5	China	4
5	Vietnam	4	Italy	5	Vietnam	3

Notes: Percentages are the share of all immigrants. Data for the United States are from 2010.
Sources: Australia, 2006 Census; Canada, 2006 Census; United States, US Census Bureau, 2010.

five years carrying 2,100 asylum seekers, according to the Australian government. Flows from Asia in the late 1970s, however, remained relatively low compared with flows into Canada and the United States, and in the following decade public attitudes in support of Asian migration were still fairly hesitant. For instance, Australian historian Geoffrey Blainey (1984, 25), in a speech to a large Rotary conference in western Victoria, argued that "an increasing proportion of Australians seem to be resentful of the large numbers of Vietnamese and other South-East Asians who are being brought in, have little chance of gaining work, and are living … at the taxpayers' expense." These attitudes continued to grow, even as Australia's Asian-born population increased from 150,000 in 1981 to 250,000 in 1986 (Jupp 1995). With the removal of remaining policies that discriminated on the basis of race, Australia saw a steep increase in migration flows from Asia. As Table 3.1 shows, the United Kingdom was the top source country for immigrants to both Australia and Canada in 2006, although the share of UK immigrants was much higher in Australia than in Canada. Between 2006 and 2011, there was a significant increase in Indian immigrants to Australia, with their share of the foreign-born population rising from 3 per cent to 7 per cent (Australian Bureau of Statistics 2011) and contributing to the rapid increase in the population of Asian immigrants in Australia over that period.

Table 3.2 shows that, by 2011, 8 per cent of Australia's population, 10 per cent of Canada's, but less than 4 per cent of the US population was born in Asia. Immigrants from Europe made up just over 8 per cent of Australia's population and just under 7 per cent of Canada's, while, as both Table 3.2 and Figure 3.1 show, unlike in Australia, a higher

Table 3.2. Immigrant Population by Source, Australia, Canada, and the United States, 2011

		(per cent of total population)	
Europe	8.3	6.8	1.6
United Kingdom	5.1	1.7	0.2
Poland	0.2	0.5	0.1
Germany	0.5	0.5	0.2
Italy	0.9	0.8	0.1
Netherlands	0.4	0.3	0.0
Asia	8.1	9.9	3.7
China	1.5	1.8	0.7
Hong Kong	0.3	0.6	0.1
India	1.4	1.7	0.6
Philippines	0.8	1.5	0.6
Vietnam	0.9	0.5	0.4
Sri Lanka	0.4	0.4	0.0
Pakistan	0.1	0.5	0.1
Cambodia	0.1	0.1	0.1

Sources: Australia, 2011 Census of Population and Housing; Canada, 2011 National Household Survey; United States, 2011 American Community Survey.

Figure 3.1. Shares of European- and Asian-born Immigrants, Australia, Canada, and the United States, 2011

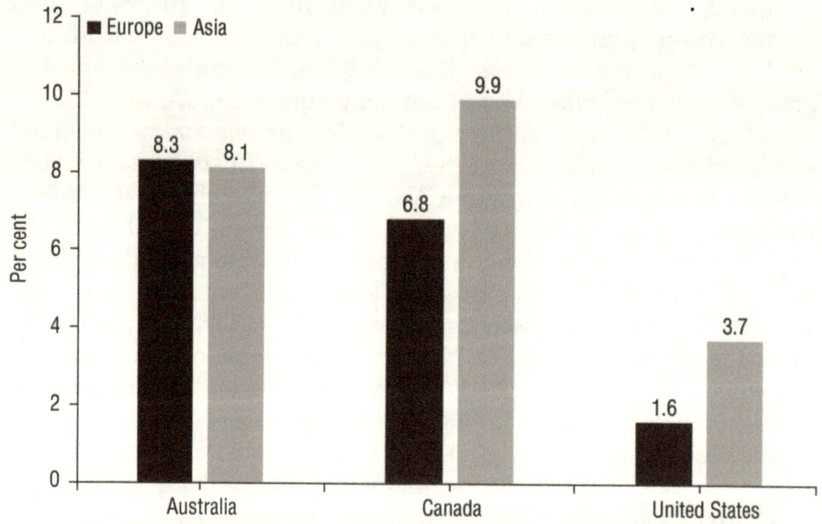

Sources: Australia, 2011 Census of Population and Housing; Canada, 2011 National Household Survey; United States, 2011 American Community Survey.

Figure 3.2. Overseas-born Population, Australia, 1971–2016

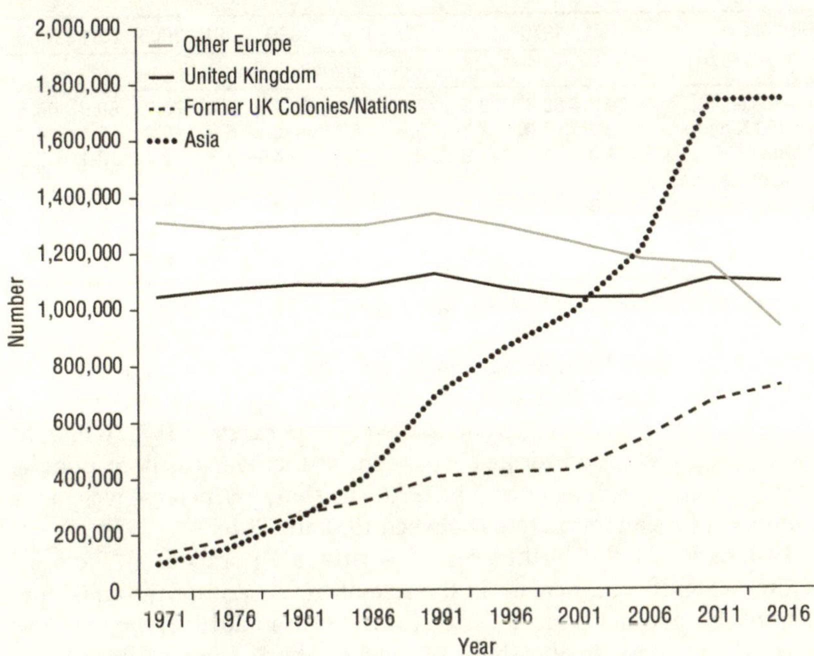

Notes: "Former UK colonies/nations" includes Canada, Ireland, New Zealand, and the United States.
Source: Australia, Census of Population and Housing, 1971–2016.

proportion of Canada's population was born in Asia than in Europe. In the United States, the share of European immigrants as a proportion of the population plunged between 1960 and 2011 as the origins of immigrants shifted from Europe to Latin America, the Caribbean, South America, and Asia.

In looking at the three countries' shared experience of Asian exclusion until the 1960s and 1970s, there is no immediate plausible explanation for the lower levels of Asian representation in Australian national politics other than the fact that Australia was delayed in opening its doors to Asian migration. In fact, in looking specifically at changes in migration trends in Australia (Figure 3.2), we see that migration flows from the United Kingdom and other parts of Europe have remained fairly steady, with a small decline between 2011 and 2016. The sharpest declines in the proportion of Australia's foreign-born population were in those from the

Table 3.3. Birthplaces of the Population, Australia, 1971–2016

Birthplace	1971	1976	1981	1986	1991	1996	2001	2006	2011	2016
	(per cent of total population)									
Australia	79.8	80.6	78.2	77.6	75.5	74.5	72.6	70.9	69.8	66.7
United Kingdom	8.2	8.0	7.5	6.9	6.7	6.0	5.5	5.2	5.1	4.6
Former UK colonies/nations	1.0	1.4	1.9	2.0	2.4	2.4	2.3	2.7	3.1	3.1
Other Europe	10.3	9.6	8.9	8.3	7.9	7.3	6.6	5.9	5.4	4.0
Asia	0.8	1.1	1.7	2.6	4.1	4.8	5.2	6.1	8.1	10.3
Other	–	–	1.8	2.6	3.4	5.0	7.8	9.2	8.5	11.3

Source: Australia, Census of Population and Housing, 1971–2016.

United Kingdom, Italy, the former Yugoslavia, and Greece. For example, in the 2016 census, the Italian-born were just 2 per cent of Australia's overseas-born population, compared with 11 per cent in 1971, while the Greek-born accounted for just 1 per cent of the overseas-born population, compared with 6 per cent in 1976. The sharpest increase was in the numbers of Asian immigrants between 1981 and 2016.

In looking at the birthplaces of Australia's population, Table 3.3 shows a significant increase in the size of the Asian-born from 0.8 per cent of the population in 1971 to 10.3 per cent in 2016. There was also a steady increase in the share of overseas-born from other regions, including the Middle East, Africa, and the Pacific islands, from 1.8 per cent in 1981 to 11.3 per cent in 2016. At the 2016 census, among Asian countries, the top sources were China, India, Vietnam, Philippines, and Malaysia, with the share of Chinese in the overseas-born population increasing from 0.7 per cent in 1971 to 8.3 per cent in 2016 (Table 3.4). There was also a significant increase in immigrants from India among the overseas-born from 1.1 per cent in 1971 to 7.4 per cent in 2016.

Census data thus show that Australia's racial and ethnic composition has gradually changed over time, with an increase in immigrants from non-European backgrounds. Although, as noted, Australia's official classification system does not measure "non-white" or "visible minority" status, in the 2016 census more than 17 per cent of Australians identified as having a Pacific islander, Asian, Middle Eastern, Sub-Saharan African, or South American ancestry, most of whom likely would be classified as "non-white" in North American classification systems. If we also include those in the "other" category, estimates of Australia's "non-white" immigrant and ethnic minority population could be closer to 20 per cent. If so, these findings suggest that up to 20 per

Table 3.4. Share of Overseas-born from Main Asian Source Countries, Australia, 1971–2016

Source Country	1971	1976	1981	1986	1991	1996	2001	2006	2011	2016
	(per cent of overseas-born population)									
China	0.7	0.7	0.9	1.2	2.1	2.9	3.5	4.7	6.0	8.3
India	1.1	1.4	1.4	1.5	1.6	2.0	2.3	3.3	5.6	7.4
Vietnam	0.0	0.1	1.4	2.6	3.3	3.9	3.8	3.6	3.5	3.6
Philippines	0.1	0.2	0.5	1.0	2.0	2.4	2.5	2.7	3.2	3.8
Malaysia	0.6	0.8	1.1	1.5	1.9	2.0	1.9	2.1	2.2	2.2
Sri Lanka	0.0	0.6	0.6	0.7	1.0	1.2	1.3	1.4	1.6	1.4
South Korea	0.0	0.1	0.2	0.3	0.6	0.8	0.9	1.2	1.4	1.3
Indonesia	0.3	0.4	0.4	0.5	0.9	1.1	1.1	1.2	1.2	0.9

Source: Australia, Census of Population and Housing, 1971–2016.

cent of Australia's population has limited "presence" in the Commonwealth House of Representatives in terms of descriptive political representation.

The underrepresentation of non-European minorities in politics is underpinned by social attitudes towards race and ethnicity in social and political institutions that are historically reproduced. Although race as a biological concept can no longer be scientifically supported, cultural and hierarchical constructions of race and ethnicity continue to be an everyday reality in politics, with the inclusion and exclusion of immigrant and ethnic minority groups at different points in time. Institutions in the settler nations of Australia, Canada, and the United States are to varying degrees shaped by traditional British beliefs, values, and social practices. The greater the distance between these traditions and those of an individual or minority group, the more likely the individual or minority group will experience social and political exclusion. This has been particularly noticeable in the adoption of citizenship tests that require considerable knowledge of English language, history, customs, and beliefs in order to pass. These differences are frequently exaggerated, with the effect of precluding any recognition of important similarities between individuals and groups that make us human. As such, immigrants and ethnic minorities continue to experience inequalities in mainstream political institutions.

The Legal-Institutional Context

The legal-institutional context provides a possible factor in explaining why "visible minority" or "non-white" immigrants struggle to achieve descriptive political representation in settler countries. One of the main barriers to immigrant and ethnic minority political representation in mainstream politics is citizenship. No democratic state can uphold a situation where a significant percentage of such groups are excluded from the political rights that come with citizenship (Koopmans and Statham 2000, 24). Core political activities such as voting or being selected for office depend entirely on citizenship status, although immigrants and ethnic minorities can participate in informal modes of participation, such as being a part of mainstream political debates, practices, and decision making. The motivation to participate in politics, however, can also be affected by immigrants' legal citizenship status (Portes and Rumbaut 2006). According to Bloemraad (2006b, 5), full citizenship can be divided into two dimensions: (i) legal citizenship in terms of naturalization; and (ii) participatory or substantive citizenship in terms of being able to engage in the adopted country's political system.

It is often assumed that immigrants who are underrepresented in politics are simply uninterested in entering politics at the national level. Political opportunity and legal structures, however, can hinder the capacity of immigrants and ethnic minorities to apply for citizenship. For example, unlike in Australia and Canada, children born in the United States to non-citizens or non-permanent residents are automatically entitled to citizenship, and tend to move quickly into the political system and participate at much higher rates than in countries where citizenship for children of immigrants is not guaranteed at birth (Hochschild and Mollenkopf 2009, 10). Among the first generation of immigrants, the pattern is very different. According to Bloemraad (2006b), Canada has a much higher citizenship take-up rate than does the United States, for a number of reasons. On the whole, Canada has taken a more interventionist approach within a framework of official multiculturalism that recognizes the benefits of ethnic minority political representation in politics. By contrast the United States has been less pro-active in encouraging new immigrants to apply for citizenship. This is partly related to the backlog of citizenship applications, involving long delays of up to a year. Applicants in the United States also need to attend an interview and pass a verbal and written test. Diverging patterns of citizenship acquisition might also be explained by different residency requirements. The United States requires immigrants to live in the country for five years as a permanent resident before they are eligible to apply for citizenship. In contrast, Canada has a residency requirement of only three years.

Figure 3.3. Citizenship Rates among Immigrants, Australia, Canada, and the United States, 2011

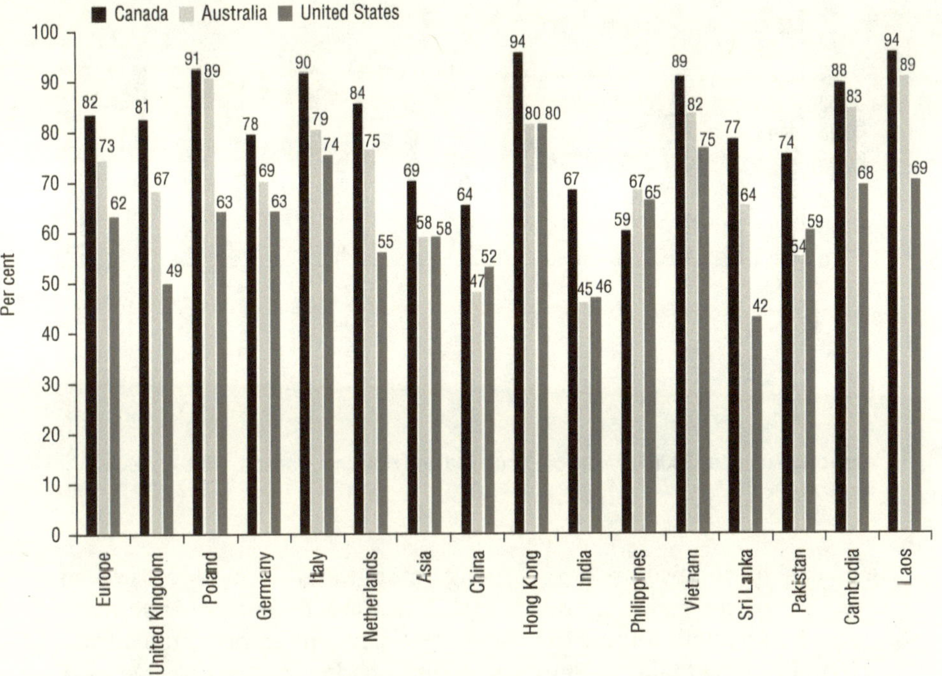

Sources: Australia, 2011 Census of Population and Housing; Canada, 2011 National Household Survey; United States, 2011 American Community Survey.

The differences in citizenship rates between Australia and Canada are more puzzling given Australia's history as a multicultural country, an important factor for explaining the differences between Canada and the United States. Figure 3.3 shows, for example, that up to 64 per cent of Chinese immigrants in Canada had taken up citizenship by 2011, whereas only 47 per cent of Chinese immigrants in Australia had done so. One possible explanation is that Australia's policy of multiculturalism has been gradually weakened since the mid-1990s in terms of resources and commitment; since then, multiculturalism has not been central to Australian government policy or to Australia's sense of national identity (Jupp and Pietsch 2017). A second explanation could be related to the two countries' different residency requirements – four years in Australia, three years in Canada. As Figure 3.4 shows,

Figure 3.4. Citizenship Rates among Immigrants with 3–4 Years of Residence, Australia and Canada, 2006

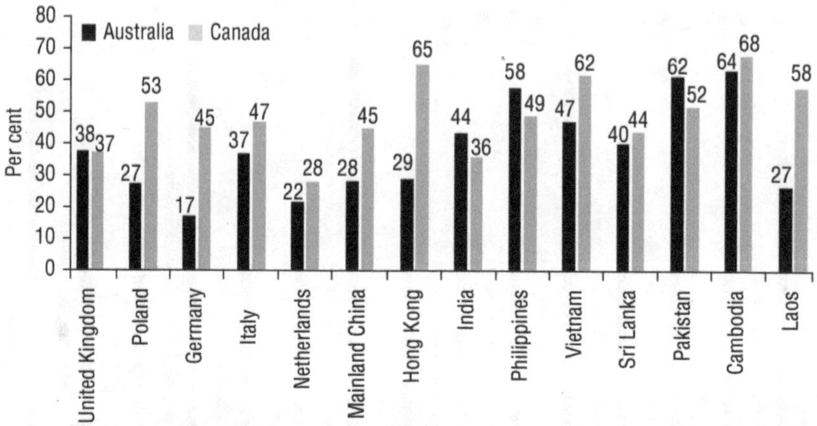

Sources: Australia, 2006 Census of Population and Housing, Canada, 2006 Census of Population.

citizenship acquisition rates among immigrants with only three to four years' residence are much higher in Canada than in Australia – for example, within three to four years 65 per cent of immigrants from Hong Kong had taken up citizenship in Canada while only 29 per cent of immigrants from Hong Kong had done so in Australia.

Given their different residency requirements and other regulatory barriers, it might be better for purposes of comparison between Australia and Canada to focus on immigrants with five to fifteen years of residence, who have had more time to adjust to their new environment and to fulfil the obligations of citizenship, such as learning English and obtaining an understanding of the history, values, symbols, and institutions of their adopted country. As Figure 3.5 shows, after such a length of time, the differences in citizenship rates between the two countries are less obvious, with some immigrant groups in Australia – those from India, Vietnam, the Philippines, Pakistan, and Cambodia – having similar rates of citizenship acquisition as those in Canada. Interestingly, in both countries, immigrants with Asian origins are more likely to take up citizenship than those with origins in the United Kingdom or Europe. Immigrant groups with the highest rates of citizenship are those that arrived in Australia either as post–Second World

Figure 3.5. Citizenship Rates among Immigrants with 5–15 Years of Residence, Australia and Canada, 2006

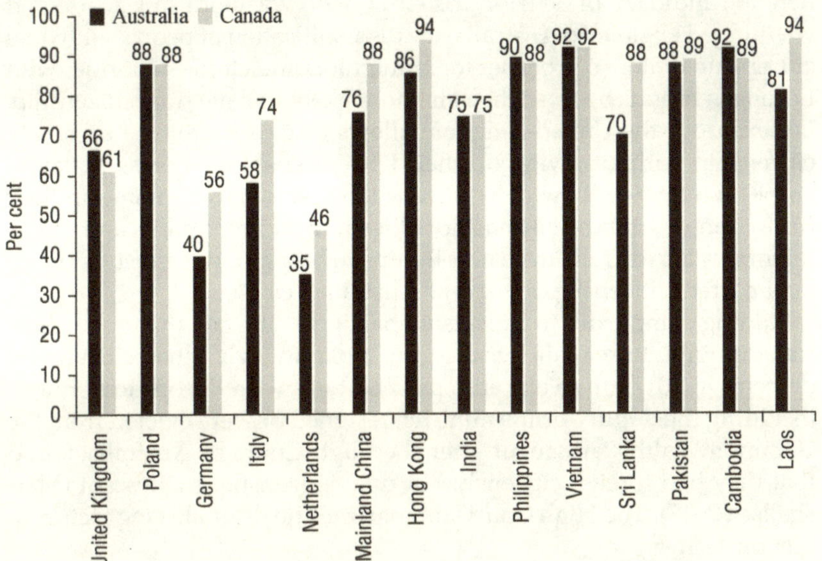

Sources: Australia, 2006 Census of Population and Housing, Canada, 2006 Census of Population.

War refugees or as refugees fleeing Indo-China following the end of the Vietnam War in 1975. In general, refugees are the most likely to take out citizenship because they see little benefit in returning home unless conditions improve. For example, after the Second World War, Australia welcomed more than 170,000 refugees, with two of the largest source countries being then-communist Poland and Yugoslavia, whose immigrants now have high rates of Australian citizenship (Refugee Council of Australia 2012).

In terms of political representation, the Australian Constitution does not allow anyone holding dual or multiple citizenship to stand for parliamentary office at the national level, while section 44 (i) of the Constitution states that those with dual nationality must prove they have taken reasonable steps to renounce their foreign nationality (Australia 2012; Odgers 2012). In Canada, in contrast, dual citizens can be elected to Parliament, while in the United States, dual citizens are disqualified only from the offices of the president and vice president, whose holders must have been born in the United States or those who were born abroad of "natural US citizens." This issue arose in 2016 in relation to the presidential candidacy of Senator Ted Cruz, who was born in Canada and was judged eligible. In Australia, the disqualification of people with dual citizenship is more of a barrier for immigrants and ethnic minorities with European origins because they are more likely to have dual citizenship. For example, the United Kingdom allows its citizens to take up a new citizenship without giving up their UK citizenship, whereas Malaysia and China do not allow their citizens to do so without giving up their Malaysian or Chinese citizenship; indeed, most immigrants and ethnic minorities in Australia from non-European backgrounds must renounce their current citizenship to become Australian citizens.

Adding complexity to citizenship barriers is the fact that many Australians with European heritage are unknowingly dual citizens by descent. In 2017, up to eleven representatives with European heritage, including the deputy prime minister, resigned or were evicted from the Commonwealth Parliament after the High Court of Australia found that they had foreign citizenship or dual citizenship by descent (Marshallsea 2017). The High Court summarized the disqualifying factors in section 44(i) as

> [a] person who, at the time that he or she nominates for election, retains the status of subject or citizen of a foreign power will be disqualified by reason of s 44(i), except where the operation of the foreign law is contrary to the constitutional imperative that an Australian citizen not be irremediably prevented by foreign law from participation in representative government. Where it can be demonstrated that the person has taken all steps that are reasonably required by the foreign law to renounce his or her citizenship and within his or her power, the constitutional imperative is engaged. (CEFA 2017)[9]

The High Court also ruled that it did not matter whether the person did not know that he or she was a dual citizen at the time of nomination for elected office: "It is necessary to bear in mind that the reference by a house of Parliament of a question of disqualification can arise only where the facts which establish the disqualification have

9 See also the ruling by the High Court of Australia, available online at http://eresources.hcourt.gov.au/downloadPdf/2017/HCA/45.

been brought forward in Parliament. In the nature of things, those facts must always have been knowable. A candidate need show no greater diligence in relation to the timely discovery of those facts than the person who has successfully, albeit belatedly, brought them to the attention of the Parliament" (CEFA 2017). Following the High Court decisions, the citizenship fiasco, which became known as the "dual citizenship crisis," affected mainly representatives with British, Greek, Italian, Canadian, and New Zealand descent. Adding to the complexity is the fact that, even if representatives find out too late that they have a second citizenship by descent, some countries make it difficult for Australian citizens to relinquish that second citizenship.

The dual citizenship crisis reflected Australia's difficulties in moving on from its past, when Australian citizenship always entailed multiple loyalties. Indeed, a sense of multiple loyalties has been an important part of Australian history (Rubenstein 2012). For instance, Australians were still considered British subjects until the Australian Citizenship Act of 1948 came into force in 1949. According to Galligan and Roberts (2004, 44), "the fact that Australians were British subjects as well as Australian citizens was not regarded as entailing a form of dual citizenship," and British subjects from Canada, New Zealand, the United Kingdom, and other Commonwealth countries could be nominated for election in Australia, while citizens of the United States and most European countries could not (CEFA 2017). Once Australian citizenship was established, however, other Commonwealth nations were finally considered "foreign."

People born in the United Kingdom continued to have dual citizenship status as British subjects for another two decades. It was not until 1973 that the Labor government of Gough Whitlam removed the special right of foreign-born British subjects to become Australian citizens, in line with requirements of other non-British immigrants (Galligan and Roberts 2004). It is perhaps for this reason that political representatives of British descent have not felt the need to disclose their dual citizenship while in political office even though it is clearly unconstitutional. Following the dual citizenship crisis, there were calls among political representatives to amend section 44 (i) of the Constitution so that the Commonwealth Parliament could better reflect the country's multicultural population. The "citizenship crisis," however, had little relevance for representatives with non-British or European heritage because in many cases their birth country has not allowed dual citizenship options.

Citizenship and Integration Policy Frameworks

Integration frameworks are another significant institutional factor that can influence the representation of immigrants and ethnic minorities in politics. For instance, an inclusive citizenship framework reflects a desire by governments to integrate immigrants and ethnic minorities as members of the national community. Once naturalized, immigrants can enjoy greater access to a range of government services and jobs and, most important, can vote for their political representatives in elections and run for public office. As mentioned, both Australia and Canada historically have supported a multicultural citizenship framework. According to Bloemraad (2006b, 237), the communities' interest in "promoting political integration relies heavily on the symbolic and material support of government as provided by policies of multiculturalism and newcomer settlement." If institutions in democratic societies are committed to the principles of equality, it is important that minority communities and their cultures are provided the means for collective political action (Rex 2000, 61). This involves symbolic and instrumental support for the maintenance of languages, minority religions, family practices, and customs.

Although Australia's policies on immigration and population growth in the 1980s broadly followed Canada's earlier initiatives in the 1970s, the two countries have since departed in their approach to multiculturalism, with Canada placing a much stronger emphasis on its institutionalization. This began in 1982 with the placement of "the Multicultural Heritage of Canadians" in the Charter of Rights of Freedoms, which is entrenched in the Canadian Constitution. Following the introduction of the Charter, ethnic groups began to mobilize and nominate leaders from their groups as candidates for parliamentary seats, which resulted in an increase in the number of MPs from visible minority backgrounds. In 1988 the Canadian Multiculturalism Act was passed unanimously and came into law. The law is situated within the broad framework of civil, political, social, and language rights in the Canadian Constitution. For instance, section 27 of the Charter provides that Canadians' multicultural heritage must be considered in interpreting other sections of the Charter, while sections 16 and 23 affirm the principle of equality of English and French as the two official languages, as well as the rights and privileges of other languages other than English and French.

The fact that Canada officially recognizes, celebrates, and financially supports ethno-cultural diversity influences immigrants' understanding of citizenship and their place in society and politics. The official endorsement of multiculturalism through legislation, according to Bloemraad (2006b), gives immigrants a normative understanding of belonging in the political system. For example, the passing of the Canadian Multiculturalism Act also aimed to address the underrepresentation in federal government institutions of minority groups that are recognized as facing persistent prejudice and discrimination. All major federal parties in Canada, regardless of their ideological orientation, support multiculturalism as official government policy. This level of support by all major parties has important implications for political participation and representation (Marwah, Triadafilopoulos, and White 2013). For instance, the successful integration and representation of immigrants in the political system relies heavily on the material and symbolic support of government through the provision of resources to community organizations that directly promote participation (Bloemraad 2006b, 125).

In Australia, meanwhile, there was little momentum to introduce legislation similar to the Canadian Multiculturalism Act at the national level despite the strong support of the Federation of Ethnic Communities Councils Australia (FECCA) – indeed, by the 1990s, multiculturalism had become too controversial to ensure the passing of such legislation in both houses of the Commonwealth Parliament (Jupp 2007). Overall, although Australia has adopted Canada's terminology of multiculturalism, it has paid little attention to the Canadian model of multiculturalism (Lopez 2000) – at the national level, Australia has only ever adopted multiculturalism in policy, rather than in legislation. In fact, since the 1990s, the Australian government has made several changes to weaken its official endorsement of multiculturalism, involving the gradual withdrawal of symbolic and instrumental assistance in response to public fears about increasing non-European migration and a changing national identity. By 2001 both Labor and Liberal governments scarcely used the word "multiculturalism," which has since gradually faded from public discourse.

This period of hostility towards multiculturalism in Australia contrasts with an earlier period of enthusiasm for an Australian version of multiculturalism. Between 1975, when multiculturalism was considered a very new concept, and the early 1990s, there were numerous government enquiries and reports on multicultural programs and services (Jupp 2007, 69). These enquiries relied on considerable research and input from immigrants and ethnic communities, as well as from academics. At the height of Australian multiculturalism, the Australian

Institute of Multicultural Affairs was established in 1979, then replaced by the Office of Multicultural Affairs (1987–96) and the Bureau of Immigration Research (1989–96) (Jupp 2007). These three agencies provided opportunities for independent publicly funded research on multiculturalism. Since then, there have been few opportunities for public enquiries or debate on multiculturalism, and few opportunities for government consultation with immigrants and ethnic communities, apart from through FECCA, which has limited resources and Commonwealth funding.

In the two decades before the demise of multiculturalism in the 1990s, there had also existed an unbroken path of Australian governments committed to making citizenship more inclusive. The government department responsible for citizenship acquisition usually provided immigrants with a great deal of support, especially in helping them answer the questions on the English test and understanding the responsibilities and privileges of Australian citizenship. To become a citizen, permanent residents had to wait only two years and the English test was relatively easy – indeed, there were active campaigns encouraging Australian immigrants to become citizens. This pattern of citizenship inclusiveness effectively ended in 2007 with the introduction of a much tougher English and "knowledge of Australia and values" test. The focus of public debate shifted from "inclusiveness" to "national security" following the 9/11 terrorist attacks in the United States, with an almost obsessive focus on maritime asylum seekers, pejoratively referred to as "boat people."

Although candidates from the major parties occasionally have pronounced Australia the "most successful multicultural country in the world," in practice, at the national level, nearly all multicultural institutions have been abolished, and policies and programs have been defunded or relegated to the subnational level (Jupp and Pietsch 2017). These institutions, policies, and programs initially were established to build a non-discriminatory policy framework for immigrants and ethnic minorities from non-English-speaking backgrounds, with the overall aim of dismantling the remnants of the White Australia policy and providing the foundations for the future social and political integration of immigrants from such backgrounds. So what went wrong, and why did Australia take such a different path than did Canada in its commitment to official multiculturalism?

The demise of multiculturalism in Australia began in the early 1990s, when family reunion migration resulted in high numbers of Asian immigrants, many of whom were unskilled. These immigrants settled in the outer suburbs of major cities and required significant government assistance with welfare and the English language (Jupp 1995). Critics of this immigration argued that the Commonwealth government was moving too far ahead of public opinion. For example, historian Geoffrey Blainey argued that Australia's immigration policy in the early 1980s was insensitive to the views of the majority of the population. In *All for Australia*, Blainey criticized Australia's multiculturalism policies and, in particular, the emergence of government rhetoric that "Australia is part of Asia" (Blainey 1984). Blainey's criticisms were echoed in the 1990s, when public opinion showed that there was some hesitation and anxiety surrounding the notion of a closer engagement with Asia (McAllister and Ravenhill 1998). Overall, findings from the 1993 and 1996 Australian Election Study showed that support among the broader Australian public for multiculturalism rapidly declined during that decade.

In 1996 Pauline Hanson, leader of the One Nation Party, capitalized on negative public sentiments about Asian immigration and multiculturalism. For Hanson, a unified, stable, and homogeneous nation was being undermined by multiculturalism (Leach 2000), a position she made evident in her maiden speech in the Commonwealth Parliament: "Immigration and multiculturalism are issues that this government is trying to address, but for far too long ordinary Australians have been kept out of any debate by the major parties. I and most Australians want our immigration policy radically reviewed and that of multiculturalism abolished. I believe we are in danger of being swamped by Asians."[10] Hanson's speech sparked a national political debate on immigration and multiculturalism. Immediately after the speech, she mobilized widespread popular support among those who felt powerless in a changing Australian society that was rapidly incorporating a large "non-white" population in response to globalization and economic competition. This populist uprising represented a rejection of multiculturalism, Asian immigration, and globalization.

In 1996, following trends in public opinion, the Liberal Party capitalized on the Pauline Hanson phenomenon by presenting the Australian Labor Party as captive to minority interests and out of touch

10 The full speech is available online at http://www.abc.net.au/news/2016-09-15/pauline-hanson-maiden-speech-2016/7847136.

with mainstream Australia. In contrast the Liberal Party argued that it was not captive to sectional or minority interests, but, rather, represented ordinary Australians and the Australian way of life (Brett 2003, 195–7). This successful campaigning, which targeted middle-class and mainly "white" Australians eventually led to the Labor Party's defeat in the 1996 federal election by a Liberal-National coalition led by John Howard. Previously Howard had made it clear that he was uncomfortable with multiculturalism. For example, in an interview in 1989 with Gerard Henderson, he stated: "The objection I have with multiculturalism is that multiculturalism is in effect saying that it is impossible to have an Australian ethos, that it is impossible to have a common Australian culture so we have to pretend that we are a federation of cultures and that we've got a bit from every part of the world" (quoted in Brett 2005, 37). At the time, there was a widespread expectation that non-European immigrants would simply assimilate into the Liberal Party's understanding of the Australian nation.

In light of its ideals, the Liberal coalition government made cuts in the areas of cultural diversity and multiculturalism, closing the Bureau of Immigration, Multicultural and Population Research and the Office of Multicultural Affairs. It also made changes in the nature of immigration to make more room for skilled immigrants who would require fewer government services. As well, new immigrants would now have to wait two years, rather than six months as before, to claim social security benefits. In 1996 nearly 69 per cent of immigrants to Australia arrived in the family stream and only 29 per cent in the skilled stream. By 2001 only 41 per cent arrived in the family stream and 57 per cent in the skilled stream (Jupp 2007, 156). This approach was economically rational, but it placed a much greater strain on immigrants who wanted to be reunited with unskilled older parents, spouses, siblings, or children still living overseas.

These policy changes, reflecting a move away from the symbolic embrace of multiculturalism, were in line with changes in Australian public opinion. Using results from the Australian Election Study, Figure 3.6 shows that, in the mid-1990s, over two-thirds of Australians favoured reducing the number of immigrants and that up to 44 per cent felt that equal opportunities for immigrants had gone too far. Negative feelings towards immigrants started to decline thereafter, but the terrorist attacks in the United States in 2001 and a subsequent focus on national and social cohesion meant that multiculturalism, in terms of

Figure 3.6. Attitudes towards Multiculturalism and Immigration, Australia, 1990–2013

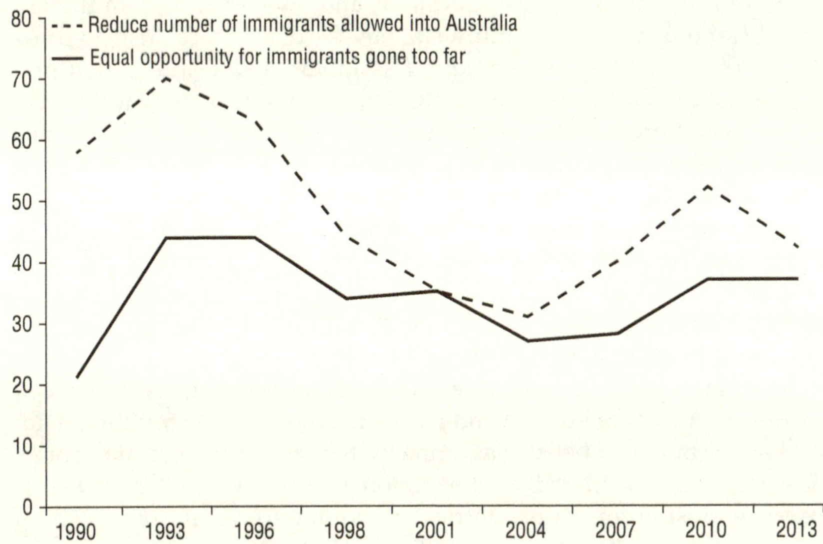

Source: Australian Election Study, 1990–2013.

symbolic and instrumental assistance and increasing immigration, was again beginning to lose public support. By 2013 as many as 42 per cent of Australians believed that the number of immigrants allowed into Australia should be reduced and 37 per cent felt that equal opportunities for immigrants had gone too far.

Since the 1990s, Australia has become heavily dependent on skilled immigrants from Asia, especially India and China. At the turn of the century, although racial prejudice was still widespread, public expressions of anti-Asian sentiment diminished in favour of a more transactional relationship with Asia as Australia became increasingly dependent on good relations with Asia for its future economic prosperity and security. After the 9/11 terrorist attacks, Asian immigrants as victims of discrimination and racial prejudice were soon replaced by Muslim communities. Many of the Muslim newcomers were also Asian, but the fear that Muslims would not integrate into mainstream Australian society further damaged any hope of renewing the early principles of multiculturalism.

The backlash against multiculturalism at the turn of the century had similarly been taking place in parts of Europe, especially in the United Kingdom, Denmark, France, Germany, and Switzerland, even though an official policy of multiculturalism never existed there. Instead these countries adopted a combination of assimilation and integration policy. Vertovec and Wessendorf (2010, 26) observe that, practically everywhere and exemplified in European countries, "there is now in this post-9/11 era a more visceral and populist attack on multiculturalism, often associated with the imputed dangers of segregation." This followed a number of serious crimes and security emergencies across Europe in the years immediately following 9/11, including the murders of Pim Fortuyn and Theo van Gogh in the Netherlands, the 2004 train bombings in Madrid, the July 2005 London bombings, and the 2005 riots in the eastern suburbs of Paris.

Australia's public debate in recent years has been largely influenced by developments in Europe, and has seen a return to the traditional liberal and republican belief that ethnicity belongs in the private sphere. The issue is not related to the notion of differentiated citizenship, because most immigrant countries are willing to accept some form of group rights for historical minorities or Indigenous peoples. Rather, the issue specifically relates to the problem of immigration and rising geopolitical insecurity (Kymlicka 2010, 43). Australia has often followed some of the geopolitical concerns of Europe as a reason to retreat from multiculturalism, without recognizing the distinctive context of Australia. In general, when large flows of immigrants are perceived as illegitimate, illiberal, or burdensome on the welfare state, support for multiculturalism is likely to wane. This does not mean, however, that there are viable alternatives to multiculturalism in countries with increasing cultural diversity. This is frequently demonstrated during periods of racial and ethnic tension involving rioting by far-right-wing political parties and anti-immigrant groups.

In 2005, for example, in a backlash against Muslim immigration, riots broke out in the Sydney suburb of Cronulla sparked by racial tensions and reports of violent assaults. Although the riots were widely condemned, they damaged public confidence in multiculturalism as a citizenship framework for Australia. Since then, debates about multiculturalism have shifted away from questions about race, language, and different standards of living; instead, differences in religious values have become the central focus and main driver of criticisms of multiculturalism. Public anxiety about the presumed threat represented by immigrants from Muslim backgrounds has raised concerns among far-right and mainstream politicians keen to exploit local tensions for political gain. These concerns instigated a parliamentary inquiry in 2011 into migration and multiculturalism. Of 513 submissions to the inquiry, which reported its findings in 2013, 212 raised concerns about Islam in Australia, with many related to fears that multiculturalism was laying the foundations for ethnic separatism or legal pluralism (Parliament of Australia 2013a).

Debates about the contemporary relevance of promoting cultural diversity mean that multiculturalism in Australia is now limited to describing a demographic fact of cultural diversity and a set of policies and programs aimed at social welfare and social cohesion. In fact, by 2016, the bureaucratic responsibilities for multiculturalism had been relegated from its former role in the Department of Prime Minister and Cabinet to the Department of Social Services. The main government advisory body to the Department of Social Services on issues relating to multiculturalism is the Australian Multicultural Council, whose six members are appointed by the government. The council's focus is primarily on improving social cohesion, particularly targeting neighbourhoods with higher levels of social and economic disadvantage than the national average. In its 2013 report, the council referred to the need for an effective multicultural social cohesion framework that targets "at risk" communities such as youth, women, and new immigrants (Parliament of Australia 2013a). Locating multiculturalism policy in the Department of Social Services thus shifted the focus to social welfare and social cohesion and away from nation-building ideas of inclusive citizenship and identity, cultural diversity, cultural rights, recognition, and representation.

On the whole, Australians are reluctant to engage with multiculturalism at a philosophical or normative level, as is seen in Canada and parts of Europe. The lack of Australian government support for an official policy and legal framework that incorporates the main guiding principles of multiculturalism has meant that the political inclusion of minority groups has stayed firmly off the agenda. Even though FECCA has made several recommendations to institutionalize multiculturalism more firmly within Australia's government institutions, this has never been realized. Cultural diversity has been encouraged, but only if political and economic structures are left intact, leaving untouched notions of political equality.

Leading up to the 2016 federal election, FECCA asked whether the major parties were prepared to develop a national legislative framework on multiculturalism. Brushing aside the significant cutbacks it made to multicultural policies and programs, the Liberal-National coalition felt that no legislation would be required to further enhance support of Australia's multicultural communities (FECCA 2016). The Australian Labor Party similarly watered down any long-term commitment to multiculturalism by supporting efforts to combat racism, re-establishing the Office of Multicultural Affairs within the Department of Social Services, investing in the Adult Migration English Program, and supporting new courses in workforce participation (FECCA 2016). Such promises failed, however, to acknowledge the overriding national importance of equality, participation, and inclusion of immigrants and ethnic minorities in Australia's representative institutions (Jupp and Pietsch 2017).

In terms of multicultural legislation, there has been more progress at the state level, which might partly explain the lack of initiative to transform national-level institutions to reflect Australia's growing cultural diversity. To date, New South Wales, Victoria, and South Australia all have specific multicultural legislation in place. This legislation, however, makes no mention of the need to enhance the participation of immigrants and ethnic minorities in formal political institutions. Instead the focus is on the recognition of cultural differences within the community and the need to uphold anti-discrimination laws and human rights. In general, successive governments in Australia have seen no real need to create a Multiculturalism Act because of general hostility towards multiculturalism and the fact that multiculturalism is viewed primarily as a set of policies and programs that, unlike legislation, allows for a degree of flexibility and adaption (Ozdowski 2015).

In the United States, unlike in Canada and Australia, multiculturalism has never been adopted as official policy. Instead there is a far greater emphasis on civil rights and constitutional protections and less emphasis on cultural maintenance (Jupp 2007, 81), with race becoming a core concept in classifying ethnic minorities and public discussions of multiculturalism subordinating cultural and linguistic differences in favour of pan-racial categories. Consequently, in the United States, ethnic claims that are at the heart of policies of multiculturalism, such as those addressing specific cultural, linguistic, or socio-economic issues have little political salience compared with race-based claims (Bloemraad 2006a, 2006b). As such, community and political leaders adopt and employ race-based forms of multiculturalism (Bloemraad 2006b, 150), and nearly all discussion of diversity is underpinned by the broad classifications of white, black, Latino, or Asian American. This is in part the result of the close association between race-based movements, such as the civil rights movement of the 1950s and 1960s, and the need to overcome a long history of oppression.

The historical marginalization and segregation of black Americans has long dominated issues of racial equality in the United States. The disproportionate number now living in poverty in low socio-economic neighbourhoods has been a constant challenge for policy makers. Indeed, according to Schmidt et al. (2013, 81), past discrimination continues to be an important influence on the high levels of poverty among black Americans and the widening gap between black and white Americans. At the political level, however, the introduction of the Voting Rights Act of 1965 and the subsequent redrawing of district boundaries were significant factors in facilitating greater political equality for black Americans and in addressing their representation in federal institutions.

As the civil rights movement gained momentum in the 1960s – particularly as it addressed discrimination and equal access to housing, employment, and educational opportunities – other racial minorities began to mobilize for greater political inclusion. By the end of the 1960s, Latinos were also requesting legislative changes to facilitate enhanced political inclusion and representation of their interests. They, like black Americans, continue to be overrepresented among the poor and tend to live in low socio-economic neighbourhoods. The discrimination that Latinos experienced was further compounded by the introduction of new laws following the 9/11 terrorist attacks (Vickers and Isaac 2012). As in Australia, in the United States the fear of homegrown terrorism meant that immigration policy became deeply entrenched with greater securitization measures, to the detriment of policies promoting political participation and representation. While some groups, especially those of Muslim background or irregular status, faced greater threats to their personal safety and well-being than others, the new counterterrorism policies had an effect on all racial and ethnic minorities, including Asian Americans.

As it has with African Americans, the United States has faced multiple challenges over the years in addressing the political inequality of Latinos, who have now, at 17 per cent of the population, become the largest racial minority group in the United States (black Americans are 13 per cent); in some electoral districts, Latinos have replaced black Americans as the majority-minority population. The Asian American population has also expanded considerably over the past few decades: between 1990 and 2005, Asian Americans increased from 2.8 per cent of the population to 4.4 per cent. Compared with Canada, however, people of Asian heritage remain a relatively small proportion of the US population, and struggle to achieve political equality with other significant racial groups (Schmidt et al. 2013). To address political inequalities, Latinos and Asian Americans have formed powerful pan-ethnic alliances to advance their status in US society. For Asian Americans, the roots of such pan-ethnic organizations lie in generations of the persistence of racial discrimination and attempts to undermine affirmative action programs and other government-funded support structures (Kim 2007; Lien 2004; Schmidt et al. 2013).

Electoral and Party Systems

In all three settler countries, the increasing political presence of immigrants and ethnic minorities in politics has no doubt been heavily influenced by changes to citizenship and integration policies. These policies can be pivotal in facilitating the effective mobilization and inclusion of minority groups with shared political interests. Other institutional factors, however, such as the design of the electoral system and rules underpinning candidate recruitment and selection to political office, also influence the effective mobilization of minority groups to improve their political representation in national-level politics (see Chapter 5). Even though Australia, Canada, and the United States share democratic ideals and bicameral legislatures, electoral systems, and party characteristics, other factors – such as minority group size, the degree of ethnic mobilization, and geographical concentration – have an impact on the representation of immigrants and ethnic minorities in mainstream political institutions.

In Canada, the House of Commons, the lower chamber of Parliament, uses a first-past-the-post, single-member plurality system, inherited from the United Kingdom and in place since Confederation in 1867, under which the candidate who wins the most votes, though not necessarily the majority, wins election to office. One advantage for immigrant and ethnic minority representation under this system is that it provides fewer opportunities than do proportional electoral systems used throughout Europe for representatives of extreme right-wing political parties to gain election – although it could also be argued that, without political representation in the national legislature, those with extreme anti-immigration views might look for other avenues to voice their protests, resulting in incidences of xenophobia and racially motivated violence (Koopmans and Statham 2000, 34).

Although the electoral system in Canada is not based on proportional representation, the existence of majority-minority ridings facilitates the election of visible minorities from groups that are large and concentrated within these ridings. The Senate, in contrast, is based on the British House of Lords and consists of members who are appointed by the governor general on the advice of the prime minister. In practice the governor general usually supports or rubberstamps the prime minister's choices. In recent years there have been moves to turn the chamber into a less partisan one that attracts candidates with a record of achievement, preferably from the public service, who can act in an independent manner (Bryden 2015). In 2016 up to 10 per cent of senators identified as visible minority.

As in Canada, the US Congress – both the House of Representatives and the Senate – uses a first-past-the-post plurality system. Senators, two for each state, are elected for a six-year term; at the end of two years, one-third of senators must face re-election or vacate their seat. The representation of immigrants and ethnic minorities in Congress has been growing for decades. Since the Civil Rights Act of 1964 and the Voting Rights Act of 1965, which focused on the election of black Americans to Congress, improvements have been made to their descriptive and substantive representation. Before these laws were introduced, however, a range of discriminatory practices – such as literacy tests, poll taxes, and whites-only primaries – blocked black Americans' access to political representation. The laws were strengthened with the passing of amendments to the Voting Rights Act in 1982 that aimed to reduce discriminatory voting results and to allow affirmative steps to incorporate racial and linguistic minorities into the political mainstream (Boyd and Markman 1983, 1374). One of the most significant changes involved a process of "racial redistricting," or the drawing of electoral boundaries to provide minority groups with descriptive and substantive representation. As a result of these reforms, most of the growth of minority representation in Congress has been attributed to membership changes in the House, where up to 20 per cent of members identify as "non-white," rather than in the Senate, where only six of the one hundred senators belong to a racial and ethnic minority group (Krogstad 2015). A significant barrier for immigrants is the fact that senators must have lived in the United States as citizens for at least nine years, a reflection of the historical view that immigrants were dangerously attached to their countries of origin – problematic given that one of the Senate's main roles is the review of foreign treaties (United States Senate 2016).

In the Australian Parliament, the House of Representatives, whose 150 members represent single-member constituencies with approximately equal numbers of voters, uses a majoritarian-preferential electoral system. The Senate, in contrast, uses a proportional representative (PR) system by single transferrable vote to elect its members. Each state, regardless of population, has twelve members and the two territories have four members each, for a total of seventy-six senators. In general Australia's electoral system is regarded as one of the most complicated in the world, leading to high rates of informal voting. Between 1919 and 1983 the rate of informal voting averaged 9 per cent per election, which declined to around 4 per cent when a new ballot paper was introduced in 1984. The new ballot paper for the Senate allowed voters to choose between voting for a party "above the line" or for candidates "below the line." The above-the-line option essentially handed control to parties, as more than 98 per cent of voters tend to vote above the line (Green 2017). The Australian Constitution gives the Senate virtually the same power to legislate as the House of Representatives, apart from initiating bills that authorize the spending of money (appropriation bills).

Immigrants and ethnic minorities are more likely to gain representation in the Senate than in the House of Representatives, for several reasons. First, the PR system has a lower threshold to be elected. Second, the tendency of Australians to vote above the line in Senate elections effectively hands control over to the parties to decide on the ordering of candidates. Third, the lower house has only a limited number of single-member electoral districts with a significant geographical concentration of immigrants and ethnic minorities; as a result, parties are more likely to select immigrant and ethnic minority candidates for the Senate. Having said this, in the 2016 election only three immigrants and ethnic minorities from "non-white" backgrounds were elected to the Senate. This suggests that, in the Australian case, in order for the PR system to bring in more representatives from these groups, political party list characteristics can make a difference.

There is much debate over whether proportional or majoritarian electoral systems are favourable for immigrants and ethnic minorities (Moser 2008). On the one hand, PR systems are by their nature more proportional to the votes they win and, in theory, should ensure that a diversity of views from different immigrant and ethnic backgrounds is represented. On the other hand, single-member plurality and majoritarian systems are more likely to encourage representatives to remain in contact with citizens and for citizens to feel there is someone in the political system who is willing to act on their behalf (Curtice and Shively 2009). In strong party systems such as Australia's, the incentive for representatives to act as citizen intermediaries might not be as large as in multi-member constituencies with open lists, as their likelihood of success depends more on the party than on the extent of their personal qualities and engagement with local electorates (Farrell and McAllister 2006; Gauja 2013; Marsh 2000). Any work in electoral districts thus might make little difference, since no candidate has a safe seat, and each candidate depends on his or her personal popularity and that of the party.

In summary, immigrant and ethnic minority representation depends not only on the type of electoral system, but also on the size and geographical concentration of minority groups within each electoral district (Moser 2008, 274). Descriptive representation is best achieved when racial or ethnic minorities are geographically concentrated and represented on a constituency basis. Yet in most Australian electoral districts, people of British and Irish origin are in the majority, which, given the majoritarian system for the lower house, means that minorities have very little chance of gaining entry to political office unless they can appeal to the majority. This contrasts with the United States and Canada, where racial and ethnic minority groups are more concentrated in marginal seats and can use group mobilization in particular localities to their political advantage (Bloemraad and Schönwälder 2013).

Under the right conditions, then, both PR and single-member plurality systems can encourage the election of immigrant and ethnic minority candidates – the former because of the lower threshold needed to win office, while the latter tend to work best in majority-minority districts where minorities, assuming they share partisanship, can mobilize in support of a minority candidate. By contrast, in PR systems, ethnic mobilization is generally manifest through parties (Moser 2008). Here, however, the success of descriptive representation of immigrants and ethnic minorities in strong party systems such as Australia's is also conditional on the behaviour and attitude of political parties. Parties often make assumptions about whether a minority candidate can overcome the various institutional barriers he or she might face. For instance, studies have shown that parties are more likely to recruit candidates who are ethnically more homogeneous than the general population, thus affecting the political advancement of immigrant and ethnic minorities (Andrew et al. 2008a; Bloemraad and Schönwälder 2013; Soininen 2011). In recruiting candidates with electoral appeal, parties strategically consider public attitudes towards minority groups.

Even though Australia's population has changed rapidly to incorporate hundreds of thousands of immigrants from non-European countries since the end of the White Australia policy, negative social and cultural attitudes persist. In the 2013 *Mapping Social Cohesion* survey (Markus 2013), for example, 15 per cent of Australians reported having negative feelings towards immigrants from Asia, and 25 per cent reported having negative feelings towards those from the Middle East. As well, legislative recruitment is highly dependent on the culture of party pre-selection committees: as Jupp (2003, 33) notes, "candidate selection rests in the hands of small numbers of local party members or state-level executives dominated by the party machines and factions." In an environment that is not conducive to multiculturalism, the pre-selectors are generally less likely to choose candidates from ethnic minority backgrounds for contestable or safe seats unless there are perceived electoral advantages – the reality of discrimination or racial prejudice among the broader electorate can result in a 10 per cent swing. Accordingly, political elites might use the negative stereotypes that immigrants and ethnic minorities face as an excuse not to field such candidates out of fear of losing seats (Maxwell 2013).

A final institutional barrier that distinguishes Australia from Canada and the United States is the Australian Labor Party's requirement that its candidates be union members. As a result, because the party depends heavily on their financial support, trade unions can have a powerful influence on the selection of candidates and in party policies. This barrier was highlighted in the 2013 Australian Election Study, in which 46 per cent of Labor supporters of Asian origin indicated they either "strongly agree" or "agree" that trade unions have too much power, 23 per cent disagreed with the statement, and 31 per cent had no opinion.

Conclusion

In summary, the historical and institutional context provides an important foundation for understanding variations in the political participation and representation of immigrants and ethnic minorities in Australia, Canada, and the United States. The pathway to achieving political representation is constrained in this context, which shapes societal values, ideas, and belief systems, and provides the means whereby individual and collective identities are formed. The citizenship and integration policy regimes of these settler societies have evolved over time, but not always in a positive direction for immigrants and ethnic minorities. In some cases, these policy regimes have helped to facilitate the political participation and representation of immigrants and ethnic minorities; in others, their involvement has been hindered through laws and policies aimed at exclusion rather than inclusion. Whether countries adopt an assimilationist or multicultural integration framework might not be as significant for political participation and representation as other institutional factors, such as whether immigrants and ethnic minorities are given the practical resources and symbolic support to participate as leaders in society and politics.

The comparison of multiculturalism in Australia and Canada is a case in point. Although both countries have adopted multiculturalism as an overarching policy framework for integrating immigrants and ethnic minorities, the two have very different understandings about what multiculturalism means in practice. Australia's understanding involves a mixture of social integration and political assimilation. Immigrants and ethnic minorities who attempt to challenge the existing racial and ethnic hierarchies in politics are usually lambasted in the media and frequently told to go back home – meaning leave Australia, where they do not belong.[11] The provision of social and cultural resources and equal access to citizenship thus does not always facilitate a pathway to entry into the political community. National symbolic gestures of acceptance and belonging are also critical to ensuring that immigrants and ethnic minorities are made to feel welcome and included.

Australia, Canada, and the United States share an overlapping history of racial exclusion, but people with an Asian background are now

11 See "Multicultural voices deserve to be heard: Tim Soutphommasane responds to 'Go back to Laos' comments," *SBS News*, 11 July 2017, available online at https://www.sbs.com.au/news/multicultural-voices-deserve-to-be-heard-tim-soutphommasane-responds-to-go-back-to-laos-comments; see also "Q&A: Jacqui Lambie and Yassmin Abdel-Magied exchange barbs over sharia law," *ABC News*, 14 February 2017, available online at http://www.abc.net.au/news/2017-02-13/jacqui-lambie-and-yassmin-abdel-magied--in-fiery-qanda-debate/8267212.

the fastest-growing racial minority group in all three countries. It is often suggested that the removal of discriminatory laws and policies in Canada and the United States sooner than in Australia is one of the main reasons Australia lags in the political representation of "non-white" immigrant and ethnic minority groups. In looking at the demographic trends and ethnic composition of the three settler countries since the 1980s, however, one must ask how long must some groups wait and to what size must they grow before their commensurate political representation in the Australian Parliament is possible? This is especially significant considering that, after decades of high-skilled migration, the barriers of a lack of English and low socio-economic status can no longer be used as an explanation, as was previously the case for post-war European immigrants from non-English-speaking backgrounds.

It is possible that party-political barriers play a significant role in directly or indirectly blocking immigrants and ethnic minorities from participating in politics. For instance, parties might prefer candidates from majority backgrounds because of their understanding of voter preferences and because voters are often more likely to vote for candidates who look like themselves (Bird 2016; Collet 2005; Hutchings and Valentino 2004; Philpot and Walton 2007). Saggar (2016, 78) observes that, in the United Kingdom, the fear of voter discrimination likely has a significant impact on parties' recruitment of ethnic minority candidates in winnable seats. Even though party representatives might personally welcome minority individuals as excellent candidates who would work hard for their communities, they implicitly worry that, at the margin, voters are more hostile or less welcoming to such candidates. This is highly significant in Australia, where few electoral districts at the national level have majority-minority status. In the next chapter, I examine some of the possible barriers to entry from the perspective of political parties and their representatives in the Australian Parliament.

PART TWO

Chapter Four

Elites and Political Representation

The comparative literature in North America and Europe on political representation reveals a number of historical, institutional, and party-political barriers that explain why Australia lags Canada and the United States in the representation of immigrants and ethnic minorities in federal politics. Much of this research has emerged from the comparison of legislative and government statistics, laws, and policies in each country. This chapter, for the first time, focuses on the individual attitudes and behaviours of MPs in the Australian Parliament regarding the political representation of immigrants and ethnic minorities, examining whether there is a strategic incentive for political parties and their representatives in Parliament to select, recruit, and promote candidates from these groups.

One way to understand more fully the individual attitudes and behaviour of MPs towards the political representation of immigrants and ethnic minorities is to draw on scholarship provided by "role theorists." Role theorists inform debates on how MPs understand their different roles, such as their party role, their representative role, their constituency role, their administrative role, and their pressure group role (Searing 1994; Wahlke et al. 1962). The scholarship on role theory in legislatures demonstrates how the attitudes and behaviour of MPs towards descriptive and substantive representation is partly conditioned by the institutional context and partly by MPs' socio-economic background, socialization experiences, and individual personalities (Saalfeld and Müller 1997; Strøm 1997).

According to Searing (1994, 1255), understanding the attitudes and behaviour of MPs is "best discovered through interviews that probe the topic with several open-ended questions." As such, this chapter draws on thirty-four semi-structured interviews with Australian MPs from all major parties. These interviews were conducted between 2015 and 2016, leading up to the federal election in July 2016, which culminated in a government formed by a Liberal-National coalition. Because of the low representation of "non-white" MPs in the House of Representatives, several interviews were conducted with "non-white" representatives in the Senate. The interview questions were informed by the international literature on racial and ethnic minority representation, with a focus on the extent to which the individual preferences of MPs are conditioned by the historical and institutional framework in which they operate.

Throughout the interviews, it was clear that MPs often felt conflicted between their own values and beliefs, those of their party, and those of the various communities they represent. This was especially a concern for MPs from immigrant and ethnic minority backgrounds. For example, MPs from such backgrounds often need to toggle between the competing priorities of ethnic communities and parties (Collet 2008). Several such MPs found themselves needing to draw at different times on several representation strategies, such as being an ethnic entrepreneur, a bridge builder, or a party delegate (Saalfeld, Wüst, and Bird 2011). Others felt a greater pressure to prioritize ethnic concerns over others because of their "marker of difference" (Nergiz 2013). The following narratives reveal some of these barriers to the representation of immigrants and ethnic minorities in Australia from the perspective of MPs.

Australian MPs' Attitudes towards Immigrant and Ethnic Minority Representation

Most MP respondents had not thought about the ethnic composition of the Commonwealth Parliament as an issue that required focused attention. This is arguably a reflection of the absence of a national discourse and legislative framework that emphasizes the importance of the representation of immigrants and ethnic minorities in Australia's national political institutions. At the beginning of the interview, each MP and senator was given the actual numbers of "non-white" immigrant and ethnic minority representatives in the House of Representatives and the Senate and relative comparisons with national-level legislatures in Canada and the United States. In many cases a deracialization perspective was adopted whereby MPs and senators preferred not to reveal a clear position on the representation of immigrants and ethnic minorities. For example, one MP responded by stating: "I don't think it's a matter to commit suicide over ... I don't think it's an alarming situation." MPs instead tended to emphasize their support for issues and values concerning human rights and refugees to appeal to a broad section of their constituency. For instance, when asked whether they felt that the descriptive representation of immigrants and ethnic minorities was important, respondents in nearly all cases subsumed the issue under other policy matters. Some respondents said they needed to follow their party line in terms of offering clearly differentiated policy positions that offer broad appeal and effective representation:

> I think our Parliament should look like who we are. It should represent women and men and in terms of disabilities, in terms of what jobs we do, in terms of a whole range of things. Ideally, the Parliament would look like who we are, so it would have all the voices of a community in it. It's not just about ethnicity; it [Parliament] also doesn't have a lot of people who come from the highly creative end of town. It has got an increasing number of people who come from security, defence, police, and the army. It's got a lot of lawyers. So there is a lot more than ethnic diversity, and if we can't put together a Parliament that has the range of perspectives from the Anglo culture in Australia, how will we put together a Parliament that has people in it with a Hindu perspective in terms of different notions of good and evil and where conversations about security and such things are profoundly different?
>
> I do think you have to be here as a representative of the broader community, not just your own personal faith.
>
> I've always thought historically that most ethnic groups become obsessed with the same issues as Anglo-Saxons around health, wages, climate change, et cetera, unless they have an abiding foreign policy interest in their own country.

Although the representation of immigrants and ethnic minorities was not considered a priority, broadly speaking most respondents felt they had a good relationship with ethnic communities in their constituencies. This was demonstrated, primarily, through attending citizenship ceremonies, associational meetings and festivities, religious and cultural events, and human rights events. The following narratives reveal the types of activities MPs covered in their role as ethnic entrepreneur:

> It is happening nearly every day. Every day I'm not in Canberra, I'm normally at something during the day or during the night, so it's full on. Multicultural politics is a very, very time-consuming enterprise.
>
> It is one of my favourite parts of the job. School kids are awesome because I get to see every day what the future of this country looks like in years to come, but also multicultural Australia and people becoming Australian citizens, and sharing that with them. Not only sharing, but also having the privilege of conveying it upon them as something that is very special.
>
> I organize a Chinese New Year event every year in my community, and I work with the university, the local councils, the local police, the local chamber of commerce, and the night noodle markets. The Confucius Institute organizes Chinese cultural and artistic performances, and it's wonderful just to bring the community together to celebrate Lunar New Year and multiculturalism.
>
> I speak regularly in the Parliament about community events that they organize. The Bangladeshi community organizes a "Biggest Morning Tea" every year for cancer research, and I will report to the Parliament on the work they have done and the amount of money that they have raised. I will also congratulate the leaders and the volunteers who have put that together. And I will do that for the Greek community as well.
>
> There is a very clear Italian community in my electorate and a community from the former Yugoslavia. I have a pretty good interactive relationship with those people. The Portuguese community is quite self-contained. They tend to not interact so much. I mean, I have been invited a couple of times to their events, and they have been really good and really welcoming, but they are not so much engaged as the [former] Yugoslav and Italian communities.

In their role as ethnic entrepreneur, MPs felt valued by their ethnic communities, especially in terms of being able to provide support and to represent individuals from different ethnic groups on certain issues, such as immigration, family visas, funding for aged care, and home country issues:

> Representatives of [southern and eastern European] communities will come to see me about particular issues that they might need help with.

> For example, they might need support for a funding application to build an aged care village for their communities. There are aged care centres in my electorate where they specialize in looking after Italian and European elderly people because they have got people who speak the languages and so forth there. It is a really nice environment, a welcoming environment. They don't exclude other people, but that is their focus. I also get people coming to me from ethnic groups from outside of my electorate because they understand that I am someone who is sympathetic and interested in their issues, so they come and see me about issues in their community or even in their home countries.

Even though it was clear from these responses that MPs in ethnically diverse constituencies valued their role as ethnic entrepreneur, one respondent stated that just attending multicultural events was not an adequate way to represent racial and ethnic minority communities: "Nothing annoys me more than multiculturalism being, you know, tokenistic – just go to a festival, tick that box, add it on the end." This sentiment is widely supported in the academic literature, which critiques top-down approaches to multiculturalism that view culture only in terms of static and internally monolithic practices, such as through dress, dance, food, and art (Vickers and Isaac 2012, 220). The focus is on the majority's tolerating cultural differences, rather than on adopting minority values and behaviour in the national discourse. Some minorities even go so far as to reject multiculturalism because it is viewed as "containing" and "managing," rather than "adopting" or "incorporating," cultural differences in mainstream social and political institutions (Ang 1993, 2001; Ang et al. 2000; Hage 1998). Stratton and Ang (1994, 126–7) argue that multiculturalism is "a top-bottom political strategy implemented by those in power precisely to improve the inclusion of ethnic minorities within national Australian culture." From their perspective, multiculturalism is viewed as policy that aims to manage and contain diversity. For instance, it is suggested that the politicization of "ethnicity" in multiculturalism in Australia has led to a containment of cultures and a widening gap between the cultures (Ang 1993, 2001).

There are often other reasons representatives embrace multiculturalism or choose to support a candidate from an immigrant or ethnic minority background, such as the strategic need to attract votes. The following respondent, for example, presented a searing insight into the motivations of political-party involvement in multiculturalism and ethnic community engagement: "You know, to put it brutally honestly, which is what I normally do, both sides of politics recruit in the hope that having someone on their ticket from that nationality will secure a tranche of votes. That's how it plays out. So, be it at local level, be it at state, federal, both parties are always trying to improve ties with different multicultural groups because sitting inside that is a subset of votes." Evidently, engagement with ethnic communities might depend on whether it is strategic to do so in terms of being re-elected. Crisp et al. (2016) assert that a legislator's willingness to focus on the concerns of immigrant and ethnic minority groups in their constituency is partly a function of whether the reputation earned by doing so is sufficient for re-election. It has been shown in other settler societies that the incentives for ethnic engagement vary across electorates according to the overall group size of ethnic constituencies.

It is widely argued in the literature on representation that descriptive representation not only has symbolic benefits, but, when there are electoral incentives, also leads to quality substantive representation in terms of policy outcomes (Crisp et al. 2016). In most cases MPs who share the experience of migration or ethnic identity with their constituents felt they could draw on their experience in understanding the needs of their communities. One MP described her own ability to represent immigrants among her electorate precisely because of her experience of life as a migrant to Australia: "I identify with my community totally because I am a migrant myself. A lot of people say, oh, but how does that work? And I say, it's very simple. I mean it is in my background, so I kind of relate directly to my constituency. They and I am a product of the same migration process, so for me I understand them psychologically as well."

MPs from established immigrant and ethnic minority backgrounds often expressed a degree of empathy and compassion for new groups of immigrants, who face stereotyping in the media and a lack of understanding among policy makers. The experience of being negatively stereotyped or racialized often gives immigrant and ethnic minority MPs a greater understanding of the effect this can have on individuals. The following MP reflected on the way her personal experience of being an immigrant helped her develop a sense of empathy, especially in relation to current debates surrounding immigrants and the radicalization of young immigrants in particular: "I guess I have a particular empathy for the debate that is going on at the moment around the so-called radicalization of young people, and I get a little bit annoyed that there seems to be a profound lack of understanding from everybody, including the media, even my own colleagues, and the decision makers. There is a profound inability to understand what the issue is about. There are seven million Australians who were born overseas, and I am pretty sure that a huge number of Australians have been through this process. We are not really drawing on that experience."

Australia's first Asian-born member of the cabinet, Senator Penelope Ying-Yen Wong, also known as Penny Wong, demonstrated the role of personal experience in policy making on racial discrimination and how it affected her family. Senator Wong was born in Sabah, Malaysia; her family migrated to Australia after her father won a Colombo Plan scholarship. She was elected to the Senate in 2001 as a Labor Party representative for South Australia; shortly afterward, her younger brother Toby died. In her maiden speech, Senator Wong spoke about how race had affected her personal life: "We have had a rather uneasy relationship with Asia for much of the post-war period. Phrases such as 'the yellow peril' and 'two Wongs don't make a White' exemplify the darker tendencies of our history. Over the years this relationship has matured as our self-perception has broadened, but this aspect of our history can still resonate today ... I want to make special mention of my younger brother Toby, who turned thirty on the day I was elected to this place, and died ten days later. Your life and death ensure that I shall never forget what it is like for those who are truly marginalized."[12]

True to her maiden speech, Penny Wong and other immigrant and ethnic minority representatives in Parliament joined forces to oppose efforts to water down section 18C of the Racial Discrimination Act of 1975, which was brought in by the Labor government in 1995. Section 18C makes it unlawful to commit an act that is reasonably likely to "offend, insult, humiliate or intimidate" someone because of their race or ethnicity. Complaints can be lodged with the Human Rights Commission, which will investigate the complaint. If a resolution cannot be found, the complaint can be taken to court; since 2014, however, less than 5 per cent of cases have made it to court (Anderson 2016). Federal politicians have debated the need to remove the words "insult" and "offend" from the legislation or even remove section 18C altogether. In an emotional response to Senator George Brandis, who claimed

12 For a transcript of Senator Wong's maiden speech, see http://parlinfo.aph.gov.au/parlInfo/search/display/display.w3p;query=Id%3A%22chamber%2Fhansards%2F2002-08-21%2F0106%22.

that "people do have the right to be bigots you know," Senator Wong responded in the following way:

> It does bring back … for people who have been the subject of racial abuse, when we are reminded of that, when we hear an echo of it in the parliament or public debate, of course it brings back some of those emotions.
>
> You remember how you felt as a child, you remember how, watching my younger brother, who was much less resilient than I, watching how he responded ...
>
> I'm thinking of the young me today, the kid who is being abused or the person on the bus … It's not just protecting me, I feel a responsibility to speak for people who don't have the platform I have or being able to stand on the floor of the parliament.
>
> You hope, on issues of race, that we have gone somewhere different as a nation and then you have a debate like this and you realise those of us who believe in acceptance, standing up against prejudice, thought we have moved on from that debate …
>
> For people who have experienced racism, it is a deeply personal debate, and it's actually a debate about real people and real hurt. (Quoted in Chan 2014b)

The responses by Senator Wong and other immigrant and ethnic minority representatives to the section 18C debate reveal the sense of personal engagement these representatives bring to debates relating to racial and ethnic discrimination. This personal engagement, which brings with it a sense of public responsibility, clearly has inspired many to be relatively outspoken, if not uniquely knowledgeable, on such issues. Several women MPs also felt that their own experiences as women in politics enabled a greater understanding of what it feels like to be marginalized in politics. Female respondents were more likely to acknowledge feelings of marginalization. Although progress was being made towards greater gender representation, there was little movement or willingness in politics to look at ethnic diversity. For example, one MP stated: "My view has always been that people should be able to see themselves in Parliament. Whether you want to be there or not, that is another issue. But you should be able to look at Parliament and see that is something you could do. White blokes were the model for a long time, and that is being knocked away slowly. However, we still have not really broken through with the area of ethnicity and people from different cultural backgrounds. People should feel that Parliament truly represents them."

In some cases, MPs from immigrant and ethnic minority backgrounds only realized the value of their role as an ethnic entrepreneur or bridge builder after they entered Parliament. Consider the following comments from a senator with South Asian origins:

> When I got into the Senate, I didn't feel that I was this person of Indian origin in the Senate and that would be my defining character, but I certainly realized it was the case among the subcontinent communities, who saw me as one of theirs in the Parliament, and I then realized how important it was that I was the only person of South Asian heritage in the Parliament. I have tried to be a role model, and I do talk to a number of people from various Asian backgrounds, including South Asians – particularly Indian, Sri Lankan, Bangladeshi, Tibetan, you name it, but also broader Asian background as well. I also talk with women from those backgrounds to say, if I can do it, you can do it, and I do not want to remain the first and I certainly do not want to be the last. I think I have tried to be a role model.

As mentioned in Chapter 1, increasing diversity in national-level legislatures brings wider symbolic benefits for racial and ethnic minorities in terms of increasing levels of political trust and feelings of national belonging. A more culturally varied legislature in a pluralist democracy is a good indicator of a more inclusive society. Even with such a legislature, however, immigrant and ethnic minority members face significant challenges in toggling between their ethnic communities and the expectations placed upon them because of their "marker of difference." For instance, one senator, reflecting on his role as an ethnic entrepreneur, described a sense of being torn between the different roles that were expected of him because of his Chinese background.

Some of the difficulties inherent in the political representation of immigrants and ethnic minorities in Australia arise from the fact that, even when ethnic minority candidates are elected, they find it difficult to speak openly about ethnic minority concerns due to the strength of political parties. This was evident in 2014 when Clive Palmer, leader of the Palmer United Party, referred to the Chinese as "mongrels" and "Chinese bastards" who shoot their own people. Senator Zhenya Wang, also known as Dio Wang, who was born in China and was elected in 2013 as a Palmer United Party senator for Western Australia, made no comment in response to the tirade of his party's leader against people from his country of birth. Clearly, Palmer's intemperate comments placed Senator Wang in a difficult position, especially because, given his obvious Chinese appearance and ancestry, there was a widespread expectation that he would stand up publicly for Chinese Australians when the need arose.

After receiving thousands of angry letters from Chinese community members, Senator Wang, while acknowledging their expectations, downplayed the importance of his Chinese background: "I think [what the Chinese community] expect of me is to do a fair job and not screw it up to give others in the Chinese community a chance at politics. It's only fair that I try my best to represent them but in the end I am here to represent [Western Australia]" (quoted in Chan 2014a).

Senator Wang's response emphasizes the difficulties ethnic representatives face in the expectation that they adhere to strict party discipline, even though they might not share the positions of the party or its leader on particular issues. In another example, a respondent observed the added pressures she did not have to contend with as a representative with European origins: "We have got a man for city council, [a] Taiwanese man. He says, "I want to represent our people, but I also want to represent everybody,' so it is almost as though they have to give a stronger message that they are representing everyone than I would. I go to all these multicultural events and they feel very pleased that I am representing them, and it is like these people [immigrant and ethnic minority representatives] have to be more than that."

In his research on Chinese representation in Australia, Kwok (2013) has found that the tense relations between mainland Chinese and Taiwanese Chinese in communities and associations could make it especially difficult for representatives with origins in mainland Chinese or Taiwan to represent both groups satisfactorily. Kwok observes that, despite these challenges, communities of immigrants from Taiwan, Hong Kong, and China have an exceptional capacity to unite on social and domestic issues in support of their representative. Given Australia's strong two-party system, characterized by internal party discipline, the ability of representatives to respond to immigrant and ethnic minority concerns might depend on the salience of the issue on the party's agenda (Klüver and Sagarzazu 2016).

In an environment where political parties compete for votes by strategically emphasizing some policy issues while downplaying others, parties often take their cues from voters by responding to the issue priorities of the broader electorate (the riding-the-wave theory) (Ansolabehere and Iyengar 1994). Political parties also might respond only to issues on which they are considered to be competent (the issue-ownership theory) (Budge and Farlie 1983; Petrocik, Benoit, and Hansen 2003). The interview examples demonstrate the difficulties for immigrant and ethnic minority MPs and senators in being responsive to ethnic concerns if they are of little interest to the party or the broader electorate.

Party-Political Barriers to Immigrant and Ethnic Minority Representation

As previously mentioned, a significant factor influencing the low participation of immigrants and ethnic minorities in Australia's two-party system is the strong role of political parties. Although discrimination is not a problem for all groups, parties often rely on perceptions that can be quite different from the reality of discrimination within electoral districts. A candidate preselected to contest a safe and contestable seat still needs to deal with discrimination and racial prejudice among the electorate throughout the campaign. Without detailed polling in each district, however, there is a lack of clarity about whether putting forward an immigrant and ethnic minority candidate would result in a political party's being penalized. Consequently, members of immigrant and ethnic minority groups are often selected for unwinnable seats and, therefore, seldom elected to the House of Representatives, even though immigrant and ethnic minority candidates are often highly suitable for preselection in winnable seats. One MP discusses the phenomenon in the following way:

> I honestly believe there are some great potential candidates out there that are just phenomenal. If we decided we were seriously going to find five, we could do it, but I don't think it would happen because the factional system would get in the way, because they would want someone who was in one faction or another. They demonstrate this by being in a faction for a while and bringing in numbers, and so you get the numbers players more than anything else.

Sobolewska (2013) has argued that, in the United Kingdom, political parties and party elites frequently act as gatekeepers or facilitators of ethnic minority political inclusion. In Australia, Jupp (2003) has similarly observed, factions in parties continue to have a significant influence on the recruitment of immigrant and ethnic minority candidates.

For instance, when asked about the role of factions in deciding who should be selected, one MP observed:

> The factions are still there. I mean, I think it is probably breaking down in terms of personal relations, but you still get situations. For example, there was one time when I was running for something, and three people said, "yes, we will support you," and then the next day they came back and said, "actually, we are not allowed." I'm going, oh, in my faction I can vote for anyone I like. But in their faction they could not. I was the one they would have supported, but they did not have support within their faction. So you still get particular seats which belong to this faction or that faction, and that is all about conference positions and ministerial positions and that sort of thing, so that creates a significant problem for ethnic diversity as well.

Another MP referred to the role of gatekeepers in exploiting new arrivals: "Unless people are organized by MPs, one finds that both political parties are having real trouble getting anyone to join, let alone getting involved. New arrivals are often exploited by factions in the political parties in struggles, rather than joining spontaneously out of civic interest."

In reflecting on how Australia compares to other similar societies, one respondent attributed the absence of "non-white" immigrant and ethnic minority representation in politics to the overall branch structure of the respondent's party and the lack of leadership:

> I think the strategy to get ethnic minorities preselected is different, and it actually needs to have leadership within the branch structure. I think something really radical needs to happen. I don't think that there is enough. There isn't like a target for individual seats – for example, look, this area has 60 per cent Chinese, we need to attract the best candidate, and why don't we have someone from a Chinese background? I actually think we are really lagging behind Canada. In Canada, they give the hardest ministries to ethnic minorities. It is great. Unlike in Australia, where they are just given token spots here and there. Instead they are given areas of big responsibility.

Even though it appears there has been a conscious effort in Canada to select visible minorities for contestable seats in the House of Commons, Erin Tolley suggests that the success of visible minority MPs might have had more to do with generally more positive attitudes towards immigrants and ethnic minorities, rather than any conscious effort on the part of the major parties (see Dharssi 2015). Indeed, in the 2015 Canadian federal election, the proportion of visible minority candidates elected to Parliament reflected the share of such candidates running for election, suggesting the existence of a broader cultural shift in social attitudes.

In deciding who would be suitable, party gatekeepers in Australia often rely on perceptions of social attitudes and the possibility of racial discrimination within the broader electorate. In the words of one MP, "Sorry, I'm not denying there's a bit of racism, too – the parties do think twice sometimes about putting forward ethnic minority candidates." This form of indirect discrimination results in different outcomes in terms of descriptive representation between the House of Representatives and the Senate. The Senate's electoral system gives party leaders more room to take risks if they feel an ethnic candidate for a seat in the House of Representatives would be penalized at the ballot box:

> A former politician once said, "you Liberals will never learn, you put your 'wogs' in the upper house and your Anglos in the lower house." And I think that theory today in Australia is still correct. Why? Because Anglo men and women appeal to the vast majority of the electorate, and multicultural Australia historically doesn't know any different. But if you put up [an Asian name] here, it appeals to a very small minority, and creates what I would consider unfortunate discussions in terms of tolerance in the broader community, which is sad but true. And the two questions are, where does the person come from, and what is their religion? There is still both open and subliminal bias in this country based around race and religion.

The fear of an electoral penalty if a candidate with a non-Anglo surname is put forward was expressed by several respondents. For example, one recalled: "There was one person we were encouraging to think about standing, Mr Wang Zhang Wei.[13] He's now the national president of his ethnic community in Australia, and I recall, when we were talking to the party head office and they thought about how you sell the notion of Zhang Wei to the electorate and about whether we could get him to

---

13 Zhang Wei is not his real name.

change his name. You know, this guy has got two kids, his kids go to Catholic schools and all that sort of stuff, community connected, so why not see if we can get him to change his name to 'Billy' or something?"

Adding to this perception that a candidate with a non-Anglo first or surname would penalize a party at the ballot box is the fact that parties are reluctant to adjust because of the perceived lack of electoral incentives. For instance, in referring to the need to recruit candidates with broad electoral appeal, one respondent observed: "Selectors do the numbers based on ethnicity, and if they're doing numbers based on ethnicity, they are not talking about putting a person in that represents everybody." Another respondent reflected on his own experience of gaining from the negative effects of discrimination and racial prejudice among the electorate in the following way: "I remember being elected to council myself, which was 1991, and it was me versus an Italian Australian and a Croatian Australian, and at the polling booth I had people coming up to me and saying, I'm voting for you because you're the white man." There is also a perception that ethnic minority candidates would not represent the interests of ethnic groups not their own. One respondent, for example, stated: "I actually think quiet racism or unintentional racism is everywhere. If you run – and again, I know this to be right; it shouldn't be – but if you run a Lebanese candidate, for example, which the Liberals did, the Chinese won't vote for them. And nor will the older Indian immigrants that have been in the area longer." Such constraints represent significant challenges for political parties, as they have to contend with the perception of racial prejudice and ethnic discrimination not only within society more generally, but also within and across ethnic communities.

A further constraint is that descriptive representation is best achieved when racial or ethnic minorities are geographically concentrated and represented on a constituency basis. This is because political parties are more likely to select minority candidates in seats with high concentrations of ethnic minorities (Saggar and Geddes 2000). Yet few federal electoral districts in Australia have large concentrations of ethnic communities; instead, ethnic communities tend to be densely populated in local government areas that are spread across different federal electoral districts. For example, Vietnamese are densely concentrated in the outer western suburbs of Sydney – in Fairfield (17 per cent) and Bankstown (8 per cent) – due to a large number of high-rise apartment buildings in a geographically small area. Indian immigrants are spread out across western Sydney, but densely concentrated in the suburbs of Strathfield (9 per cent), Holroyd (9 per cent), Parramatta (9 per cent), and Blacktown (8 per cent). Several respondent MPs identified the lack of ethnic concentration in federal electoral districts as a significant barrier for ethnic minorities' being elected or their ability to mobilize votes, compared to other settler countries:

> The government has to get a majority of voters, not just niche markets, right. The parties have to gain a majority or broad spectrum of people, and it is compulsory. In the United States, interest groups can basically be overrepresented, including concentrated ethnic groups, so if you have got a lot of Koreans in South San Francisco, they are going to be politically relevant if they can be mobilized, do you know what I mean? It is a lot easier in the United States in that way I think ... and because it isn't compulsory, if you can get your people to think, well, Mr Wong is running and Mr Wong will help us when he gets there, then that provides an incentive.

> The real difficulty is that you're talking about a majority system where you've got single-member electorates. For a proportional system in the states and for the Senate, I would say the selection of an ethnic candidate absolutely would make a material difference to the votes. For single-member electorates, I just don't think so. I don't think that is possible.

In Canada, due to higher concentrations of ethnic constituents in numerous ridings – in some cases, more than 50 per cent – political parties traditionally have been more strongly motivated to court their votes. Since the early 1980s, political strategists in the major parties have recognized the significance of ethnic minorities in particular areas (Stasiulis and Abu-Laban 1991); in the 2011 federal election, up to forty swing ridings had sizable ethnic minority populations, and the Conservative Party specifically targeted up to ten of these seats (Payton 2012). In the United States, parties similarly court black, Latino, and Asian voters due to their high concentrations in particular districts and their long history of mobilization and experience in party-political work.

Experience as a Barrier to Immigrant and Ethnic Minority Representation

The lack of experience in party-political work is perceived as a key barrier to the selection of ethnic minority candidates in national-level politics. In *Politics as a Vocation*, Max Weber (1965) first described the process of "political professionalization," which has since become a universal trend in Western democracies (Borchert 2003). Gaining a career in the national legislature and, ultimately, a spot at the cabinet table is usually the primary goal of would-be politicians who rise through the ranks, usually beginning with involvement in local-level politics. Australia's party-political system rewards those who have worked for a party at the grassroots level over an extended period, indicating an overall pattern of the professionalization of party politics, while the roots of the political class in the Commonwealth Parliament are firmly within the major political parties, and traditionally have been drawn from within the ranks of the Australian-, British-, or Irish-born (McAllister 2003, 37).

The requirement in Australia of participation in party work over a long period naturally disadvantages those in new and emerging communities who have not had time to establish professional networks or the necessary social and political capital to enter politics. This is demonstrated in the following commentary, where, in reflecting on why there is no momentum inside their party to improve ethnic representation, respondents observed the following:

> There is no reason why we don't run ethnic minority candidates. There is no reason why parties wouldn't have done better in the Senate, except that I would say, as an insider in the party, that quite often when they do look at who they might put up for the Senate from one ethnic background or another, it is actually a person who has been working within the party, not in the broader community.

> It is much harder to get preselected federally than it is to get preselected in any other sphere of government. There are fewer positions, there are about thirty federal seats in my state, about eighty-nine state seats and there are literally hundreds of councils. So it is firstly a scarcity issue, the more scarce something is, the harder it is to get preselected. Therefore, you must have a combination of very good luck and a body of support behind you in that party … and that is something that takes a long time to do.

Another respondent indicated the importance of participation at the local branch level and an overall demonstration of commitment to the party over an extended period, particularly if one is to be considered for preselection: "In the [Australian Labor Party] it is rare for someone to get preselected if they haven't been involved in the party over a period of time. So there is a party process you have to go through. You join branches, you get involved, you support campaigns and you go to fundraisers. You know, you are part of the party, and that can be either through your branch engagement or through your union engagement." One respondent acknowledged that the requirement of experience as either a party member or employment in the party did not always produce the most suitable candidate: "For me, in my seat, the people who would put their hands up first and who would be front runner would be people who spent the previous five or six years playing the politics of the party. I personally would not pick them. I would pick others but I would not pick them. They would put themselves forward, they have created structures, and they have given themselves titles."

Relating to experience is the expectation that, to be preselected, candidates need to develop a reputation and identity working outside the party in the local area. One respondent observed that this was important if one intended to be preselected for the House of Representatives, even more so than for the Senate:

> People join political parties and use the parties as their way of developing status, and quite often they are the ones who end up getting preselected or being on the list for preselection when they have no status outside the party. Their status that entitles them to run comes from within the party … and we have Anglo people in the party who are like that as well. Traditionally, within the party, Anglo people like that end up in the Senate, that is where they go. They don't end up in the lower house because in the lower house you actually have to win your seat. I suspect that when the Australian people vote for a person who speaks with an accent, or clearly comes from a subcontinent country or whatever, even if they are born here, that vote will be easier if that person has a status of their own, outside of the party.

Studies in the United Kingdom have similarly found that voters' preferences for candidates are driven by evidence of long-term experience working within the local community. For example, Campbell and Cowley (2014) find that voters are likely to rate the candidate's occupation and place of residence as an important shortcut when evaluating a list of candidates. Other studies have also shown that, with the decline in partisanship and class alignment, voters are increasingly likely to look to candidates' local neighbourhood experience or professional occupational characteristics (Denver et al. 2002; Denver and Hands 1997; Johnston et al. 2004; Russell et al. 2007).

In my interviews with Australian MPs, the importance of long-term neighbourhood experience – active membership in a range of community, religious and sports organizations – was clearly evident. One MP, reflecting on his own success in politics, felt that the personal experience of living among his electorate, over several generations, and being involved in the local community was crucial: "And I am completely typical of people in my electorate, irrespective of whom they vote for. I have grown up there, went to school there, played sport there, go to church there, my kids are now doing the same, my parents did the same before me. You know, I have got good grassroots – three generations of networks that span the length and the breadth of the electorate. When I do speak out on something, from a personal perspective, it often will strike a chord strongly with the clear majority of the electorate."

Some groups, however, have been waiting longer than others to become descriptively and substantively represented in the Commonwealth Parliament. Growing strength in numbers appears to have worked well to increase the political representation of racial and ethnic minorities from Europe, but not necessarily that of minority groups such as the Vietnamese and Chinese. Rather than pointing to the constraints in the electoral landscape, some MPs felt that the main reason for the lack of representation of some ethnic minority groups was unwillingness of some groups to get involved in politics:

> My point with a lot of the communities is that the Greeks, the Italians, the Turks, whose arrival was principally late 1940s, 1950s and 1960s, have actually been pretty successful but it took them twenty years. The issue with other groups such as the Vietnamese, historically, is an unwillingness to involve themselves in organizations, particularly when uniforms are involved. This is a real issue for them because of the nature of what that meant back home, regardless of your politics. We do see that.

> We have got a culture of engaging with a political party. If you are from a country where it is dangerous to engage with a political party, or it is something that only a certain group of people do, if you are from the less egalitarian country, if you haven't got a family history or a civic history of knowing that people do this all the time, then I can see why joining a political party wouldn't be the first thing that would come to mind. It is not the sort of thing that just occurs to you.

> Parties are hopeless at giving opportunities to people. You have got to really fight for opportunities in political parties. They are not just given to people, and so if you have got cultural or linguistic impediments to

> engage with the structure or with the people, then that is just an added obstacle, an added barrier to getting those opportunities. No one just gets an opportunity in a political party. You must be forthright.

> Some communities are not as desirous to become politically active. I think in the 1970s immigrants were very politically active. It was a very dynamic period and it did inspire a lot of people. Today it's very different.

> Yes, look, the Chinese don't come in. Again, the longer they have been here, the less they come. The Chinese don't very much at all. The subcontinent does a lot. The Indian community in particular does a lot.

A local candidate from a South Asian background confirmed the effect of homeland politics and cultural barriers. Although cultural pressures did not stop him from wanting to go into politics, in the interview he raised them as a constraint that he needed personally to overcome: "When I rang my mother and said, look, I am running for local council, I thought that she would be excited, but rather than congratulate me, her first reaction was to ask who got me involved in politics. The connotation was that I was doing something bad; I was getting involved in something bad because all this back home is very bad. It means you have to be a master of thugs and all this sort of thing. So the understanding is that good people don't get into politics."

Despite such constraints, are parties doing all they can to encourage racial and ethnic minorities in their communities to see themselves represented in democratic politics? Is the lack of representation due to individual barriers or to the lack of opportunities for minority groups within political parties? As the following respondent observed:

> The question is whether candidates are not coming forward or the political parties are not giving space for the candidates to come forward. There has got to be an opening there to be able to put your hand up for something. I think political parties can do more work in the space, I really do, but I would like to see more work to encourage candidates from diverse backgrounds to come forward, and I am not sure if any political party is doing that very well at the moment.
>
> You know, because they arrive in Australia without their networks, sometimes it is only later that you realize that they have run government departments in three continents and their father was a politician and they have been in politics all their life, but they don't bring any of that with

them. Unless you look for it, you don't find it. So sometimes they remain invisible, and that is a casual and unintentional form of racism.

One way to encourage immigrant and ethnic minority candidates to come forward and for political parties to recruit, nominate or select more such candidates would be through the adoption of racial or ethnic quotas, which could help overcome existing barriers of casual or unintentional forms of racism. Such quotas have already been introduced in more than twenty countries (Htun 2004; Krook and O'Brien 2010; Reynolds 2005). The adoption of gender quotas, in addition, could improve outcomes for ethnic minority women, whose representation is abysmally low (Hughes 2011, 616; Mansbridge 1999).

Quotas and party strategies to improve representation are often introduced as a fast-track way to address the uneven balance in national legislatures of politically underrepresented groups, which can lead to unprecedented historical leaps in their representation (Dahlerup and Freidenvall 2003). In some cases, party competition can create a chain reaction where, once one party has implemented strategies to increase the numerical representation of an underrepresented group, rival parties will feel pressured by the much higher numbers and seek to emulate it (Matland and Studlar 1996). Although many culturally diverse countries have adopted quotas, laws, or policies to rectify persisting racial or ethnic inequalities, in Australia diversity quotas, either in the form of reserved seats or voluntary party quotas, are widely unpopular in political parties. As one MP respondent argued, "Our political system doesn't require attention to quotas. It's kind of an open [policy], well open, and in a sense it is what makes us stand out a lot, so I don't think we necessarily need to look to the Canadians or the Americans, I think we're very different." Although MPs and senators acknowledged that Australia has persistent racial and ethnic inequalities that are institutional or culturally based, it seems there is little momentum within the country's political parties to rectify these inequalities either by actively seeking and recruiting minority candidates or by introducing laws, policies, or strategies to increase their number in politics.

Conclusion

In summary, the interviews revealed that, despite Australia's strong party system, there is a great variety of views among MPs towards immigrant and ethnic minority representation. Overall the respondents were upfront about the existence of discrimination and racial prejudice in their party and in society more generally. In some cases, there was discomfort with the way things are and an acknowledgment that parties are not doing enough to encourage racial and ethnic minorities to put themselves forward as potential candidates. In other cases, MPs felt that there was nothing to be concerned about because Australia differs from Canada and the United States and, as such, the introduction of policies and legislation aimed at encouraging greater cultural diversity in its political institutions was unnecessary.

Talking about race and ethnicity with MPs in the Australian Parliament was admittedly a fraught domain. It generated uncomfortable conversations about Australia's history of racial discrimination, when skin colour and other racial characteristics were used to insult, ridicule, and harass people because of their physical differences. It also encouraged interviewees to reflect on the extent of inclusiveness in their own party and whether enough was being done to reach out to culturally and politically marginalized communities. On the one hand, there was a sense of defeatism about the strong role of political parties and the role that factions and party gatekeepers play in blocking the entry of immigrant and ethnic minority candidates. On the other hand, personal experiences of immigrants and ethnic minorities among their own constituents as politically disengaged, inappropriately strategic, inexperienced, and constrained by homeland cultural and political origins provided fertile ground to attribute responsibility elsewhere for the obvious representation gaps in Australian politics.

Even though overt forms of racism based on skin colour are decreasing, the significant gap in politics between the descriptive representation of those with European origins and those without suggests that underlying, low level, but pervasive forms of discrimination persist in Australian society. In the absence of a "liberal wave," immigrants and ethnic minorities will continue to face considerable social and political barriers to entry into Australia's political class. The next chapter examines whether these common experiences of social and political exclusion are enough to generate in Australia the kind of "pan-ethnic consciousness" that exists in Canada and the United States and that could be an important resource for mobilizing immigrants and ethnic minorities around important policy issues.

Chapter Five

Pan-ethnic Identity and Political Behaviour

Immigrants and ethnic minorities are underrepresented in national-level politics in Australia compared to their situation in Canada and the United States. Several historical, contextual and party-political factors explain differences among the three settler countries; however, it is commonly thought that political underrepresentation might be closely correlated to electoral conditions that make it difficult to mobilize immigrants and ethnic minorities or to the absence of a collective political identity on the part of these groups that might be mobilized. To examine this proposed explanation in more depth, in this chapter I focus specifically on Asian immigrants and ethnic minorities as a group, which, although they are collectively the fastest-growing racial group in all three settler countries, have achieved lower levels of political representation in Australia than in either Canada or the United States.

As discussed in Chapter 1, international research has identified the existence of shared political identities among immigrant and ethnic minority groups through the study of partisanship, voting behaviour, and political preferences. Even though the average citizen holds several identities based on age, class, gender, and religion, evidence from cross-national studies suggests that common experiences of social, cultural, and political disadvantage disproportionately affect some immigrant and ethnic minority groups more than others. For example, "non-white" or "non-Western" immigrants in Australia appear to be more exposed to negative stereotyping and to institutional forms of social exclusion (Booth, Leigh, and Varganova 2012). Before a future that is characterized by the political inclusion of diverse immigrant and ethnic interests can be achieved, however, a key question to be addressed is whether a "pan-ethnic" identity or broad pattern of distinctive political behaviour can be mobilized to meet the needs and circumstances of immigrant and ethnic minority groups.

Partisanship and Pan-ethnic Politics

Asian pan-ethnicity in Western democracies has emerged as a new field of inquiry. Several recent works have noted that, even though present-day Asian immigrants in settler societies are heterogeneous with respect to their national origins, they still represent a meaningful category when it comes to political behaviour (Heath et al. 2013; Wong, Lien, and Conway 2005). Earlier studies of Asian pan-ethnicity in Australia suggested the possibility of a pan-ethnic political identity based on a shared experience of racialized exclusion (Ang et al. 2000). Do Asian immigrants and ethnic minorities with diverse migration histories and socio-economic backgrounds share a common political identity?

Some key aspects of the Asian experience of political exclusion in Australia might be expected to have produced similarities in voting behaviour and issue preferences. First, Australia did not fully open its immigration program to Asian immigrants until 1975, more than one hundred years after the Chinese first arrived in the New South Wales and Victorian goldfields and once it became clear that the White Australia policy had to be rejected in the interests of Australia's foreign policy interests.[14] Although some concessions were made for non-European business immigrants before this time, on the whole immigration policies were aimed at preserving a homogeneous population. Immigrants from the British Isles were favoured because they were viewed as being able to integrate more quickly.

Second, although the first generation of refugees from Southeast Asia had access to citizenship rights, they had little in the way of social capital or political resources, resulting in significant socio-economic disadvantages among both the first and second generations. Despite some evidence of socio-economic mobility, discrimination remains a significant constraint for those from "non-white" ethnic minority backgrounds. Third, as discussed, Australia's electoral and strong party systems have resulted in lower levels of representation of Asian immigrants, particularly in single-member, majority-minority districts. Finally, compared

14 For example, anti-Chinese riots occurred at the Burrangong goldfields in Young, New South Wales, in 1861, and a violent attack at Lambing Flats, New South Wales, in 1905 forced about a thousand Chinese miners to flee the area.

Table 5.1. Respondents, by Birthplace, 2013 Australian Election Study

Birthplace	Respondents	
	(per cent)	*(number)*
Australia	78.5	2,819
UK/Ireland	9.0	322
Other Europe	6.0	214
Asia	6.6	238
Total	100.0	3,593

Source: 2013 Australian Election Study.

with other minority groups in Australia, Asian immigrants from a variety of national origins share common experiences of discrimination because of their skin colour, ethnicity, or religion (Markus 2013).

Some of these experiences are shared by ethnic minorities in, for example, the United Kingdom, which also has a significant Asian population. Saggar (2016, 63–4) finds that ethnic minorities – which in the United Kingdom broadly speaking refers to immigrants and their offspring from Commonwealth countries such as India, Pakistan, Bangladesh, and those in Africa and the Caribbean – are more likely to experience discrimination and racial prejudice, social and economic disadvantage, their educational qualifications and skills are more likely to deliver lower outcomes in labour markets, and they tend to have poorer health experiences than their white peers.

Whether pan-ethnic identity matters might depend on the size and power of particular immigrant and ethnic groups in electoral politics. For example, where such groups are large and mobilized, one might expect ethnic party formation or ethnic bloc voting for an existing party that champions the interests of ethnic groups alongside other group interests (Chandra 2011). To determine whether immigrant and ethnic minority groups display distinctive voting behaviour, this section draws on findings from the 2013 Australian Election Study, focusing specifically on comparisons between first-generation immigrants from different groups (the numbers of second-generation immigrants in the AES are too small for reliable comparisons).

Table 5.1 shows the number of respondents born in each of the broad categories used for comparison. In each of these categories there is a great deal of variation in terms of socio-economic background, age, length of stay, and country of origin. The table shows there were 238 Asian-born respondents who participated in the 2013 AES. Drawing on this sample, the following analyses in this chapter explores whether

Table 5.2. Party Identification, by Birthplace, Australia, 2013

	Australia	UK/Ireland	Other Europe	Asia
	(per cent of respondents)			
Liberal-National	43.3	40.1	37.4	26.0
Australian Labor Party	34.7	37.9	44.9	41.6
Minor party	10.0	10.9	7.5	4.2
No party	12.0	11.2	10.3	28.2
Total (n)	(2,819)	(322)	(214)	(238)

Source: 2013 Australian Election Study. The question was: "Generally speaking, do you usually think of yourself as Liberal, Labor, National or what?"

pan-ethnic and internally heterogeneous groups such as the Asian group selected from the AES share an over-riding political identity with shared attitudes and behaviour.

An important aspect of political identity is party identification, which is central to explaining how people vote in democratic countries (Campbell et al. 1960). This is particularly the case in Australia, where party identification remains an enduring explanation of electoral behaviour. Australia's complex electoral system places several demands on voters in terms of the amount of information they need to absorb. Compulsory voting in state and federal elections requires Australian citizens to participate in a poll on average nearly every eighteen months using a variety of majoritarian and proportional representation systems, as in the elections for the House of Representatives and the Senate in the Commonwealth Parliament (McAllister 2011). To cope with this complexity, voters often rely on party identification.

Table 5.2, which presents data on party identification, shows that in 2013 Asian immigrants were significantly less likely to identify with the Liberal-National coalition than were people born in Australia, the United Kingdom, and elsewhere in Europe. Those born in the United Kingdom were 14 per cent more likely to identify with the Liberal-National coalition than were Asian immigrants, who were also slightly less supportive of minor parties, with only 4 per cent doing so. By far the biggest difference between the comparison groups is not in levels of support for the Australian Labor Party, as is often assumed, but in the numbers of respondents with no party identification at all: just over 28 per cent of Asian immigrants had no such affiliation, compared with between 10 and 12 per cent of respondents in all other categories.

In looking at differences by country of origin, Table 5.3 shows that, although immigrants from the five main Asian source countries were

Table 5.3. Party Identification, by Asian Birthplace, Australia, 2013

	India	China	Vietnam	Malaysia	Philippines
	(per cent of respondents)				
Liberal-National	30.5	23.3	28.1	31.5	29.2
Australian Labor Party	44.8	25.3	54.4	32.9	44.4
Minor party	1.0	4.7	1.8	9.5	7.0
No party	23.8	46.7	15.8	26.0	19.4
Total (n)	(105)	(150)	(114)	(73)	(72)

Source: 2013 Australian Election Study. The question was: "Generally speaking, do you usually think of yourself as Liberal, Labor, National or what?"

more likely than those born in Australia and Europe not to identify with any party, immigrants from China were the most likely (47 per cent) not to do so; immigrants from Vietnam were the most likely (54 per cent) to identify with the Australian Labor Party.

There are several explanations for these findings. The fact that so many Asian immigrants who participated in the study did not identify with a political party might be linked with a perception of discrimination and resultant feelings of alienation and disengagement from national politics. This might especially be the case for immigrants whose early years in Australia were the mid- to late 1990s, when racism targeting Asian immigrants was widespread in the Australian media and political landscape. A further explanation might be the invisibility of Asian immigrants in the House of Representatives.

Immigrants' cumulative exposure to Australian politics might be expected to lead to increasing identification with a party over time, but even among Asian immigrants who had lived in Australia for several decades, a high proportion (over 20 per cent) still did not identify with any political party (Figure 5.1). The proportion increased with new arrivals, of whom up to 40 per cent did not identify with any party. In contrast, only 13 per cent of newly arrived immigrants born in the United Kingdom did not identify with a party; it is possible that such immigrants are more familiar with Australia's political traditions and find it easier to transfer their political loyalties from one country to the other (Pietsch and McAllister 2016). Immigrants from countries with political systems dominated by a single party, such as China, Vietnam, Malaysia, and Singapore, might have more difficulty developing an attachment to a party within Australia's two-party system (Pietsch 2015). This does not, however, explain why, as Table 5.3 shows, 24 per

Figure 5.1. UK and Asian Immigrants' Lack of Party Identification, by Length of Residence, Australia, 2013

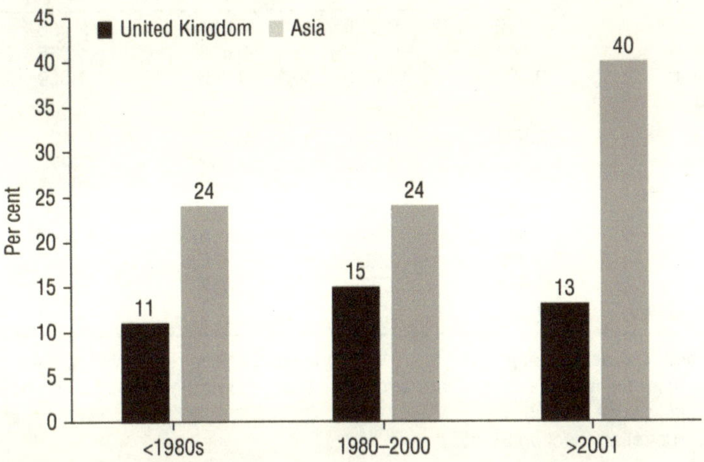

Source: 2013 Australian Election Study.

cent of immigrants from India and 19 per cent of those from the Philippines, both of which have multi-party systems, did not identify with a political party.

Length of stay and experience of discrimination have been identified as possible reasons for the lower levels of party identification among Asian immigrants than among immigrants from the United Kingdom. A long-established literature demonstrates, however, that the interests and motivations of immigrant voters can be explained by traditional class-based theories (Saggar 1998, 2000, 2016). Based on previous studies of race, ethnicity, and party identification, it is anticipated that race and ethnicity will fall away as significant determinants of party identification when other important variables, such as class, length of stay in the host country, and social background, are taken into consideration.

To explore this in more detail, the model presented in Table 5.4 includes a range of independent variables that are likely determinants of party identification. The findings reveal that, to a statistically significant degree ($p = 0.004$), Asian immigrants are more likely than immigrants born in the United Kingdom and elsewhere in Europe to have no party identification at all. The difference holds up as significant even adjusting for several other variables that predict party identification, such as length of stay, class, and social background. Most important,

Table 5.4. Estimating the Probability of Having No Party Identification

Race	B	SE.	Sig.	Exp(B)
Asia	0.899	0.311	**0.004**	2.456
Discrimination	−0.064	0.152	0.673	1.066
Year of arrival	0.009	0.011	0.393	1.009
Background				
Education	0.525	0.279	**0.060**	1.69
Income (scale)	−0.022	0.022	0.332	0.978
Occupation (scale)	0.005	0.006	0.403	0.995
Age (in years)	−0.014	0.011	0.220	0.986
Gender	0.395	0.249	0.113	1.485
Urban	0.246	0.266	0.356	1.279
Constant	−20.612	22.006	0.349	
Nagelkerke r square	0.161			

Note: **statistically significant at p < .01, *p < .05, two-tailed. Logistic regression results showing parameter estimates and standard errors predicting the probability of having no party identification at all. N=525.
Source: 2013 Australian Election Study.

being Asian in Australia is revealed to be an important predictor of the absence of party identification.

In general, it is expected that people's vote choice will follow their party identification (Heath et al. 2013). It is anticipated that Asian immigrants are more likely to vote for the Labor Party or to have no party preference. For those who do not identify with a political party, it might also be the case that, at election time, they have become disillusioned with the party with which they previously identified: in the 2013 general election, following national trends, slightly more than 46 per cent of Asian respondents voted for the Liberal-National coalition and 12 per cent voted for a minor party.

The figures in Table 5.5 suggest that those who do not identify with a party are inclined to vote for a party, rather than place no mark on their ballot paper, with only 2 per cent of Asian immigrants casting an informal vote. At the 2013 federal election, 46 per cent voted for the Liberal-National coalition, 40 per cent for the Labor Party, 12 per cent for a minor party, and 2 per cent registered an informal vote. Whether the Liberal-National coalition will retain the loyalty of these voters remains to be seen. Clearly, however, there are parallels between partisanship and the vote among Asian immigrants. Despite a broad national swing to the Liberal-National coalition, Asian immigrants were still the most

Table 5.5. Voters' Preferences, 2013 House of Representatives Elections, by Birthplace

	Australia	United Kingdom	Other Europe	Asia
	(per cent of respondents)			
Liberal-National	47.5	46.1	42.2	46.4
Australian Labor Party	31.5	31.5	36.6	40.1
Minor party	19.4	21.5	16.9	11.8
Informal vote	1.6	0.9	4.2	1.7
Total (n)	(2,815)	(321)	(213)	(238)

Source: 2013 Australian Election Study.

Figure 5.2. Trends in Labor Party Voting at Federal Elections, Australia, 1993–2013

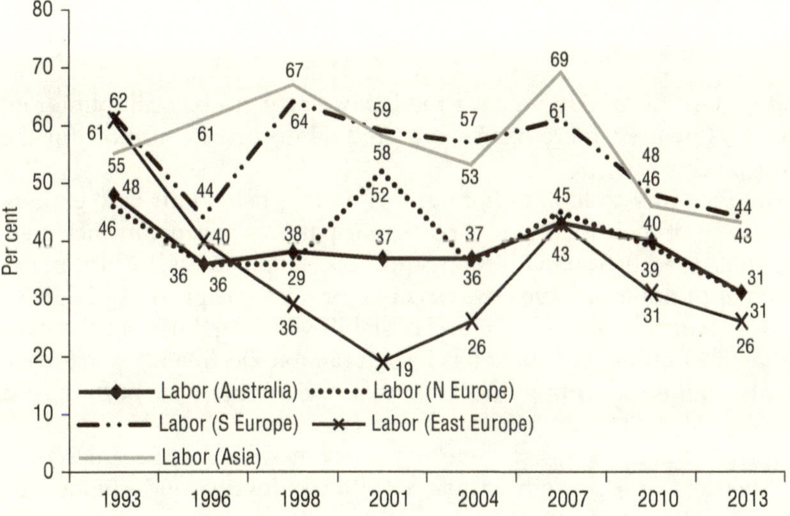

Sources: 1993–2013 Australian Election Study. The question was: "In the Federal election for the House of Representatives on [date], which party did you vote for first in the House of Representatives?"

likely to vote for the Labor Party, a finding similar to that in the United Kingdom, where ethnic minorities historically have been more likely to vote for the Labour Party, which is perceived as more liberal on issues of immigration and more welcoming of ethnic minorities (Saggar 2016, 71). As Figure 5.2 shows, immigrants born in Asia and southern Europe have been consistently more likely than those born in northern

Table 5.6. Patterns of Lifetime Voting for the Same Party, by Birthplace, Australia, 1993–2013

	1993	1996	1998	2001	2004	2007	2010	2013
	(per cent of respondents)							
Australia	56	52	49	47	47	43	53	50
Northern Europe	54	46	44	49	45	44	47	52
Southern Europe	67	59	54	54	58	38	68	59
Eastern Europe	40	52	50	38	63	44	50	36
Asia	64	57	46	36	44	38	51	43
Total (n)	(2,966)	(1,796)	(1,865)	(1,979)	(1,969)	(1,873)	(2,214)	(3,955)

Sources: 1993–2013 Australian Election Study. The question was: "Before this current Federal election for the House of Representatives, had you always voted for the same party, or had you sometimes voted for different parties?" The figures report those who stated that they "always voted for the same party."

and eastern Europe to vote for the Labor Party. Among all immigrant groups, however, there has been a gradual decline in support for the party since 2007.

Another way to look at immigrants' voting behaviour is to explore the extent of their loyalty to a particular party over time. In each election year, the Australian Election Study asks respondents, by birthplace, whether or not they have always voted for the same party. As Table 5.6 shows, there has been a high level of stability among those born in Australia and Europe, but there has been a notable decline (21 percentage points) in lifetime voting for the same party among those born in Asia (see also McAllister 2011, 52).

These findings suggest there is some potential for the emergence in Australia of a pan-ethnic Asian political identity, underpinned by lower levels of party identification and similar voting patterns indicating a higher likelihood than other groups of voting for the Labor Party. The mobilization of this identity would allow for a pan-ethnic stand on social policy issues such as citizenship, care for the aged, family visas, and racial and ethnic discrimination, to name just a few. Asian voters collectively are also more likely to prioritize certain major policy issues more than does the rest of the population. For example, the 2013 AES found that Asian immigrants were more likely than other major groups to value the election issues of taxation, the economy, and education as extremely important and less likely to view the issue of asylum seekers as important (see Table 5.7).

Table 5.7. Issue Preferences of Voters, by Birthplace, Australia, 2013

	Australia	UK/Ireland	Other Europe	Asia
	(per cent of respondents)			
Economic issues				
Taxation	32.6	34.9	39.6	55.4
Management of the economy	69.3	79.8	70.7	76.3
Industrial relations	29.2	30.9	32.8	31.8
Immigration and asylum seekers				
Immigration	44.5	47.9	43.1	43.3
Refugees and asylum seekers	48.5	52.4	39.6	39.7
Environmental issues				
Environment	43.0	44.3	38.9	41.4
Global warming	32.6	34.2	33.5	30.6
Carbon tax	36.3	38.1	35.8	35.3
Health and education				
Education	62.7	67.4	58.0	71.8
Health and Medicare	68.8	75.9	77.4	71.4
Total (n)	(2,770)	(307)	(208)	(234)

Source: 2013 Australian Election Study. Percentages are of those who replied "extremely important" to the question, "In deciding how you would vote in the election, which was most important to you?"

Why, then, has this potential for a shared political identity with similar policy preferences not yet led to group pressure for greater policy sensitivity to the needs and circumstances of Asian immigrants and ethnic minorities in Australia? Their relatively low levels of party identification perhaps represent a degree of detachment and alienation from Australia's party system and from politics in general. Alternatively, it is possible that neither of the major parties has offered a clear policy platform that represents the aggregate interests of Asian immigrants. For example, the declining support of Asian immigrants for the Labor Party might reflect their concerns about the party's positions on issues they are more likely to prioritize, such as taxation and the management of the economy. While supportive of the Labor Party's stance on education, Asian immigrants are more than twice as likely as the rest of the population to favour reducing government expenditure in most policy areas, a view more consistent with that of the Liberal Party.

According to Ratcliff (2017, 237), Australia's major political parties traditionally have been characterized as interest aggregators representing different constituencies. For instance, the Liberal-National coalition traditionally has represented the middle class and owners of capital, while the Labor Party has represented workers and, since the 1980s, immigrants from non-English-speaking backgrounds. It is possible that it has now become difficult for both the Liberal-National coalition and Labor to meet the interests of, say, highly skilled middle-class Asian immigrants, particularly those who operate their own business, who might prefer the Liberal-National coalition on economic policies, but Labor's stance on education. Pan-ethnic organizing might be less effective in Australia than in Canada or the United States because ethnic groups in Australia tend to organize along the cleavages that dominate the wider party system when average group preferences do not align along the same issues. To help us further understand this phenomenon, in the next section I look at how pan-ethnic organizing is achieved in the United States and Canada.

Pan-ethnic political organizing appears to be much stronger in the United States than in Australia even though the two countries have similar Asian immigration histories. The spate of research on the political behaviour of Asian Americans in the United States reveals that, even though present-day Asian Americans are heterogeneous in terms of their national origins, they represent a meaningful category when it comes to racial classification and political participation. As with Asians in Australia, Asian Americans are significantly less likely to identify with conservative politics, with only 15 per cent identifying with the Republican Party (30 per cent of "white" Americans do so), while 46 per cent had no party identification at all in 2008 (Ramakrishnan et al. 2012).

In the United States, the civil rights infrastructure provides the platform for building solid racial and ethnic blocs, of which there are no equivalents in Australia. Asian political behaviour in the United States is shaped by a shared experience of discrimination, as it has been in Canada and Australia, but there is more evidence of political mobilizing among Asian voters in the United States (Khalid 2016; Ramakrishnan 2016). Some of the reasons for this have been discussed in earlier chapters, such as the fact that racialized exclusion of Asian immigrants ended sooner in the United States than in Australia, and was never as firmly entrenched there as it was in Australia through its White Australia policy. Political citizenship was available to Asian immigrants in the United States in the 1950s, whereas it was not open to most Asian immigrants in Australia until 1969, and then only to those who could read and write English proficiently. Party organizations are stronger and more influential in Australia than in the United States, which makes it difficult for minorities to break into party structures that are steeped in tradition.

Greater support for Democrats than for Republicans among Asian Americans also can be attributed to several push factors from the Republican side, such as anti-immigrant and anti-Muslim rhetoric and the rise of Christian conservatism. The 2012 Pew survey for instance, found that Asian American support for the Democratic Party was strongest among Hindus, Muslims, and those who claim no religious affiliation. The Democratic Party has also boosted its outreach to Asian Americans – for example, in 2009 President Barack Obama established the White House Initiative on Asian Americans and Pacific Islanders and nominated a number of Asian Americans to cabinet posts (Ramakrishnan 2016).

In a similar pattern of voting behaviour to that found in Australia and the United States, in Canada Asian immigrants are much less likely than the rest of the population to identify with a political party. The 2011 Canadian Election Study revealed that 36 per cent of Canadians born in Asia did not identify with any political party, compared with 20 per cent for the rest of the Canadian population. Asian immigrants in Canada are similarly more likely (47 per cent) to identify with a party on the left of the political spectrum (Fournier et al. 2011).

Another finding is that both Asian Australians and Asian Canadians are less likely than Asian Americans to mobilize through a process of pan-ethnic group-based collective action. There are three possible explanations for the lower levels of pan-ethnic organizing in Canada and Australia. First, the sheer size of the Asian American population, compared with much smaller numbers in Canada and Australia, allows greater opportunity for political coalition-building across ethnic groups. Second, unlike in Canada and Australia, in the United States the civil rights infrastructure has generated a framework for political coalition-building across communities of divergent ethnic origins with shared political concerns. Third, pan-ethnic political organizing in the United States is often motivated by a perception of inequality within a racial hierarchy in which Asian Americans have generally been perceived to be somewhere in the middle, between whites at the top and blacks at the bottom (Feagin 2001). In Canada and Australia, racial and ethnic groups are not stratified in a top-down hierarchy, even though there is evidence of a hierarchy in terms of ethnic and political stratification. Canada, in fact, stands apart from both Australia and the United States in having depoliticized immigration as an issue: unlike in the other two countries, no major political parties in Canada have engaged in recent years in anti-immigration rhetoric, shifting immigrant voters towards left-of-centre parties (Winnick 2015).

Group Size and Concentration

One of the most significant differences between Australia and the two North American countries is their respective size and geographic concentration of immigrants and ethnic minorities in electoral districts. For example, contributing to the more enhanced political integration of minority interests in Canada is the greater electoral strength of immigrants and ethnic minorities in the country's single member plurality electoral system. This has been enabled by the geographical concentration of immigrant groups in politically important urban ridings. Within this electoral system, minorities can capitalize on the existence of large ethnic or pan-ethnic voting blocs in swinging ridings. Although Australia, in contrast, does not have many electoral districts with significant groups of pan-ethnic and mobilized voters, a growing number, especially in Sydney and Melbourne, have that potential. In marginal seats, in particular, political representatives are having to pay closer attention to their voters' concerns in order to remain competitive.

One way to observe this phenomenon more closely is to look at the competitive seats in the 2013 federal election with relatively high pan-ethnic concentrations of immigrants (Table 5.8). The findings show that, among seats with more than 30 per cent of the population born overseas, 17 were marginal Labor seats and 8 were marginal Liberal. In several marginal Labor seats – Kingsford Smith, Parramatta, Bruce, Chisholm, Greenway, Isaacs, Moreton – more than 15 per cent of the population was Asian-born. A few marginal Liberal seats – Reid, Banks, Barton – also had a significant population of Asian constituents. Thus, the potential exists in Australia for pan-ethnic political mobilization on social policy issues, such as racial and ethnic discrimination and skilled and family migration, that cross ethnic lines.

Although there is potential for mobilization on pan-ethnic social or political issues, this is still a relatively new idea, and is occurring in the context of Australia's sensitivity to race following the removal of the White Australia policy. In the next section, I explore some of these differences to see why it is difficult for Asian and other "non-white" immigrant and ethnic minority groups to achieve descriptive representation in Australian federal politics.

Pan-ethnic Political Mobilization

The US tradition of grassroots organizing has provided a workable model for Latinos and, later, Asian Americans and Pacific Islanders.

Table 5.8. Population by Birthplace, Marginal Seats, 2013 Australian Federal Election

Seat	Australia	NZ	Pacific Islands	Northern Europe	Southern, Eastern Europe	North Africa, Middle East	Asia	Other	Total
				(per cent)					(number)
Banks	54.6	1.7	1.0	2.7	5.9	3.5	23.7	7.0	147,762
Barton	51.7	1.8	1.0	2.8	11.8	4.9	17.4	8.7	142,067
Greenway	58.5	1.9	1.9	3.8	3.7	3.0	20.2	7.0	154,739
Kingsford Smith	52.6	2.2	0.8	7.2	6.4	2.7	16.3	11.8	157,480
McMahon	53.5	1.5	1.5	2.7	7.7	12.6	12.6	7.9	143,450
Parramatta	44.4	1.7	1.3	2.5	3.0	6.7	30.7	9.5	164,653
Reid	44.9	1.4	0.8	3.2	5.4	4.9	30.1	9.4	166,485
Werriwa	58.0	2.3	4.6	3.5	5.5	4.7	12.0	9.4	148,306
Bruce	44.5	1.5	0.7	4.3	9.0	3.0	28.8	8.3	135,282
Chisholm	53.4	1.3	0.3	4.2	5.4	1.1	27.5	6.8	139,669
Deakin	68.0	1.4	0.3	6.1	3.5	1.0	13.9	5.7	126,671
Isaacs	62.4	1.8	0.6	6.7	5.1	1.5	13.9	7.9	155,990
Melbourne	53.0	2.6	0.2	5.5	3.9	1.8	19.3	13.7	177,631
MelbPorts	58.2	2.8	0.2	8.4	6.2	1.8	9.8	12.6	153,146
Forde	69.3	8.6	1.2	8.1	1.5	0.3	3.3	7.7	144,964
Griffith	67.9	3.8	0.7	6.7	2.5	0.9	8.1	9.4	142,643
Moreton	57.8	3.4	1.4	4.9	2.5	1.4	20.1	8.5	145,978
Oxley	61.9	6.4	2.6	6.8	1.6	1.2	11.3	8.2	144,524
Rankin	61.3	8.2	2.0	5.4	2.0	0.9	9.9	8.8	167,865
Adelaide	64.0	0.9	0.2	6.6	5.3	1.3	13.8	8.0	150,023
Hindmarsh	70.3	0.7	0.2	7.5	6.5	1.0	7.5	6.3	137,653
Brand	63.8	4.5	0.2	17.8	1.3	0.3	2.7	9.3	155,740
Fremantle	63.8	2.8	0.2	11.6	5.7	0.6	6.3	9.1	144,412
Hasluck	62.9	3.7	0.2	12.8	1.9	0.7	8.3	9.5	149,329
Perth	55.3	2.8	0.2	10.3	5.2	1.3	13.7	11.3	145,063
Solomon	66.4	2.1	0.7	5.5	1.9	0.8	10.2	12.4	103,115

Note: The Australian Electoral Commission views a marginal seat as one held by a margin of less than 6 per cent.
Source: 2011 Population and Housing Census.

Latinos initially focused their efforts on institutionalized harassment and police inaction, struggles for better housing, improvements in public education, and access to higher education. More recently, Latino-based organizations and protest groups have focused on issues affecting new immigrants and on unauthorized and undocumented migration (Schmidt et al. 2013, 138). Organizing by Asian Americans and Pacific Islanders gained momentum in the 1960s to lobby against racial oppression (Espiritu 1992; Lien 2001; Vickers and Isaac 2012). Since then, there has been a surge in programs and activities to mobilize Asian Americans politically on common issues that cross ethnic boundaries, such as racialized discrimination and violence, voting rights, affirmative action, labour rights, and bilingual education programs (Lien 2001; Schmidt et al. 2013). In Australia these same issues are either addressed top-down through the Department of Social Services or through government-funded institutions such as the Australian Multicultural Council or the Federation of Ethnic Communities Councils Australia (FECCA). It is this top-down approach that led Vickers and Isaac (2012, 205) to conclude that race relations in Australia are characterized by dependency and marginality.

In the United States, most funding for race or ethnic group interests comes from private sources. It is often suggested that dependence on government funding will dampen grassroots mobilization and political participation. The crowding-out argument, for instance, suggests that government-funded organizations crowd out civil society grassroots organizations, which are not at risk of being co-opted into the dominant political structure. Underpinning this argument is an assumption that smaller grassroots organizations can serve as a counterforce to the unchecked power of government actors. Research also finds, however, that civil society organizations also can play a role in legitimating, rather than challenging, the status quo (Bebbington, Hickey, and Mitlin 2008). For instance, in Australia several ethnic minority community leaders, particularly those with business links, have been able to garner political influence through their financial ties to political parties (O'Malley, Wen, and Koziol 2016). Furthermore, it is also the case that immigrant and ethnic minority groups do not necessarily view participation and direct representation in politics as "co-optation" (Bloemraad 2006b, 178).

In Canada, there have been significant cuts to funding for the Canadian Ethnocultural Council and a history of less dependence on government agencies as the sole source of funding. Minority groups have become more reliant on a mix of government agencies, philanthropic think tanks, and private sources in the absence of a clear peak body (Boucher 2014). It is possible that the diversity of funding sources in Canada has allowed for much greater opportunities for the political participation and representation of minority interests. According to Bloemraad (2006b, 162), however, the model of structured mobilization suggests the opposite – namely, that government support should increase local organizational capacity by providing legitimacy, material resources, and technical support. In this sense the government lays down the foundations for immigrant and ethnic minority groups to expand and organize collectively.

The decline of government-funded support programs for immigrants and ethnic minorities has become a significant problem for Australia since the decline of multicultural citizenship as a model for successful integration (Jupp and Pietsch 2017). Jupp (1993, 1997, 2003) argues that a combination of government restructuring and cuts to the funding of immigrant and ethnic minority organizations has diminished any substantive representation in policy making that such groups might once have had. In support of the structured mobilization argument, the main umbrella organization, FECCA, located centrally in Canberra, just five kilometres from Parliament House, has provided valuable resources for smaller organizations by tracking legislative changes of concern to their members, and by calling upon members to mobilize around particular legislative debates. In this regard, the involvement of these groups in legislation and policy making is perhaps the most effective means by which immigrant and ethnic minority communities can have a meaningful voice in Australian federal politics.

FECCA has been particularly vocal on issues affecting cultural diversity and social equality for immigrants. In the parliamentary inquiry into migration and multiculturalism in Australia, FECCA argued that, as a consequence of political rhetoric discrediting multiculturalism and its emphasis on social justice, racial intolerance is now both more acceptable and less visible because people no longer feel empowered to complain (Parliament of Australia 2013a). Perhaps this points to a larger problem: indications of a sense of denial that racialism still exists in a systematic form (Vickers and Isaac 2012). Table A.1 in the appendix shows the main proposed legislative changes between 2014 and 2016 that FECCA members felt would have an impact on immigrant and ethnic minority groups in Australia, and FECCA's responses to these changes.

On legislative and policy issues relating to a broad array of pan-ethnic related concerns, FECCA has the resources and political capital to mobilize its members and to generate political engagement and participation. Other immigrant and ethnic minority community associations, however, are less able to engage in the political process. This is especially the case for those that focus on meeting the specific welfare needs of their communities. These associations depend heavily on "top-up" government funding, and therefore target their programs in line with government policies aimed at service provision. Grönberg (1993) shows that governments are more likely to cooperate with non-profit organizations in instances where service provision is needed. For example, one of the most successful ethnic service provision organizations in Australia is the Chinese Australian Services Society (CASS), based in the Sydney suburb of Campsie and employing up to 170 full-time staff. Although the CASS initially focused on Chinese communities, its membership has since expanded pan-ethnically to include other Asian communities in Sydney and Melbourne. The organization focuses on six key areas that were once funded by the federal and state governments: child care, health, aging, and disability services; cultural programs; settlement services; community capacity-building; and Chinese-language schools. As a service provider, its role as an advocator is limited, however, by its heavy dependence on government funding. Any criticism of government might result in the withdrawal of funds for important community services. Overall, the CASS's submissions to government focus on lobbying for the subcontracting of affordable housing, child care, language training, and aged care services to smaller, ethnically based service providers.

In terms of service provision, the CASS's approach is highly effective, as the ethnic or pan-ethnic community organizations most likely to be funded are those that focus on social welfare and service provision, rather than on political concerns. This is part of an overall trend in Australia involving smaller government, smaller bureaucracies, and the subcontracting of government services to non-governmental organizations, which, in terms of multicultural services, risks co-optation and depoliticization, whereby groups might be reluctant to mobilize politically on sensitive issues or in areas of particular concern to racial and ethnic minorities, thus limiting their capacity to advocate on their community's behalf (Bloemraad 2006b; Chaves, Stephens, and Galaskiewicz 2004).

A much smaller but more political organization is the Chinese Australian Forum (CAF), established in 1985 to provide the Chinese and other Asian communities with a voice in the political process on sensitive and potentially divisive issues such as race relations, immigration, citizenship, discrimination, multiculturalism, and social justice. The CAF is an independent, not-for-profit organization that consults with government and political parties on a regular basis. In contrast to the CASS, however, the CAF does not have an administrative office or much in the way of resources – in fact, it often relies on the CASS to provide the facilities to mobilize and lobby government on policy issues. Government support, it appears, is more likely to go to ethnic or pan-ethnic organizations that are apolitical, non-partisan, and prepared to oversee previously government-run services. Nevertheless the process of applying for grants opens up opportunities for networking with government representatives and policy makers and the capacity to raise concerns about various settlement, cultural, immigration, and humanitarian issues that otherwise might not gain attention on the overall legislative and policy agenda, where interest groups compete for attention.

Aside from political organizations, there is a great deal of ethnic community and associational life in Australia's major cities in the form of ethnic and social clubs, many of which receive small amounts of government funding for festivals or special events through competitive grant schemes. The scholarly literature on social capital and pan-ethnic self-organizing suggests that the funding of immigrants' associations is beneficial for the political incorporation of immigrants and ethnic minorities by providing institutional channels for their participation in policy making (González-Ferrer and Morales 2013; Morales and Giugni 2011). The capacity of these associations to engage in the policy process often depends, however, on significant financial funding and human resources (González-Ferrer and Morales 2013), which are not readily available for most ethnic associations in Australia. Despite such limitations, a few ethnic associations are providing the necessary social, political, and financial resources for the preselection of local candidates, particularly at the local and state levels, where the selection of ethnic minorities is more likely.

At the local level, constituency engagement in ethnic and community associations is important in improving a candidate's chances of preselection. It is perhaps one reason immigrants and ethnic minorities from European backgrounds, with their longer history of involvement in ethnic community associations, have achieved higher levels of descriptive representation. European immigrants traditionally organized around work and employment conditions through the trade union movement, another pathway into politics in Australia. Between 1947 and the 1970s, European immigrants were mainly working class, and found homes in neighbourhoods close to large factories, while their leaders in ethnic community associations were middle class. For example, in the early 1970s in Sydney and Melbourne, Greek, Jewish, and east European communities were very active in ethnic community associations (Jupp 2007). Several MPs from immigrant European backgrounds interviewed for this book mentioned that they were initially involved in an ethnic community association or a trade union, which then facilitated their transition into national politics.

Notwithstanding the progress made among European immigrants' in transitioning from ethnic organizations or trade unions into politics, most such organizations have limited involvement in political affairs, and focus instead on providing opportunities for their members to connect with one another and with the broader Australian community. For instance, in Canberra a long list of clubs and associations is an important source of social capital for immigrants and ethnic communities, including the Australia Croatia club, the Polish White Eagle Club, Spanish Australian Club, Russian Canberra, Canberra Irish Club, Canberra Swiss Club, Hellenic Club, Austrian Australian Club, and Harmonie Germany Club. Other associations aim at forming links between ethnic and religious communities and the rest of Australia, such as the Chinese Australian Historical Society, the Australian Turkish Cultural Platform, Brazilian Association of Canberra, Canberra Africa Association, and Canberra Islamic Centre.

Further complicating the role of associations and ethnic advocacy groups in mainstream politics is the extent of associational fragmentation across Australia, particularly on home-country political issues. Community representatives are often concerned about having one individual leader speak on their behalf, especially on contentious home-country issues that have divided ethnic and religious communities. It is perhaps for this reason that FECCA chooses not to comment on immigrant and ethnic minority homeland issues, so as to maintain the trust of ethnic communities across Australia. But it is not only home-country politics that can fragment ethnic communities. For example, within the Chinese communities, the Hong Kong and Singapore-born Chinese, who have higher socio-economic status on average, tend to support the Liberal Party; mainland Chinese and Indonesian Chinese, however, with generally lower socio-economic backgrounds, tend to support the Labor Party (Kwok 2013).

The perception of major points of difference in party loyalties and the potential for conflict over home-country issues – such as the cross-strait tensions between mainland Chinese and Taiwanese Chinese – has implications for ethnic community associations. On the one hand, interest in home-country politics can provide the necessary glue for political mobilization; on the other, in the Australian context, involvement in home-country politics has the potential to undermine bridging forms of social capital based on cross-ethnic alliances. In short, ethnic candidates and representatives, unless they run as an independent, are frequently under considerable pressure not only to take the party line, but also not to take sides on home-country issues.

Conclusion

Where ethnic groups are relatively small and dispersed, pan-ethnic mobilization is essential for the political participation and representation of immigrants and ethnic minorities. There are, however, possibilities for pan-ethnic political organizations in Australia to achieve policy sensitization, designed to better meet the needs and circumstances of different groups. Overall, the potential for political mobilization is underpinned by groups' distinctive political behaviour and their growing numbers in densely populated electoral districts in inner cities and metropolitan areas across Australia.

The question, therefore, is why pan-ethnic groups have not used this potential to the same extent as such groups have in Canada and the United States. In those two countries, immigrants and ethnic minorities are supported by a strong multicultural framework and by the cumulative experience of grassroots civil society movements that have grown in size and diversity and accumulated considerable social and political capital. Without such a framework, ethnic associations and organizations with limited financial capital struggle to gain influence in mainstream politics in Australia.

One possible avenue for participation in mainstream Australian politics is through political party membership. Immigrants and ethnic minorities often find it difficult, however, to break into a party-political culture that has become increasingly professionalized and dependent on long-established community networks and ties. Similar findings in the United States reveal that mainstream party organizations are not always critical sources of mobilization for "non-white" immigrants (Jones-Correa 1998; Lien, Conway, and Wong 2004). Adding to this is widespread disaffection for political parties more generally as a suitable mechanism by which citizens can participate in politics. Therefore, government intervention in activities that build both social and political capital and advocacy capacity would help ensure a diversity of voices of immigrants and ethnic minorities in the political process. The receipt of public funds would enable ethnic organizations to survive and to join large umbrella organizations such as FECCA, which has the capacity to monitor legislative changes that affect immigrants and ethnic minorities.

Chapter Six

Home-Country Politics and Political Attitudes

Interest and participation in politics is a necessary precondition for the political inclusion and representation of immigrants and ethnic minorities in national-level politics. One of the recurring themes raised in the interviews with Australian political representatives is the enduring influence of the ties that immigrants and ethnic minorities retain with their countries of origin, irrevocably influencing their levels of political interest and participation in politics. One way this can be examined in more depth is by looking at levels of interest in Australian and home-country politics, as well as other political attitudes and behaviour, such as levels of political knowledge, trust, and efficacy.

People migrate for many reasons. They bring with them not only their labour skills and capital, but also a variety of political histories, skills, and learning experiences that can have an influence on their levels of political interest and engagement in politics. For example, those who enter under a skilled migration program, as opposed to those accepted for humanitarian reasons, are often more likely to maintain positive ethnic and political ties with their country of origin, which might influence the process of their political integration into their country of destination. This group is exemplified by recent skilled immigrants from India and China to Australia, Canada, and the United States, who in many cases have come from the highest echelons of their respective societies and might have benefited from the regime in their country of origin (Bueker 2005). By contrast, those migrating as refugees and asylum seekers are often fleeing political persecution, and are thus unlikely to be supportive of the political regime in their country of origin.

Some highly skilled and family immigrants might have been enabled by the political circumstances of the regime in their country of origin to progress in terms of socio-economic mobility before their decision to migrate. Others, however, might have decided to leave, or been forced to leave, because they faced persecution or were dissatisfied with the government. Although skilled immigrants are, in general, likely to have an active interest in and engagement with politics in their home country, that engagement might be characterized by political activism against – or disappointment in – the ruling home-country elite, rather than by support for the regime. Once settled in their new country, however, immigrants' interest in their home-country politics is expected gradually to diminish and for engagement in the politics of the host society to grow, especially for those who are unable to return because they fear persecution.

Even though people from non-democratic countries might not want to return to their home country or show much interest in its politics, it still might take time to become fully comfortable with the democratic politics of their new country because of the enduring influence of their political socialization. Research has shown that political orientation is often shaped by the premigration experience of growing up in an authoritarian country (Bilodeau, McAllister, and Kanji 2010; Jacobs and Shapiro 2000; Linz and Stepan 1996; Pietsch and McAllister 2016; Stevens, Bishin, and Barr 2006). Children and youth often receive the authoritarian and democratic values of their society through family, educational, and political institutions, and, in the process of their migration, carry their political learning from one political setting to another. Consequently one might expect those who emigrate from democratic countries to be better able to understand and become more engaged with the democratic politics of their new country.

The societal and political-institutional context of the receiving country is also an important influence in both the maintenance of old political orientations and the formation of new political orientations. As Østergaard-Nielsen (2003, 767) observes, "only the crudest analysis would ascribe political orientations among immigrants to the agency of the sending country." For example, as mentioned in Chapters 3 and 5, a country that encourages multiculturalism might encourage the engagement of immigrants and ethnic minorities in politics by giving resources to community organizations. Canada exemplifies this in its policy of multiculturalism, which encourages the retention of ethnic identity, viewing it as compatible with Canadian identity. The opportunity structures in a host society also might determine immigrants' and ethnic minorities' sense of either optimism or pessimism about their future economic and social well-being, which, in turn, might influence their political orientation. In general, even among new immigrants who are not financially well off, a vision of a brighter future can instil confidence in the host-country government and engender a positive political outlook. On the other hand, immigrants who feel that their future is bleak might be less likely to demonstrate much interest in politics.

Finally, experience of racial or ethnic discrimination in the host society can diminish any sense of belonging and willingness to engage in its politics. As I discuss in more detail in Chapter 7, Asian immigrants in Australia are more likely to have experienced discrimination and unfair treatment than are immigrants of European origin. It is unclear, however, if the experience of discrimination holds as a significant determinant of political orientation once other premigration experiences are considered. These factors might interact with the likelihood that immigrants will cleave to home-country politics and thus delay the process of their political integration into the new society.

Interest in Politics

Within any group there are always some who are entirely disengaged from electoral politics, for reasons related to lifestyle factors such as study, work, or family commitments and the availability of free time, or to the lack of civic skills such as English-language ability or an understanding of how politics works in practice (Verba, Schlozman, and Brady 1995, 289). Are there other factors, however, that might disproportionately affect the disengagement of immigrants and ethnic minorities from Australian politics?

An advantage of compulsory voting in Australia is that voters are not only exposed to party symbols, but also required to think about alternative party policy platforms and make an informed political decision. Whether this leads to a greater sense of empowerment and support for the voting system, however, is another matter. Table 6.1 shows that those born in the British Isles were the least likely among the different comparison groups to support compulsory voting, while 47 per cent of Asian-born immigrants strongly favoured compulsory voting. In the absence of compulsory voting, however, it is predicted that British/Irish and other European immigrants would be more likely to vote than would immigrants from Asia. This suggests that Asian immigrants might not feel a sense of efficacy or empowerment when it comes to exercising their vote. In addition, Australia's voting system is one of the

Table 6.1. Support for Compulsory Voting, by Birthplace, Australia, 2013

	Australia	UK/Ireland	Other Europe	Asia
		(per cent of respondents)		
Strongly favour compulsory voting	50.1	43.0	46.2	47.0
Definitely would have voted if voting was not compulsory	67.1	69.7	60.4	51.2
Total (n)	(2,798)	(321)	(212)	(236)

Source: 2013 Australian Election Study.

Table 6.2. Interest in Politics, by Birthplace, Australia, 2013

	Australia	UK/Ireland	Other Europe	Asia
		(per cent of respondents)		
Discuss politics with others in person	75.7	74.0	69.7	68.6
Discuss politics with others online	13.4	12.0	14.0	20.6
Total (n)	(2,748)	(308)	(196)	(228)

Source: 2013 Australian Election Study. Percentages are of those who answered "frequently" or "occasionally" to the question, "Here is a list of things some people do during elections. How often did you do any of these things during the recent election?"

most complicated in the world, with different electoral systems operating at state and federal levels that immigrants from non-English speaking and non-democratic backgrounds are likely to find more difficult to navigate (McAllister 2011; McAllister and Makkai 1992).

The 2013 AES (Table 6.2) also revealed an untapped potential of engaged, yet possibly disempowered, voters: during the 2013 federal election campaign, more than two-thirds of Asian immigrants discussed politics with others in person; moreover, Asian immigrants were more likely than other groups to discuss the election with others online. The study also asked a series of questions to determine if immigrants had an interest in the politics of their home country. As Table 6.3 shows, Asian and UK/Irish immigrants were more likely than those from the rest of Europe to maintain an interest in home-country politics, while Asian immigrants were slightly less likely than other immigrants to have an interest in Australian politics. Immigrants from Vietnam had the least interest, but among immigrants from India there was a very high level of interest in Australian politics, with 77 per cent reporting they had a "good deal" or "some" interest.

Table 6.3. Interest in Home-Country and Australian Politics, by Birthplace, Australia, 2013

	Interest in Home-Country Politics	Interest in Australian Politics	Total
	(per cent of respondents)		*(number)*
Australia	n.a.	80	2,813
UK/Ireland	44	85	316
Other Europe	30	80	213
Asia	48	74	236
India	59	77	112
China	67	53	152
Vietnam	46	47	119
Philippines	46	66	74

Sources: 2013 Australian Election Study and 2013 National Survey of Asian Australians. The percentages given are of those who indicated "a good deal" or "some" in questions relating to their interest in politics.

As Table 6.3 indicates, paying attention to the politics of their country of origin does not appear to be associated with whether immigrants and ethnic minorities take an interest in Australian politics. It is possible that, in the Australian context, compulsory voting has generally promoted a healthy engagement in politics, whether in immigrants' countries of origin or in Australia. Another finding is that immigrants from China and India demonstrated a much higher level of interest in what was happening in their birth country than did immigrants from Vietnam and the Philippines.

Several background factors might account for the differences in levels of political interest among immigrants and ethnic minorities in Australia. Most Indian immigrants are among the very recent wave of highly educated and skilled from India and have good English-language ability. They have also come from one of the world's largest democracies, and thus are likely to be familiar with elections and democratic processes. Filipino immigrants are also more likely to be highly skilled and well educated, so it is not surprising that they too demonstrate a high level of engagement in Australian politics. They are less interested than Indian immigrants, however, in political events in their country of origin, perhaps related to entrenched corruption and money politics in the Philippines (Aspinall and Sukmajati 2016).

Chinese immigrants, meanwhile, are a mixed group in terms of skills level, education, and length of stay in Australia. It is to be expected that language barriers might prevent many from developing an interest in and understanding of Australian politics. Unlike India, China – even though it has elections at the local level – is not a democracy where active engagement in politics is encouraged. This could explain why Chinese immigrants are generally less interested in politics. Lack of experience with democratic processes could also explain the disengagement from politics among immigrants from Vietnam. It is possible that growing up in a regime that discourages dissent and provides few opportunities to practise civic skills might discourage people from engaging with the democratic politics of their new host society. Other likely explanatory factors are related to the local context and socio-economic status of many Vietnamese immigrants, who face significant barriers in terms of employment opportunities and who are more concerned with making a decent living for themselves and their families than with engaging with the Australian political process.

In the United States, a similar pattern prevails to that in Australia in terms of the level of South Asian immigrants' interest in domestic politics. Again, research suggests the relatively high level of interest among Indian immigrants might be related to their higher-than-average levels of education and political knowledge of democratic processes. Political interest among Vietnamese immigrants in the United States is high, however, unlike in Australia, where as I explore in Chapter 7, Vietnamese have struggled to gain a foothold in terms of occupational and social mobility.

In Canada the 2011 Canadian Election Study revealed relatively low levels of interest in Canadian politics across the broader population. Interestingly, however, immigrants tend to have much higher levels of interest than the rest of the population. Respondents were asked to rank on a scale of 0 to 10 their interest in the federal election. After pooling all respondents who scored between 6 and 10 as the measure of political interest, only 55 per cent of Canadian-born respondents reported an interest in Canadian politics, while much higher percentages of those born elsewhere did so (Asia, 65 per cent; Europe, 69 per cent; the United Kingdom, 79 per cent). Although the study did not measure interest in home-country politics, these findings indicate that Canada's well-entrenched policy of multiculturalism encourages interest in domestic politics (Bloemraad 2005, 2006b).

Two further enablers in immigrants' maintaining an active interest in their home-country politics are the availability of news media in languages other than English and the wide variety of ethnic community organizations, which allow immigrants to keep informed about

Table 6.4. Use of Non-English News Services, by Asian Immigrants, Australia, 2013

News Source	Respondents Using	
	(per cent)	*(number)*
Media services delivered in a language other than English	37.2	201
Radio	33.3	67
Newspaper	42.8	86
Television	46.3	93
Website	43.8	88

Source: 2013 National Survey of Asian Australians.

Table 6.5. Interest in Country of Origin, Asian Immigrants, Australia, 2013

Level of Interest	Respondents Reporting	
	(per cent)	*(number)*
General interest in participating in ethnic organization in community	37.8	204
In the past 12 months, have you ...		
Closely followed news about politics in country of origin	58.7	263
Sent money to people in country of origin	31.5	170
Paid close attention to Australian foreign policy towards country of origin	43.3	234

Source: 2013 National Survey of Asian Australians.

political developments in their country of origin. In the 2013 National Survey of Asian Australians, respondents were asked if they got their news from media services delivered in a language other than English and, if so, which type of media they used. As Table 6.4 shows, more than a third of Asian respondents said they got their news from a non-English-language service. Television and online services were the most popular options, with 46 per cent using the former and 44 per cent the latter to keep up to date with the latest news from Australia and around the world.

The 2013 National Survey of Asian Australians also asked respondents how much interest they had in participating in ethnic community organizations and in maintaining contacts with relatives, friends, and organizations in their country of origin. As Table 6.5 shows, nearly 38 per cent of respondents indicated an interest in a local ethnic community organization, even though they did not necessarily have time to be an active member. Importantly, in terms of maintaining close social and political ties with their country of origin, 59 per cent said they closely followed news about home-country politics, 43 per cent said they paid close attention to Australian foreign policy, and 32 per cent said they sent money to people in their country of origin.

Similar patterns have been identified in research elsewhere, such as that of Lien (2001, 34), who notes that, in the United States after 1911, Chinese immigrants, while dissatisfied with political developments back home, were keen to strengthen the existing political regime in China and to provide financial contributions for its rebuilding. Ethnic and racial communities frequently have come together over time to work to solve a problem or discuss political developments in their place of origin and, in so doing, also work towards solving a problem in their country of destination. This has been demonstrated particularly in the United States, with its large racial and ethnic minority communities, where, for example, thousands of Asian Americans participated in the armed forces in both World Wars despite government policies of exclusion and discrimination. Participation in home-country political issues in the United States often led to greater involvement in domestic politics, especially as they related to issues of inclusion, citizenship, and equal treatment. Japanese and Chinese immigrants could extract support from their home country and from ethnic communities in the United States in their struggle for social and political equality. According to Lien (2001, 41), their struggle for inclusion "set many precedents in the civil rights, immigration, and naturalization litigation of the United States and, in turn, changed the social structure and identity of the ethnic community." Through their experiences, Asian Americans were able to forge new ethnic American identities that cut across ethnic, class, and religious boundaries.

Political Empowerment and Belonging

Having established that Australia's largest "non-white" pan-ethnic group, the Asian-born, demonstrates an interest in participating informally in Australian politics while maintaining an active interest in home-country politics, the next area of investigation is to find out whether this group's interest in participating in Australian politics is matched with a sense of empowerment and belonging. Based on comparative research in Canada and the United States, the descriptive representation of immigrant and ethnic minority groups in politics has the capacity to improve overall feelings of efficacy, trust, and support with respect to the political system. Conversely, such representation is

Table 6.6. Political Efficacy and Trust, by Birthplace, Australia, 2013

Birthplace	High Political Efficacy	High Political Trust	Total *(n)*
	(per cent of respondents)		
Australia	67	36	2,782
UK/Ireland	62	30	310
Other Europe	61	37	209
Asia	63	41	236
India	72	39	112
China	59	41	151
Vietnam	53	49	119
Philippines	56	54	71

Sources: 2013 Australian Election Study; 2013 National Survey of Asian Australians. The question relating to political efficacy was: "Some people say that no matter who people vote for, it won't make any difference to what happens. Others say that who people vote for can make a big difference to what happens. Using the scale below, where would you place yourself?" Percentages given are of those who chose "4" or "5" on a five-point scale. The question relating to political trust was: "In general, do you feel that the people in government are too often interested in looking after themselves, or do you feel that they can be trusted to do the right thing nearly all the time?" Percentages given are of those who chose "3" or "4" on a four-point scale.

almost impossible if these groups lack such a sense about formal political institutions.

As Table 6.6 shows, there were few differences among the main comparison groups in terms of their levels of political efficacy and political trust, according to the 2013 AES. Looking closer at the effects of birthplace, however, reveals significant differences between immigrants who were born in India, 72 per cent of whom showed high levels of political efficacy, and those born in China, Vietnam, and the Philippines, of whom only 59 per cent, 53 per cent, and 56 per cent, respectively, exhibited such efficacy. Interestingly, Asian immigrants with low levels of political efficacy tended to be more trusting of the political system than were the Australian-born.

It is possible that levels of political efficacy and trust are shaped by levels of political knowledge, especially given Australia's complex voting system and the fact that many immigrants come from non-democratic countries. To determine levels of political knowledge, the 2013 AES and 2013 National Survey of Asian Australians asked respondents six questions about Australian political institutions and processes (Table 6.7). The surveys found that the Australian-born and UK/Irish immigrants were able to answer more questions correctly than were respondents

Table 6.7. Political Knowledge, by Birthplace, Australia, 2013

Birthplace	Political Knowledge (3–6 questions correct)	Political Knowledge (0–2 questions correct)	Total
	(per cent of respondents)		*(n)*
Australia	31	69	2,819
UK/Ireland	36	64	322
Other Europe	25	75	214
Asia	27	73	238
India	44	56	34
China	26	74	50
Vietnam	3	97	31
Philippines	19	81	37

Sources: 2013 Australian Election Study; 2013 National Survey of Asian Australians.

born in the rest of Europe or Asia. The differences were small, however, just 9 percentage points between Asian and UK/Irish immigrants and 11 percentage points between UK/Irish immigrants and those from elsewhere in Europe. Overall, immigrants from Vietnam and the Philippines had more difficulty answering the political knowledge questions than did other immigrants. Interestingly, a much higher percentage of Indian immigrants than the Australian-born could answer the political knowledge questions.

Thus far I have proposed that a range of factors other than the nature of home-country politics can lead to positive or negative political orientations and the likelihood of participating in politics. In summary, previous research has suggested that it is to be expected that the politics of an immigrant's country of origin might delay the development of interest and engagement with politics. Some of these effects might be overshadowed, however, by the positive effect, in Australia, of compulsory voting, which can lead to higher levels of political trust, efficacy, and knowledge. It is also to be expected that experience of an authoritarian regime and contextual factors, such as experience of discrimination and pessimistic economic evaluations, might have a dampening effect on an immigrant's interest in Australian politics. Socio-economic background is also likely to have an influence, as one might, for example, expect immigrants with higher levels of education and English-language ability to show more interest in Australian politics.

The mode of migration is also likely to have an effect on immigrants' interest in Australian politics. It might be expected, for example, that those who arrived as political refugees will be more interested in

Table 6.8. Reasons for Migration, Australia, 2013

Reasons for Migration	Poverty	Family	Freedom	Student
Poverty in country of origin	**0.74**	−0.09	0.13	−0.18
Earn money	**0.71**	0.14	−0.07	0.19
Accompanying or joining family	0.19	**−0.81**	−0.05	−0.08
Better life	0.31	**0.73**	−0.02	−0.10
Persecution in country of origin	0.08	−0.07	**0.80**	0.00
Freedom	0.28	0.21	**0.61**	0.34
Turmoil in country of origin	−0.19	0.01	**0.47**	−0.25
To be a student	−0.04	−0.03	−0.02	**0.89**
Eigenvalue	1.32	1.27	1.26	1.06
Variance explained *(%)*	16.45	15.83	15.74	13.28

Note: The table presents the results of a factor analysis using a varimax rotation of items in the Australian Election Study on reasons for migration.
Source: 2013 Australian Election Study.

Australian politics than those who arrived as students. Table 6.8 presents the results of a factor analysis that shows the reasons for migration. Factor analysis is useful for examining broader themes or concepts that are not easily measured with single items (or in this case reasons for migration). Four main concepts emerged. The first concept, "poverty," includes two items, "poverty in country of origin" and "earn money"; the second concept, "family," includes "accompanying or joining family" and "better life"; the third concept, "freedom," includes items relating to "persecution" and "turmoil in home country"; and the fourth concept is a single item, "student."

The next stage of the analysis is to look at whether interest in home-country politics influence an immigrant's level of interest in Australian politics after controlling for a range of other individual and contextual factors. The regression analysis presented in Table 6.9 shows that interest in home-country politics and Australian politics is not mutually exclusive. In fact, the more interest immigrants and ethnic minorities have in political events in their country of origin, the more likely they will show an active interest in Australian politics. Political efficacy also matters – that is, the more immigrants and ethnic minorities feel that their vote will make a difference, the greater their interest in Australian politics. For the Asian-born, the reasons for their migration and their English-language ability are also important factors. An important finding is that political interest can be influenced by whether immigrants have experienced discrimination or unfair treatment, as I discuss in

Table 6.9. Factors Affecting Asian and European Immigrants' Interest in Australian Politics, 2013

	Asian Immigrants		European Immigrants	
	Interest in Australian Politics			
	(b)	(beta)	(b)	(beta)
Constant	23.27		12.92	
Political resources				
Interest in home-country politics	0.19	0.25***	0.16	0.20**
Political trust	0.02	0.03	0.05	0.07
Political efficacy	0.17	0.24***	0.15	0.21**
Political knowledge	0.04	0.09	0.13	0.29***
Democratic satisfaction	0.08	0.08	−0.09	−0.08
Democratic experience	0.09	0.06	0.20	0.12
Contextual-level factors				
Experience of discrimination	−0.13	0.16*	−0.15	−0.16*
Egocentric economic evaluations	0.03	0.02	0.05	0.04
Sociotropic economic evaluations	−0.15	−0.13	−0.15	−0.12
Individual-level factors				
Length of stay	0.01	0.10	−0.00	−0.02
Reasons for migration				
Poverty	−0.22	−0.14*	−0.10	−0.07
Family	0.12	0.10	0.06	0.04
Freedom	0.23	0.17*	0.11	0.08
Student	0.19	0.09	−0.35	−0.06
Controls				
Gender	0.00	0.00	0.16	0.10
Age	0.01	0.10	0.01	0.11
Education	0.16	0.11	0.21	0.10
English language	0.26	0.24***	0.18	0.12
Income	−0.01	−0.06	0.00	−0.02
Adjusted R^2	0.35			0.23
Total (n)	(190)			(173)

Note: Results are from ordinary least squares (OLS) regression. b: unstandardized regression coefficient. beta: standardized regression coefficient. p value p < .05 = *, p < .01 = **, p < .001 = ***.
Source: 2013 Australian Election Study.

Chapter 7, with such experience associated with lower levels of interest in Australian politics.

Political Origins and Support for Democracy

In terms of overall support for the democratic system, while much is known about the broader Australian population, little is known about the experience of Asian and European immigrants and ethnic minorities and whether engagement with home-country politics has an influence on their overall satisfaction with democracy. There is widespread concern that multiculturalism might undermine the commitment of immigrants and ethnic minorities to the democratic politics of their host countries, and is one reason support for multiculturalism has declined both in Australia and throughout Europe. The analysis presented in Table 6.10 reveals, however, that interest in home-country politics has no effect on immigrants' overall satisfaction with democracy in Australia.

Table 6.10. Effects of Home-Country Politics on Immigrants' Satisfaction with Democracy, Australia, 2013

	Asian Immigrants		European Immigrants	
	Satisfaction with Democracy			
	(b)	(beta)	(b)	(beta)
Constant	2.98		31.40	
Political resources				
Interest in Australian politics	0.09	0.09	−0.07	−0.08
Interest in home country politics	0.00	0.00	−0.03	−0.04
Political trust	0.11	0.16*	0.14	0.22**
Political efficacy	0.04	0.06	0.20	0.32***
Political knowledge	0.02	0.04	0.02	0.05
Democratic experience	−0.21	−0.15*	−0.21	−0.15*
Contextual factors				
Experience of discrimination	−0.07	−0.09	−0.10	−0.12
Egocentric economic evaluations	0.11	0.09	0.03	0.03
Sociotropic economic evaluations	0.13	0.11	0.02	0.02
Individual-level factors				
Length of stay	−0.00	−0.08	0.01	0.13
Reasons for migration				
Poverty	0.07	0.05	−0.04	−0.04
Family	0.00	0.00	0.05	0.05
Freedom	−0.08	−0.06	−0.09	−0.07
Student	−0.18	−0.09	−0.21	−0.04
Controls				
Gender	0.12	0.08	0.02	0.01
Age	0.01	0.11	0.01	0.17
Education	−0.16	−0.11	−0.01	−0.01
English language	0.11	0.10	0.02	0.01
Income	0.02	0.15	0.00	0.00
Adjusted R^2	0.12			0.22
Total (n)	(190)			(173)

Note: Results are from ordinary least squares (OLS) regression. b: unstandardized regression coefficient. beta: standardized regression coefficient. p value $p < .05$ = *, $p < .01$ = **, $p < .001$ = ***.
Source: 2013 Australian Election Study.

Rather, what seems to have a greater effect is a sense of political trust among Asian and European immigrants, those who are more trusting of government are more likely to feel satisfied with democratic politics.

Democratic experience also affects satisfaction with democracy, but not in the way that the literature on the effect of authoritarian political origins would lead one to expect. Immigrants and ethnic minorities with more experience of democracy are less satisfied with democracy in Australia than those from authoritarian countries. This supports the "critical citizen" argument that, although support for democracy as a principle is widespread, many citizens have become critical of the way democracy performs (Dalton 2004). Consequently, those born in democracies are likely to have much higher expectations of government and are more likely to be dissatisfied when governments fail to meet their expectations, particularly in Western countries with struggling economies (Inglehart and Welzel 2005).

Conclusion

Asian immigrants in Australia collectively have the desire to engage and participate in politics to the same extent as European immigrants do, yet they have low levels of political efficacy and thus feelings of empowerment. Barriers to political participation exist for immigrants from some Asian countries, but the prediction that one's immigrant and ethnic background is a significant determinant of one's political disengagement is not born out in the Australian context. If there is no variation among immigrant and ethnic minority groups in their political engagement and participation, questions need to be asked about why levels of the descriptive representation of Asian and other "non-white" immigrants and ethnic minorities in formal Australian politics are low. For example, why is it that Chinese Australians have marginal political status despite high levels of socio-economic achievement and well-developed political networks? From the evidence in this chapter, there is little support for the idea that Asian immigrants are not interested or engaged in politics, as some of my political interviewees suggested; rather, quite the opposite is the case.

Australia's institutional setting of compulsory voting has led to high levels of political interest and trust among immigrants and ethnic minorities, but low levels of political efficacy; compulsory voting also might explain the higher levels of interest in domestic politics among Asian immigrants in Australia than those in the United States and Canada. Contrary to expectations, immigrants from countries with democratic governments are less likely than those from countries with authoritarian regimes to feel satisfied with democracy. High levels of trust and efficacy also contribute to satisfaction with democracy. Importantly, maintaining an interest in home-country politics among those with experience of authoritarian origins has no detrimental effect on their levels of satisfaction with democratic government, as is often assumed.

So far, there is little evidence to suggest that Asian immigrants and ethnic minorities are less likely than their European counterparts to become engaged in Australian civic and political life. There is also little support for the idea that low levels of descriptive representation of Asian Australians can be explained by the much shorter time they have lived in Australia than have their counterparts in Canada and the United States. In fact, length of stay has an effect only in the opposite direction – in other words, Asian immigrants who have lived in Australia longer are *less* engaged in politics than newer arrivals.

One way to address these issues is to look at whether the ongoing experience of discrimination plays a role in discouraging or even blocking the participation of "non-white" immigrants and ethnic minorities in national-level politics. It appears that one major difference between Australia and the United States is immigrants' experience of discrimination, which is a predictor of low political interest in Australia, but appears not to be in the United States (Lien 2001). My interviews with Australian parliamentarians revealed that perceptions of racial and ethnic discrimination in society more generally might be contributing to the reluctance of parties to recruit immigrant and ethnic minority candidates for public office. For this reason, in the next chapter, I examine racial and ethnic discrimination as a critical factor in explaining low levels of immigrant and ethnic minority representation in Australian politics.

Chapter Seven

Discrimination and Unequal Outcomes

Australia, Canada, and the United States differ in their institutional makeup, but they are similar in the sense that, historically, race and ethnicity have been used to discriminate against minorities. The consequences of this history underlie the continuing racialization of "non-white" immigrants and ethnic minorities in all three societies. Although some minorities have managed to join mainstream society through generations of assimilation and socio-economic mobility, others continue to experience the symbolic effects of racialization and discrimination.

This case study has established that, in Australia, Asian immigrants have struggled to enter formal national-level political institutions to a degree not experienced by their counterparts in Canada and the United States. In exploring the reasons for the low representation of Asian Australians, the findings show that several institutional barriers exist, some of which are underpinned by systemic forms of discrimination. It is clear, however, that low levels of Asian political representation do not reflect lower levels of political engagement by Asian immigrants than the rest of the population. This suggests the possible existence of direct and indirect forms of discrimination and racial prejudice that make it difficult for immigrants and ethnic minorities to use their education, skills, and experience. This is especially relevant in an increasingly professionalized political domain, where candidates typically are selected based on such qualifications.

There is no doubt that forms of discrimination and racial prejudice are all too prevalent in immigrant societies. Inequalities based on skin colour are reproduced through a variety of practices stemming from new forms of racism. Although research acknowledges a great diversity of experience among different immigrant and ethnic minority groups, it is still the case that some experience – or perceive they experience – various forms of discrimination and racial prejudice more often than others. In all three countries, Asian immigrants from diverse socioeconomic backgrounds reported experiencing higher levels of discrimination than did European immigrants, which, given their similar skills and qualifications, suggest that ascriptive characteristics and place of origin are the basis of the discrimination Asians face.

The two main types of discrimination are interpersonal (discriminatory interactions between individuals) and institutional (policies or practices embedded in organizational structures) (Karlsen and Nazroo 2002, 64). The latter form in particular is often less visible and difficult to prove because it might be embedded and normalized in the culture and institutions of society. Perpetrators of both types of discrimination often act unfairly towards members of a particular group in order to reinforce relations of dominance and subordination (Krieger 1999). The two are not always mutually exclusive. The forms of racism and prejudice that individuals display might be underpinned by larger institutional values or organizational structures of the society of which they are a part.

Evidence from the Australian Election Study reveals that people from "non-white" backgrounds are more than twice as likely as those of European origin to experience discrimination and/or racial prejudice (see also Markus 2013). This finding suggests that pervasive forms of discrimination and racial prejudice based on stereotypes are possible factors underpinning the participation gap of Asian Australians in national politics. Such stereotypes are one way historical forces affect contemporary life, by being built up over the history of a society and thus influencing how people relate to one another and how they function – for instance, by avoiding situations in which they perceive they will be stereotyped. One obvious place where this is likely to happen is in the political domain, where talk of citizenship, national belonging, and national identity is ever-present. Even though overt forms of discrimination and racial prejudice have been discouraged through various education and legislative reforms, it is possible that people are simply finding new and subtler ways to discriminate.

Perceptions of Discrimination in Australia

In Chapter 3 I discussed the history of racialized discrimination in Australia for much of the nineteenth century and the first half of the twentieth. What might have gone unremarked was the semblance of hope that racial discrimination targeting Asian immigrants and ethnic minorities would cease with the official end of the White Australia Policy in 1973 and the introduction of the Racial Discrimination Act in 1975. Although progressive reform was introduced in the 1960s and 1970s to put an end to racial discrimination, negative stereotypes – often historically produced and based on cultural superiority – are persistent influences. Racial prejudice directed towards Asian immigrants surged in 1998 when Pauline Hanson initiated a national discussion about Asian immigration and multiculturalism. Hanson's One Nation Party polled well in state elections leading up to the 1998 federal election, after which the Australian Election Study asked several questions about whether Australians were comfortable living and working with Australians of Asian origin. Of Australian-born respondents, 63 per cent reported they would be uncomfortable if their boss was from Asia and 67 per cent said they would feel uncomfortable if a relative married an Asian.

During the subsequent decade, the global environment changed considerably. Fears about terrorism in Australia following the 9/11 terrorist attacks in the United States in 2001 and the Bali bombings in 2002 turned negative attention towards immigrants from Muslim backgrounds, many of whom became new targets of public hostility. Racial tension peaked in 2005 when anti-Muslim riots broke out at Cronulla Beach in Sydney that attracted international attention. The vast majority of Muslim Australians are also members of "non-white" immigrant and ethnic minority groups from Asia, Africa, and the Middle East. Several studies have since shown that minority groups from these regions, particularly those of Muslim background, face various forms of racial and ethnic prejudice in their daily lives (Dunn and Forrest 2007; Dunn and Nelson 2011; Dunn, Pelleri, and Maeder-Han 2011; Forrest and Dunn 2007).

To look more closely at the persistence of racial discrimination in Australian society, in the 2013 AES respondents were asked whether they had experienced discrimination in the preceding five years. As Table 7.1 shows, respondents from Asia, Africa, and the Middle East were significantly more likely to have experienced discrimination in the previous five years than were immigrants born in New Zealand, United Kingdom, Ireland, and the rest of Europe. In fact, Asian immigrants were 31 per cent more likely than UK/Irish immigrants and 22 per cent more likely than those born in the rest of Europe to report

Table 7.1. Immigrants' Experience of Discrimination, by Birthplace, Australia, 2013

	UK/Ireland	Other Europe	Asia	Africa, Middle East
	(per cent reporting discrimination in 5 years preceding survey)			
Often	1.3	2.8	9.4	9.4
Sometimes	7.6	14.6	30.5	31.3
Rarely	16.1	23.9	36.5	21.9
Not at all	75.1	58.7	23.6	37.5
Total (n)	317	213	233	32

Source: 2013 Australian Election Study.

experience of discrimination. A high proportion of respondents from Africa and the Middle East (41 per cent) also felt they had experienced discrimination. Similar findings were obtained in the 2013 Mapping Social Cohesion Survey, which asked respondents: "Have you experienced discrimination in the last 12 months because of your skin color, ethnic origin or religion?" Over 40 per cent of respondents from Malaysia, Singapore, India, and Sri Lanka, and 39 per cent from Indonesia, China, and Hong Kong, felt they had done so, compared with only 12 per cent of respondents from the United Kingdom and Ireland (Markus 2013, 23).

Since the 1970s studies on immigrants and ethnic minorities in Australia generally have been limited to examining distinctions between those from English-speaking and non-English-speaking backgrounds. The experiences of immigrants from post-war Europe, however, stem from issues that are very different from those experienced by immigrants from Asia, the Middle East, and Africa, most of whom are fluent English speakers. Post-war European immigrants were largely invisible in politics and other areas of influence throughout much of the 1960s. Their visibility improved little in the 1970s, as many immigrant children from post-war Europe had left school with low attainment levels, attributable to their difficulties with English, and had entered the manufacturing sector. In more recent immigration programs, English-language proficiency has been addressed by a points system that gives preference to applicants with English fluency and high qualifications. This has reduced poor English-language fluency as a reason for discrimination, but concerns about cultural and religious differences now seem to be at the heart of racial and ethnic prejudice.

Australia has more than a hundred different ethnicities, and prides itself as a country that has moved beyond race. As mentioned in

Table 7.2. Perception of Discrimination among Asian Australians, 2013

Nature of Discrimination	Respondents Reporting	
	(per cent)	*(n)*
Unfairly denied a job	10.4	56
Unfairly denied a promotion at work	13.5	73
Unfairly treated by police	10.7	58
Unfairly prevented from renting or buying a house or apartment	4.3	23
Treated unfairly at restaurants or stores	16.3	88
Treated unfairly at airports by customs officials	10.0	54
Been called an offensive name based on race or ancestry	33.9	183

Source: 2013 National Survey of Asian Australians.

Chapter 1, Australia refrains from using racial categories such as "white," "Asian," "black," or "visible minority" in official statistics to identify minorities that might be more vulnerable to discrimination, but if discrimination based on race, ethnicity, and skin colour continues to have a noticeable effect on opportunities for immigrants and ethnic minorities, some form of positive discrimination might be necessary.

The 2013 National Survey of Asian Australians (NSAA) asked several questions about perceptions of discrimination that might have a serious effect on well-being, such as being fired or unfairly denied a promotion. The survey asked respondents whether they had been treated unfairly in Australia because of their own or their parents' Asian background, and to indicate whether they felt they had ever been discriminated against in certain situations. As Table 7.2 shows, in all but one situation, over 10 per cent of respondents reported they had been treated unfairly because of their Asian origins.

The most common form of discrimination, reported by 34 per cent of survey respondents, was being called an offensive name based on race or ancestry, a form of discrimination that stems from practices and beliefs consistent with the oppression of one group by another (Quillian 2006, 301). With the ubiquity of mobile phones with cameras, incidents of verbal racial abuse are now frequently captured by bystanders and circulated for public viewing. In 2014, for example, an Asian Australian woman travelling on an inner-city Sydney train found herself the victim of sudden and unprovoked racial abuse. The incident was caught on camera, but most are hidden from public scrutiny and simply internalized by the victim. Tim Soutphommasane, having experienced racism growing up in Australia and having heard the concerns of many in the community in his role as race discrimination commissioner, observes

Table 7.3. Immigrants' Perception of Discrimination, by Ascribed Characteristics, Australia, 2013

	Perceptions of Discrimination	
	(b)	(beta)
Constant	–23.84***	
Ascribed characteristics		
Race (Asian)	0.45	0.24***
Gender (male)	0.03	0.02
Age (in years)	0.01	0.13*
Resources		
Location (urban)	0.01	0.00
Education (university)	0.07	0.04
Income (scale)	–0.01	–0.10**
English language	–0.14	–0.07
Religious attendance	0.04	0.09**
Year came to Australia	0.01	0.11*
Adjusted R^2	0.23	

Note: Results are from ordinary least squares (OLS) regression. b: unstandardized regression coefficient. beta: standardized regression coefficient. p value p < .05 = *, p < .01 = **, p < .001 = ***. The variables (race, gender, location, education, English language and religious attendance) have been specified in simple binaric dummy variable form. Total N=540.
Source: 2013 Australian Election Study.

that, "those exposed to racist abuse will testify that it can inflict mental and physical harm. It can wound your very dignity as a person. It is something that diminishes people's freedom and their ability to participate in society" (Soutphommasane 2014).

Are Asian Australians more likely than immigrants of European origin to perceive discrimination? Table 7.3 presents an analysis of whether this is so, taking into consideration a range of control factors that might interact with perceptions of discrimination. The dependent variable of perceived discrimination stems from the following question in the 2013 AES: "In the past five years, how often do you feel that you have experienced ethnic discrimination or unfair treatment in Australia?" The study revealed that Asian immigrants are much more likely than others to feel they have experienced discrimination in the past five years.

A considerable body of research in the United States has investigated differences in perceived individual and group-level discrimination. Although Table 7.3 presents findings that relate to perceptions of individual-level discrimination, immigrants might also perceive group-level discrimination. Accordingly, the analysis presented in Table 7.4

Table 7.4. Effects of Immigrants' Characteristics on Perceptions of Prejudice, Australia, 2013

	Perceptions of Ethnic Group Discrimination		*Perceptions of Racial Group Discrimination*	
	(b)	(beta)	(b)	(beta)
Constant	0.18		4.36	
Ascribed characteristics				
Race (Asian)	0.11	0.09**	0.23	0.09**
Gender (male)	0.03	0.03	−0.03	−0.01
Age (in years)	−0.00	−0.08	0.00	0.03
Location (urban)	−0.05	−0.04	0.02	0.01
Resources				
Education (university)	0.12	0.10**	0.37	0.15***
Income (scale)	0.00	0.05	−0.00	−0.01
English language	−0.04	−0.03	−0.13	−0.05
Religious attendance	0.02	0.05	0.01	0.02
Year came to Australia	0.00	0.05	−0.00	−0.04
Adjusted R^2	0.02		0.04	

Notes: results are from ordinary least squares (OLS) regression. b: unstandardized regression coefficient. beta: standardized regression coefficient. p value p < .05 = *, p < .01 = **, p < .001 = ***. The variables (race, gender, location, education, English language and religious attendance) have been specified in simple binaric dummy variable form. Total N=540.
Source: 2013 Australian Election Study.

draws on two items in the 2013 AES that measured perceptions of racial and ethnic prejudice and discrimination. The questions asked were: "Do you think there is a lot of ethnic prejudice in Australia nowadays, a little or hardly any?" and "Do you agree that 'white' Australians are advantaged over others in applying for jobs?" The responses indicated that not only is being Asian a predictor of group discrimination, but so is education.

In contrast to studies in the United States that show low socio-economic status as a predictor of perceived discrimination, having a university education appears to matter most in perceptions of group discrimination. This is undoubtedly because highly educated people from non-European backgrounds are more sensitive to the difficulties inherent in gaining employment than those of European origins. According to Valtonen (2001, 430), discrimination in this context is defined as "a situation in which the immigrant is accorded worse treatment than members of the majority population in spite of the fact that her/his education, qualification and work experience are equivalent to that of candidates from the main population." The results presented in Table 7.4 confirm not only that there are concerns among Asian immigrants about the existence of racial and ethnic discrimination, but also that the discrimination tends to result in more favourable outcomes in employment opportunities for "white" Australians.

In Australia it has been found that, although there are occasional public displays of hostility or racial abuse, the discrimination and racial prejudice that affect levels of socio-economic achievement and overall political integration are, overall, practised much more subtly, and often by well-mannered, well-intentioned people but who prefer to work alongside people who speak and look like them. The outcome of such subtle and more individualized discrimination is that racialized groups often unfairly attribute their failure to themselves, thus reducing their capacity for the collective mobilization often necessary to address racial and ethnic inequalities.

Discrimination and the Professional Class

To be a full member of society, immigrants and ethnic minorities need opportunities not only to participate, but also to shape the future of society by using their education, skills, and experience, all of which are vital for success in the political arena. One significant barrier for such groups is a growing demand for linguistic assimilation in terms of English-language proficiency, as well as the adoption of local accent, style, and pronunciation, which some researchers view as a form of racial discrimination (Colic-Peisker 2005; Creese and Kambere 2003; Hill 2008). Piller and Takahashi (2011, 371) observe, in fact, that "social inclusion policies are often blind to the ways in which language proficiency and language ideologies mediate social inclusion in linguistically diverse societies." For instance, in Australia and other diverse English-speaking multicultural societies, immigrants wishing to attain citizenship must demonstrate language proficiency by passing a citizenship test written in the official language.

In applying for a professional job or position of leadership, some immigrants and ethnic minorities also need to overcome social bias due to attributes such as place of birth, skin colour, and distinctive accent. Although it is not always possible to know a person's place of birth, visible and audible markers such as skin colour and accent are often used to practise social bias (McCrone and Bechhofer 2008). For those with such ascribed characteristics, full social and political integration might be an unreachable goal. Although research has detected a general pattern of upward socio-economic mobility over time, some immigrants and ethnic minorities are less likely than others to experience such mobility, which suggests evidence of discrimination; indeed, some minorities might experience downward mobility because of various social and institutional barriers (Basran and Zong 1998). Weber (1978) referred to this phenomenon as a form of "social closure," whereby one group excludes another from scarce resources so as to maintain the dominant group's privilege and social position.

Research has also found evidence that race and birthplace can influence whether some groups will experience upward socio-economic mobility (Bauder 2003; Frank 2013; Saggar 2016; Weeden 2002). This has been shown to be the case for "non-white" ethnic minorities who, despite having very high levels of education, are particularly vulnerable to discrimination and ultimately exclusion. For example, with an overall shift from unskilled to skilled migration, higher levels of socio-economic status as well as access to professional and managerial occupations are to be expected among first-generation immigrants to Australia. This assumes, however, that skilled new immigrants do not face direct or indirect discrimination in the workforce. Inglis and Model (2007) find that, in contrast to people with European ancestry, "non-white" immigrants and ethnic minorities often remain disadvantaged for several generations. To examine whether this pattern is occurring in Australia, the next section looks at the labour market outcomes – in terms of income and occupational status – of Asian and European immigrants with similar education backgrounds and length of stay in Australia. All things being equal, it is expected that the labour market experiences of the two groups should be similar.

To demonstrate the diverse socio-economic outcomes of European and Asian first-generation immigrants in Australia, Table 7.5 presents comparisons in the education, income, and occupation of three separate immigrant cohorts from the United Kingdom, elsewhere in Europe, and Asia, as determined by Australian census returns. The findings reveal that a higher proportion of immigrants from Asia than from other countries holds a bachelor's or postgraduate degree, which could be attributed to the greater proportion of recent immigrants being highly skilled people who have met the requirements of the competitive points system. Nevertheless, even when the education levels of those who arrived before the 1990s are taken into account, Asian immigrants are still more likely to hold a university qualification than are immigrants from other countries.

Table 7.5. Immigrants with a University Education, by Birthplace and Date of Arrival, Australia

Birthplace	Date of Arrival			
	1990 and Earlier	1991–2000	2001–14	
	(per cent with university education)			*(n)*
United Kingdom				
England	20	30	22	125,778
Scotland	18	32	27	16,388
Wales	23	36	31	4,692
Northern Ireland	21	42	34	3,366
Other Europe				
Italy	5	21	24	7,300
Former Yugoslavia	6	17	12	12,493
Germany	14	28	26	11,016
Greece	5	11	9	4,328
Netherlands	12	31	23	7,061
Ireland	22	37	29	8,535
Poland	23	37	48	10,655
Malta	4	14	12	1,494
Asia				
China	28	41	48	54,866
India	36	58	60	66,376
Vietnam	20	13	17	25,532
Philippines	38	34	36	40,418
Malaysia	48	47	38	25,815
Sri Lanka	34	40	40	19,974
South Korea	40	42	32	10,901
Indonesia	31	44	37	8,445

Source: Australian Census of Population and Housing, 1990–2014.

Given the much higher levels of educational attainment among immigrants born in Asia, one would expect there to be a higher proportion of Asian immigrants than European immigrants in high-income professional occupations, particularly among those groups who arrived in the 1990s. As Figure 7.1 shows, however, two groups from different regions with similar education and period of arrival in Australia nonetheless have diverse outcomes, indicating that some groups face barriers to reaching their full potential. Asian and UK immigrants who arrived in Australia before the 1990s have fairly similar incomes – indeed, over time, Asian immigrants catch up to and even overtake other groups, such as those from other parts of Europe. For new immigrants, the story is very different. Those from the United Kingdom tend to receive a much greater return on their education than do new immigrants

Figure 7.1. Share of Immigrant Citizens Employed in Highest Income Bracket, by Birthplace and Year of Arrival, Australia, 2011

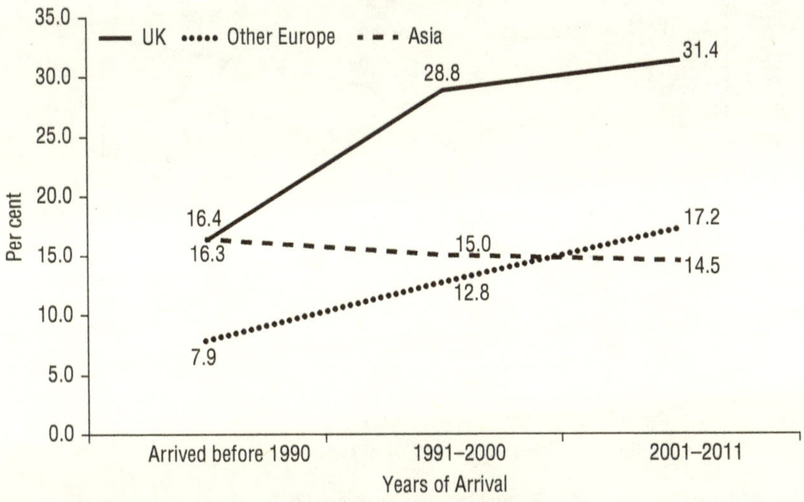

Source: Australian Census of Population and Housing, 2011.

from Asia. Over 30 per cent of recent arrivals from the United Kingdom, but only 14 per cent of new immigrants from Asian countries, are employed in the highest income bracket. The heightened emphasis on English-language ability might explain some of this difference, but since university-educated immigrants from Asia are usually fluent in English, other factors, such as skin colour and accent, likely play a role.

Figure 7.1 looks only at immigrants who have obtained Australian citizenship. Many Asian immigrants, however, are not citizens, but students; as Figure 7.2 shows, only 6 per cent of recent arrivals from Asia without citizenship earn a high income, while 28 per cent of those from the United Kingdom and 19 per cent of those from other parts of Europe do so. Asian immigrants who arrived before 1990 end up doing comparatively better, but it appears that it takes them longer to achieve similar or better outcomes than their European counterparts.

The differences in outcomes might be explained by a number of other factors. For example, it is possible that the Asian immigrants who arrived before 1990 came from different countries than those who arrived later – for example, we might expect those from English-speaking Hong Kong to have better outcomes than recent arrivals from

Figure 7.2. Share of Immigrant Non-citizens Employed in Highest Income Bracket, by Birthplace and Year of Arrival, Australia, 2011

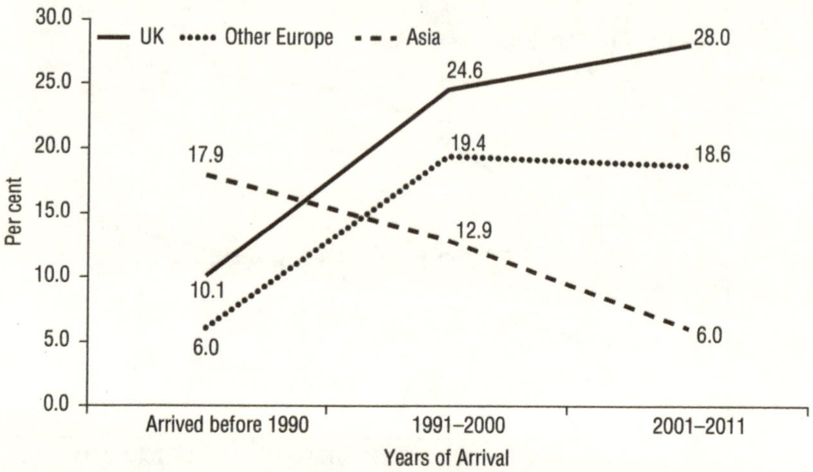

Source: Australian Census of Population and Housing, 2011.

non-English speaking countries in Asia. There are also likely to be differences among those from English-speaking northern European countries and those from countries in southern and eastern Europe where English is much less widely spoken. To explore this in a little more detail, I conducted an analysis, controlling for background factors such as education, age, and gender, to see if there was a correlation between country of origin and income status. From the results presented in Table 7.6, it is clearly evident that immigrants from South Asia and Northeast Asia, as well as those from southern and eastern Europe, are less likely to earn a high income than immigrants from the United Kingdom and northern Europe. Newer arrivals are also less likely to earn a high income than immigrants from previous migration waves.

Up to 45 per cent of the total sample of South Asians and 70 per cent of new arrivals from South Asia had completed a bachelor's or postgraduate degree, compared with 38 per cent of the sample of Northeast Asians and 70 per cent of new arrivals from Northeast Asia. Among northern Europeans, in contrast, only 24 per cent had completed a bachelor's degree or higher, and among the new arrivals only 55 per cent had done so. With such differences in education qualifications between those from Asia and those from northern Europe, one would expect a

Table 7.6. Effects of Immigrants' Characteristics on Income Achievement, Australia, 2011

	Determinants of a High Income	
	(b)	(beta)
Constant	2.61	
Birthplace		
South Asia	−0.68	−0.09***
Northeast Asia	−1.22	−0.16***
Southeast Asia	−0.04	−0.01
Southern and eastern Europe	−0.67	−0.07***
Ancestry of parent 1		
Southern and Central Asia	0.27	0.04
Northeast Asia	0.26	0.04
Southeast Asia	0.39	0.04
Southern and eastern Europe	0.35	0.04*
Ancestry of parent 2		
Southern and Central Asia	−0.17	−0.01
Northeast Asia	−0.38	−0.01
Southeast Asia	0.68	0.02**
Southern and eastern Europe	−0.07	0.00
Language spoken at home		
Southern Asian language	0.44	0.06*
Eastern Asian language	0.59	0.08*
Southeast Asian language	−0.10	−0.01
Southern European language	0.55	0.07***
Northern European language	1.28	0.10***
English proficiency		
Very well or well	1.44	0.12***
Time of arrival		
2000 or before	1.02	0.17***
2001–05	0.71	0.08***
Background		
Age	−0.09	−0.09***
Education	0.53	0.23***
Gender	1.37	0.22***
Citizenship	0.84	0.13***
Adjusted R^2	0.18	

Notes: results are from ordinary least squares (OLS) regression. b: unstandardized regression coefficient. beta: standardized regression coefficient. p value p < .05 = *, p < .01 = **, p < .001 =***. N=11,979.
Source: Australian Census of Population and Housing, 2011.

positive relationship between Asian country origin and income status. Instead, the opposite is the case, indicating the possible existence of racial or ethnic discrimination.

A similar outcome was found in terms of occupational status. Since a higher percentage of immigrants from Asia in the sample had a university education than did immigrants from northern Europe, one might expect a higher percentage of the former to be employed in a professional occupation. As Table 7.7 indicates, however, the opposite is true: immigrants from South Asia and Northeast Asia are less likely to be employed as professionals than those from northern Europe even after controlling for language spoken at home, English proficiency, time of arrival, education, age, and citizenship status. Moreover, the analysis suggests that immigrants from the United Kingdom and northern Europe, despite having lower levels of educational attainment, are more easily able to move quickly into high-income professional occupations after their arrival in Australia.

These findings reveal that there are several barriers to high income and occupational status among new immigrants, even for those with high levels of education, resulting in racial and ethnic labour market segmentation. In terms of income, new immigrants from Asia are less likely to enter professional or managerial positions with a high income than are new immigrants from northern Europe. Because the census survey does not ask if immigrants obtained their educational qualifications in Australia, however, it is difficult to determine, as we will see, if there is an issue with the recognition of overseas qualifications or if racial and ethnic discrimination is affecting the socio-economic outcomes of immigrant groups. As to the former, research in Canada has shown that employers tend to favour immigrants from English-speaking countries with comparable training systems (Hawthorne 2007). Consequently visible minorities often find that their skills are either not recognized or devalued. A similar phenomenon occurs in Australia, given that the qualifications and requirements to work in the country depend on the type of occupation. In some occupations, requirements must be met before one can start working, and might be required by law. Industry-representative bodies, individual employer organizations, professional associations, and responsible authorities in each state and territory determine and assess the educational criteria for employment. Occupations that require specialized knowledge and skills in Australia have registration, licensing, professional membership, or other industry requirements that must be met before an immigrant can start working. If employment in a certain occupation does not depend on meeting such requirements, however, it is up to the employer to decide if the overseas qualification is appropriate for the job.

The Australian government performs educational or qualification assessments for Australian citizens, permanent residents, and

Table 7.7. Effects of Immigrants' Characteristics on Occupation, Australia, 2011

	Determinants of a high-Income occupation			
	B	SE	Sig.	Exp(B)
Constant	–4.06	0.21	0.00	0.02
Birthplace				
South Asia	**–0.93**	**0.14**	**0.00**	**0.40**
Northeast Asia	**–0.70**	**0.23**	**0.00**	**0.50**
Southeast Asia	–0.12	0.22	0.57	0.88
Southern and eastern Europe	–0.08	0.15	0.59	0.92
Ancestry of parent 1				
Southern and Central Asia	**0.53**	**0.17**	**0.00**	**1.70**
Northeast Asia	0.24	0.21	0.26	1.27
Southeast Asia	0.08	0.23	0.73	1.08
Southern and eastern Europe	–0.05	0.16	0.75	0.95
Ancestry of parent 2				
Southern and Central Asia	0.00	0.29	0.99	1.00
Northeast Asia	–0.13	0.37	0.73	0.88
Southeast Asia	0.07	0.24	0.79	1.07
Southern and eastern Europe	–0.43	0.23	0.06	0.65
Language spoken at home				
Southern Asian language	0.03	0.19	0.89	1.03
Eastern Asian language	**0.61**	**0.26**	**0.02**	**1.84**
Southeast Asian language	–0.26	0.26	0.32	0.77
Southern European language	**0.26**	**0.12**	**0.03**	**1.30**
Northern European language	**0.81**	**0.13**	**0.00**	**2.25**
English proficiency				
Very well or well	**1.30**	**0.18**	**0.00**	**3.66**
Time of arrival				
2000 or before	**0.32**	**0.09**	**0.00**	**1.37**
2001–05	**0.21**	**0.08**	**0.01**	**1.24**
Background				
Age	0.02	0.01	0.11	1.02
Education	**0.70**	**0.02**	**0.00**	**2.02**
Gender	**0.14**	**0.05**	**0.01**	**1.15**
Citizenship	**0.27**	**0.07**	**0.00**	**1.31**
Nagelkerke R^2		0.25		

Note: **statistically significant at p < .01, *p < .05, two–tailed. Logistic regression results showing parameter estimates and standard errors predicting effects of immigrants' characteristics on occupation. N=8,386.
Source: Australian Census of Population and Housing, 2011.

non-residents seeking employment in a number of occupations, but these assessments are advisory only, with a view merely to help the prospective employer understand the level and quality of the overseas training. When all is said and done, assessing overseas qualifications for employment purposes is usually a separate process from applying for a job, where, as in all occupations, the employer decides whom they will employ. This tends to ensure that, as in Canada, employers in Australia can devalue legitimate qualifications and skills – the human capital – held by "non-white" visible minorities.

Comparative research has also shown that employers tend to be less inclined to hire an immigrant than a local-born candidate (Heath and Cheung 2007; Lindbeck and Snower 1988). These forms of discrimination are thought to originate from the idea that people generally identify more with people who look like themselves (Lancee 2012). For example, Becker (1971) argued that "personal preferences" or "tastes for discrimination" on the part of employers and organizations was the main reason for labour market discrimination. Racial and ethnic discrimination, therefore, might prevent highly educated immigrants from gaining professional employment opportunities with high incomes and potential leadership opportunities.

Another approach to explaining labour market differences is to consider social capital theory, which implies that immigrants who are equipped with social resources – social networks and the resources of others – perform better in the labour market (Aguilera 2002; Flap and Völker 2004; Franzen and Hangartner 2006). Such social capital provides an important gateway into the labour market and even more so into politics. One way to understand the influence of social capital is by distinguishing between "bonding" and "bridging" capital (Leonard and Onyx 2003; Putnam 2000; Schuller 2007; Woolcock and Narayan 2000). Bonding capital refers to social networks formed within groups, while bridging capital refers to social networks formed between groups. According to Lancee (2012, 159), the acquisition of bridging capital tends to result in higher income and occupational status, whereas the acquisition of bonding capital (such as those formed by family or co-ethnic networks) does not. Given that the majority of employers and employer organizations, including party officials, tend to have European origins, the capacity of "non-white" immigrants and ethnic minorities to build bridges between their own group and a resource-rich group such as those with European origins is likely to yield positive returns in the labour market. Newer Asian immigrants might have greater difficulty, however, tapping into resource-rich networks that have been established over many generations. For instance, research has shown that, for immigrants to succeed, they must acquire country-specific skills such a local education qualification and

English-language proficiency, as well as general experience in the local labour market (Borjas 1994; Duleep and Regets 1999; Friedberg 2000; Zeng and Xie 2004). This was evident in my interviews, when MPs talked about their own well-established social networks, connections, and local skills.

In examining these results more closely, on the surface it seems that immigrants from countries with similar cultural, political, and historical ties to those of Australia's European majority are more quickly and more easily able to transfer their education, skills, and experience. This might partly explain why Asian immigrants face greater challenges in gaining meaningful employment in line with their qualifications and skills. It does not, however, explain the whole picture, since many Asian immigrants have in fact gained appropriate qualifications since arriving in Australia or hold quality qualifications from internationally recognized higher education institutions in Western democracies. Alternatively many might have been successfully awarded qualification recognition by the Australian government or by a peak industry body for holding one or more qualifications from internationally recognized institutions in their country of origin. Regardless of education qualifications and how they are assessed, however, the ability to work in Australia depends on the occupation and on the assessment of local employer organizations. At the end of the day, employers alone decide who they will employ, regardless of applicants' qualifications and skills, leaving new immigrants with limited social networks highly vulnerable to the attitudes of employers.

In the United States, citizens tend to place far greater emphasis on race-based, rather than ethnicity- or language-based, discrimination because access to economic resources and educational opportunities is determined by how individuals identify with their race rather than with their ethnic group (Bashi-Bobb and Clarke 2001; Waters 2001). Since some groups at the top of the social hierarchy have more access to resources than those at the bottom, evidence is mixed as to whether experience in the United States of perceived and actual discrimination is diminishing over time, with some scholars finding that discrimination is declining (Kaiser et al. 2009; Wilkins and Kaiser 2013), while others argue that widespread discrimination and racial prejudice persists (Sellers and Shelton 2003). An example of its persistence is the 2014 flare-up of racial tension in Missouri following the police shooting of an unarmed African American teenager. Asian Americans and Latinos joined in the ensuing protests, drawing attention to their shared experience of racial profiling and police brutality.

In Canada, less emphasis is placed on race than is apparent in the United States, but more emphasis on skin colour as a marker of discrimination. Although Canada is recognized for its progressive stance on multiculturalism and immigration, racial and ethnic minorities continue to experience discrimination and racial prejudice. As in Australia, overt forms of discrimination are practised through social discrimination and limitations on employment entry and promotion opportunities. In a survey on racism and creating a sense of belonging, Canadians expressed a great deal of support for multiculturalism as a national philosophy, but felt that there was still a level of "racism beneath the surface" (United Nations Association in Canada 2008, 16). The survey found that nearly two in three Canadians were concerned about rising racism, while 53 per cent felt there had been a rise in anti-immigrant sentiment. In another survey, over a quarter of British Columbians of Chinese and South Asian origin felt they had experienced a moderate or significant amount of discrimination because of their ethnicity, 28 per cent felt they had been denied a potential employment opportunity because of their ethnic background, another 24 per cent felt they had been mistreated in the workplace, and 25 per cent said they had experienced verbal harassment because of their ethnicity (Todd 2014).

The perceptions of discrimination and racism in Australia, Canada, and the United States is perhaps grounded in general public attitudes towards immigration and public fears about job security in the host society. For instance, based on the World Values Survey, Figure 7.3 shows that 47 per cent of Americans, 40 per cent of Australians, and 38 per cent of Canadians believed government should place strict limits on the number of immigrants coming into the country to work. In Australia and Canada, half of the population supported immigration for work as long as there were jobs available, while in the United States only 36 per cent did so.

Whether attitudes towards immigration more generally affect the likelihood of employing "white" versus "non-white" immigrants and ethnic minorities is difficult to assess with the current measures available in cross-national surveys, which focus on broad categories, rather than subgroups, of immigrants. Nevertheless, it is possible that having a surname that indicates possible membership of a racial or ethnic minority can be a significant hurdle when applying for a job. In a 2012 study on ethnic discrimination in Australia, Booth

Figure 7.3. Public Attitudes towards Immigration, Australia, Canada, and the United States

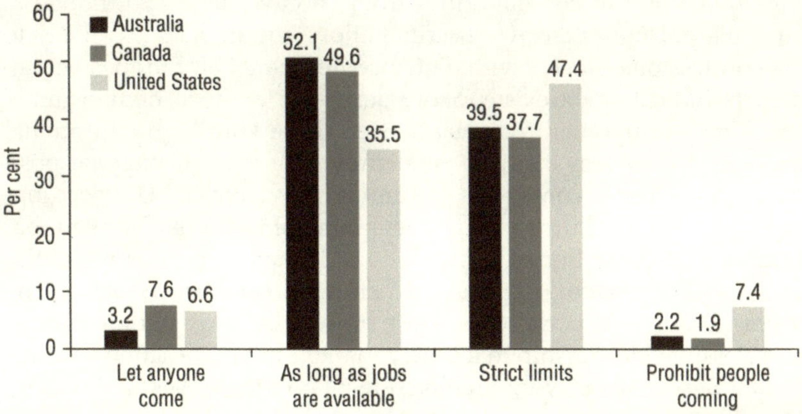

Source: World Values Survey, 2010–2014. The question asked was: "How about people from other countries coming here to work. Which one of the following do you think the government should do?"

and her colleagues compared public attitudes towards Australians of UK/Irish background with those towards Indigenous Australians, Italian Australians, Middle Eastern Australians, and Chinese Australians (Booth, Leigh and Varganova 2012). As part of their experiment, the researchers applied for entry-level jobs using surnames that were distinctively from these cultures and discovered that applications submitted with names from the British Isles had a mean callback rate from potential employers of 35 per cent, those with Italian surnames had a slightly lower callback rate of 32 per cent, and those with distinctively Chinese and Middle Eastern surnames had callback rates of 21 and 22 per cent, respectively. Chinese applicants in Sydney hoping to get an interview would have to put in 92 per cent more applications than applicants with British or Irish names (Booth, Leigh, and Varganova 2012, 567). Given this level of discrimination in securing entry-level employment and the general attitudes towards immigrants found in surveys, it is reasonable to assume that immigrants and ethnic minorities will have much more difficulty entering mainstream Australian politics than will those with a European heritage due to a general phenomenon of "taste-based" discrimination by those in positions of influence.

Conclusion

Immigrants and ethnic minorities from "non-white" backgrounds in Australia not only perceive discrimination, but are also less likely to have professional careers with high incomes than their European counterparts, indicating the existence of a pervasive low-level of discrimination. New immigrants from Asia – even those with high educational attainment – are less likely to enter professional or managerial positions with a high income than are immigrants from the United Kingdom and northern Europe. At the beginning of the book, I argued that the underrepresentation of immigrants and ethnic minorities in politics is a symbolic indicator of broader structural inequalities in society. The greater difficulty, especially for those from Asia, in reaching positions of professional leadership in a timely manner might be acting as a significant barrier to entry into national-level politics in Australia, where becoming part of the professional political class frequently depends on structural preconditions, such as having a reliable source of income, available time for campaigning, professional networks, and a professional career to fall back on if not re-elected.

There appears to be sufficient evidence of the existence of racial hierarchies in Australia, Canada, and the United States that ultimately affect the extent to which immigrants and ethnic minorities feel a sense of social and political inclusion in their respective new societies. Heath (2007, 640), for example, finds a consistent pattern whereby groups from northwest European origins are at the top, followed by those from other European origins, while at the bottom of the hierarchy are those from non-European origins. Traditionally, this pattern of racial and ethnic stratification has been explained by the fact that immigrants from northwest Europe tend to have higher-than-average education levels, reflecting patterns of class reproduction, while those from elsewhere in Europe are less likely to have such education. Furthermore, Heath (2007) finds that, in similar studies in other countries, most groups from non-European origins continue to experience disadvantage and ethnic penalties in later generations despite having similar, if not higher, levels of education than those from northern European origins. This suggests that factors other than class might be contributing to their disadvantage and marginalization.

Chapter Eight

Conclusion

Given the limited examination of immigrants and ethnic minorities and their social and political outcomes in Australia, this research began with an overriding puzzle: why, despite high levels of socio-economic achievement, immigrants and ethnic minorities – mainly from "non-white" backgrounds in Asia, the Pacific Islands, the Middle East, and Sub-Saharan Africa – have not achieved the same level of representation in Australia's formal social and political institutions as have those with European origins. The bulk of this analysis has been devoted to comparisons with visible minorities in Canada and "non-white" groups in the United States. In a nation of immigrants, with established multicultural institutions, one would expect roughly similar levels of racial equality within formal institutions, particularly in a system that mandates political participation through compulsory voting.

By drawing on existing theories that predominantly stem from research conducted in Canada, the United States, the United Kingdom, and elsewhere in Europe, I have used a variety of research methodologies to work backwards to find answers as to why Australia's Commonwealth Parliament is so "white" or "European" despite several decades of population change that is rapidly transforming the country's racial and ethnic composition. Traditional theories based on socio-economic resources, which explained the delayed entry of post-war European immigrants into Australia's political institutions, could not be transferred easily to the experiences of highly educated English-speaking immigrants from non-European backgrounds. Looking beyond traditional resource-based explanations, the research project explored other avenues for an explanation of the underrepresentation in Australian politics of immigrants and ethnic minorities compared with their experience in Canada and the

United States, such as migration history, the legal-institutional context, party-political barriers, home-country political origins, ethnic group size, ethnic concentration, pan-ethnic identification, political behaviour and attitudes, and, finally racial and ethnic discrimination.

The argument articulated in Chapter 2 began with the empirical fact of "non-white" descriptive underrepresentation in national legislatures relative to the size of each immigrant and ethnic minority group across the three settler countries, observing differences in the political representation of immigrants and ethnic minorities from "non-white" backgrounds in Australia compared to Canada and the United States. In explaining these empirical differences, in Chapter 3 I explored the institutional context in terms of history and opportunity structures, with a focus on demographic flows, citizenship access, and electoral system constraints. The underrepresentation in Australia of immigrants and ethnic minorities from "non-white" backgrounds can be explained partly by the fact that the largest "non-white" group, Asians, was allowed into the country in significant numbers only after the end of the White Australia policy in 1973. But other factors also play a role.

In more recent years, the shift towards skilled migration has witnessed the arrival of waves of immigrants from high socio-economic backgrounds, with immigrants from India, in particular, well equipped with a combination of democratic experience and high levels of socio-economic achievement to engage in Australian politics. In fact, in their interviews for this research, parliamentarians discussed the enthusiastic engagement and political experience of Indian citizens in their electorates. Australia's system of compulsory voting also ensures that citizens from immigrant and ethnic minority backgrounds become quickly familiar with democratic politics and the processes necessary for political integration. Yet, nearly four and a half decades after the arrival of large numbers of Asian immigrants began, how long do groups need to wait and to what size must they grow before their political descriptive representation in Australia's national-level politics is not only achievable but becomes the norm? With the election of the first Indigenous woman to the national legislature only in 2016, it appears that some groups will need to wait a very long time.

A multitude of barriers besides recent arrival, in fact, make it more difficult for immigrants and ethnic minorities to participate actively in Australia's political system and play a role in making laws and policies that will influence the lives of everyday citizens. In Chapter 3 I presented evidence demonstrating the differences in attitudes towards multiculturalism in Australia and Canada, with the latter actively embracing a "strong" multiculturalism through legislation and specific policies aimed at addressing racial inequalities in mainstream politics. Drawing on census data, I also demonstrated that new arrivals – Asian groups, in particular – have higher rates of citizenship in Canada than in Australia. I also showed how the electoral system for the federal House of Representatives in Australia is not advantageous for the election of immigrant and ethnic minority candidates to public office unless the groups to which they belong are geographically concentrated, sufficiently large in size, and politically mobilized. The geographical dispersion of immigrants and ethnic minorities sets Australia apart from Canada and the United States, where majority-minority electoral districts facilitate the successful election of minority candidates to public office.

In Chapter 4 I considered the role of party representatives in the Commonwealth Parliament in discriminating against potential immigrant and ethnic minority candidates. Unlike in Canada and the United States, the strong party system in Australia tends to block such individuals from party leadership ranks, leading to feelings of disillusionment about the role of party gatekeepers and factions in keeping out newcomers, who might make ideal political representatives of their communities – for instance, it was acknowledged among immigrant and ethnic minority representatives that their own experience of being a minority in Australia enhanced the quality of representation in their own electoral district. In general, political representatives actively embraced multiculturalism, but only if political structures were left untouched. There was no support for quotas, policies, affirmative action legislation, or strategies to bring in high-performing, and high-skilled immigrants from traditionally underrepresented groups. Instead Australia's "informal" and more "flexible" approach to recruitment, which relies on loyalty, social networks, local engagement in the community, and long-term service to the party, was the preferred option among most of those I interviewed.

In Chapter 5 I tested the waters on pan-ethnicity to see if in Australia there was any possibility for mobilization, already widely practised in the United States, to rally behind ethnic political candidates or to affect policy outcomes of concern to immigrants and ethnic minorities on account of their race, religion, culture, or immigrant status. The research found overlapping political behaviour and room for mobilization in electoral districts with high concentrations of Asians, Australia's largest pan-ethnic group. As well, surveys have found that Asian Australians are more likely to vote for the Australian Labor Party or to identify with no party than those born in the United Kingdom, Ireland, the rest of Europe, or Australia. At present, however, Australia still does not have the infrastructure or political culture to facilitate bottom-up racial and ethnic political mobilization, other than through the Federation of Ethnic Communities Councils Australia, which is hampered in its ability to discuss homeland issues and address specific ethnic concerns.

Evidence further suggests that low levels of political efficacy, trust, and confidence in the political system lead to lower rates of political participation and representation, which are also affected by the closeness of ties to immigrants' home countries. As is often theorized, however, there is limited evidence for the low engagement in politics of immigrants and ethnic minorities from "non-white" backgrounds or of any detrimental effect on engagement in home-country politics. Even though some groups of Asian immigrants were slightly less likely than comparison groups to demonstrate an interest in Australian politics, paying attention to the politics in one's country of origin and engagement with ethnic media did not appear to have an influence on whether racial and ethnic minorities follow Australian politics.

There is, as well, no significant relationship between authoritarian socialization experiences and interest in Australian politics. What matters more is whether immigrants and ethnic minorities feel a sense of efficacy and trust in politics, whether they are interested in their home-country politics, and whether they have a strong command of the English language. Importantly, for Asian immigrants and ethnic minorities, the experience of racial and ethnic discrimination has a negative effect on their interest in Australian politics. This is to be expected given the association between experiences of racial or ethnic discrimination and feelings of national belonging. The experience of discrimination, when all other factors are controlled for, also has a negative effect on satisfaction with democracy in Australia.

In Chapter 7 I presented a great deal of evidence of low-level discrimination in terms of both perceptions and actual practice. The English-language skills and qualifications of Asian immigrants are similar to those possessed by European immigrants – in fact, the recent wave of Asian immigrants is more highly qualified than those from Europe. Structural barriers, however, make it more difficult for those from "non-white" backgrounds to gain entry to high-income professional occupations. For example, when it comes to income earnings, new immigrants from the United Kingdom and the rest of Europe tend to receive a much greater return on their education, qualifications, and experience than do immigrants from Asia, regardless of proficiency in English. The existence of significant structural and social barriers to the economic mobility of Asian immigrants might be the reason many choose to find employment in smaller firms or family-run businesses outside of formal institutions.

In summary, the underrepresentation of "non-white" immigrants and ethnic minorities in Australian politics is a symbol of structural and social inequalities. These inequalities facilitate the maintenance of racial and ethnic hierarchies, as well as various forms of social and political closure. This raises many questions for reflection in terms of the overall representativeness, responsiveness, and accountability of democratic institutions in a multicultural plural society such as Australia and more, broadly Canada and the United States. In addressing these issues, research on political participation and representation is now becoming an important part of cross-national research in immigrant scholarship.

Returning to the theoretical model in the introductory chapter, the research conducted for this book demonstrates that political engagement and participation in Australian politics is determined by a wide variety of contextual, institutional, and individual factors. Most important, the many theoretical explanations for the persistent racial and ethnic gap in Australian politics are not empirically supported by the available qualitative and quantitative data collected for this research. Rather, the findings reveal a very engaged and knowledgeable citizenry among immigrants and ethnic minorities. Given their high levels of socio-economic achievement, it is expected that skilled immigrants and ethnic minorities one day will account for a larger share of the Australian Parliament. It is hoped that this will take place when the persistent structural and social barriers identified in this research are broken down.

Finally, comparative research in Australia, Canada, the United States, the United Kingdom, and elsewhere in Europe has established the importance for democracy of a "politics of presence" of underrepresented groups in terms of improving overall trust and confidence in the political system. In Australia, in particular, "non-white" immigrants and ethnic minorities are underrepresented in national-level politics despite their long presence in the country. This participation gap undermines the future of representative democracy at a time when confidence in national institutions is declining. As such, the issue of immigrant and ethnic minority representation requires significant attention in the field of political science, as well as future legislation and policy making.

APPENDICES

Table A.1. Responses of the Federation of Ethnic Communities Councils Australia (FECCA) to Events and Government Legislation and Policies relating to Multiculturalism and Immigration

Event or Announcement by Year	FECCA Response
2014	
Proposed cuts to community radio	FECCA joins the National Ethnic and Multicultural Broadcasters' Council and other ethnic community broadcasters in voicing strong opposition to the recommendation of the recently released Commission of Audit Report proposing to cut funding for the Community Broadcasting Program. FECCA chair Joseph Caputo said: "It is important for the government to fully comprehend that pursuing cuts to the Community Broadcasting Program would present a major roadblock for this important sector and would result in a significant setback to the promotion of diversity in our multicultural society."
Mixed outcomes for Australians from cultural and linguistically diverse (CALD) backgrounds in the federal budget	FECCA is extremely disappointed over the decision to reduce the number of human rights commissioners. FECCA chair Caputo says: "The Australian Human Rights Commission plays an integral role in the promotion of human rights and multiculturalism in Australia. The importance of dedicated portfolios for each of the present Commissioners is vital to ensure adequate attention is paid to issues that impact on all Australians, including those from CALD backgrounds." FECCA is concerned that the government does not see the value in maintaining the Commonwealth Human Rights Education Program and has announced its discontinuation. Caputo says: "The Programme has played an integral role in promoting community awareness and understanding of human rights and the responsibilities of individuals as members of a tolerant, inclusive society." FECCA is also concerned by the announcement to cease funding for the Connection Interviews and Job Seeker Workshops offered by Job Services Australia, citing this as an important program through which to enable access and equity and to facilitate job-readiness for CALD Australians.
Abduction of girls in Nigeria by Boko Haram	FECCA calls on the Australian government to join international efforts and take a strong position to secure the safe release of the abducted girls.
The hidden cost of dowries	FECCA is concerned over the increasingly adverse effect of demands related to the payment of dowry on immigrant women in Australia.

Cuts to the Refugee Council of Australia (RCOA)	FECCA is extremely disappointed by the government's decision to cut the core funding for the RCOA despite its allocation in the 2014–15 budget. FECCA senior deputy chair Eugenia Grammatikakis says: "RCOA has played a critical role in advocating for the rights of refugees and asylum seekers in Australia and internationally."
Proposed merger of the Australian Broadcasting Corporation and the Special Broadcasting Service (SBS)	FECCA senior deputy chair Grammatikakis says: "The proposed changes, whilst looking broadly at cost efficiency measures to reduce expenditure, are undermining the delicate fabric of multiculturalism in Australia. SBS is a unique service that broadcasts in over 74 different languages, providing an invaluable source of news and community information to ethnic communities in Australia, as well as the broader community. FECCA believes that the potential merger will not present any actual savings, given the detrimental long-term risk of SBS losing its core multicultural focus, providing a major impediment to advancing Australia's multiculturalism."
Refugee Week 2014, "Restoring Hope"	FECCA senior deputy chair Grammatikakis says: "Refugee Week is a time to celebrate the significant contributions and notable achievements that refugees have made to Australian society."
Release of "Enabling Equality: Disability and Diversity in Australia"	FECCA announces the release of *Australian Mosaic*, issue 37, entitled "Enabling Equality: Disability and Diversity in Australia."
Launch of Second Action Plan of the *National Plan to Reduce Violence against Women and Their Children*	In its submission to inform the development of the Second Action Plan, FECCA highlights the need for greater focus on particularly vulnerable groups such as Indigenous, CALD women, and women with disabilities.
Paid Parental Leave	FECCA advocates for a more balance approach to Paid Parental Leave. FECCA women's chair Pallavi Sinha says: "The costs of childcare are particularly damaging on families from CALD backgrounds who are often the lowest income earners, and this needs to be factored more into the current debate regarding [Paid Parental Leave]."
Celebration of National Aborigines and Islanders Day Observance Committee (NAIDOC) Week	FECCA senior deputy chair Grammatikakis says: "NAIDOC Week is an opportunity to recognise and celebrate the historical and significant contribution Aboriginal and Torres Strait Islander peoples and cultures continue to make in building a stronger and socially cohesive multicultural community in Australia."

Table A.1. Responses of the Federation of Ethnic Communities Councils Australia (FECCA) to Events and Government Legislation and Policies relating to Multiculturalism and Immigration (Continued)

Event or Announcement by Year	FECCA Response
2014	
Release of 2013–14 Access and Equity Report	The report provides a summary of the perspectives and broader feedback received through FECCA's consultations with culturally and linguistically diverse communities and service providers around Australia regarding the design and delivery of Australian government services.
Government abandons proposed changes to Racial Discrimination Act	FECCA welcomes the government's decision not to proceed with amendments to the racial vilification provisions of the Racial Discrimination Act. During FECCA's consultations, the overwhelming community and institutional response from our constituency was opposed to the proposed amendments. People expressed a real fear that the proposed changes were a threat to the social cohesion of Australia, as it stripped protections for the most marginalized members of our society.
Celebration of International Youth Day	FECCA has advocated the need for increased funding to support further engagement of interpreters and bicultural workers and their employment across all fields of mental health care to improve service delivery for CALD youth. FECCA has also highlighted the need for more community education and outreach programs to counter stigma and other barriers that CALD youth face in engaging with mental health services. In particular, FECCA has advocated that such initiatives should focus on particularly vulnerable groups, such as newly arrived youth, and those from refugee and humanitarian backgrounds.
Moves to scrap specialist job service providers for disadvantaged job seekers	FECCA chair Caputo questioned the benefit of the proposed recommendation to culturally and linguistically diverse job seekers, observing that "job services need to be more targeted, tailored and culturally competent in order to address the complex needs of individuals looking for sustainable employment opportunities."
Freedom of cultural and religious expression	FECCA calls on the presiding officers of Parliament House to reconsider the recently proposed rule changes concerning access restrictions for people wearing facial coverings.

2014 federal budget measures to reduce poverty	As Anti-Poverty Week 2014 comes to a close, FECCA warns that the challenges for people from multicultural communities who live below the poverty line linger on, with continued uncertainty around the 2014 federal budget measures.
Death of former prime minister Gough Whitlam	FECCA pays tribute to a visionary leader whose vast intellect and remarkable service to this country set the nation on the path to multiculturalism. Whitlam created the fundamentals of multiculturalism, promoted cultural diversity, and, in his final months as prime minister, introduced the Racial Discrimination Act.
Rise of racially based attacks	FECCA calls on the government to promote due recognition of the benefits of multiculturalism in order to remove the barriers created by racism and discrimination and, conversely, "nurture a diverse and inclusive Australian."
White Ribbon Day	FECCA chair Caputo says: "Domestic violence is a significant issue in some of the CALD communities in Australia. Although anecdotal evidence shows that the rate of violence perpetrated against women from CALD backgrounds is very high, the issue tends to remain hidden because most of the abuses committed against women within these communities are not reported due to a range of cultural and structural obstacles."
Anti-Muslim event in Sydney	FECCA joins with the Islamic leadership and the broader community in calling for calm and unity in the days following the tragic event in Sydney overnight.
2015	
Release of *Review of Australian Research on Older People from CALD Backgrounds*	FECCA releases its landmark *Review of Australian Research on Older People from Culturally and Linguistically Diverse Backgrounds*. The review highlights that older people from CALD backgrounds are not a homogeneous group, and therefore meeting their needs is highly complex. Many older people from CALD backgrounds have higher levels of disadvantage and other risk factors than older Australians with origins in the British Isles.
Reclaim Australia rallies	FECCA chair Caputo says he found the presence of these rallies across the country deeply disconcerting as they pose a risk to social cohesion and harmony. In recent months, there has been a rise in racially and religiously motivated attacks against members of Australia's multicultural communities.

Table A.1. Responses of the Federation of Ethnic Communities Councils Australia (FECCA) to Events and Government Legislation and Policies relating to Multiculturalism and Immigration (Continued)

Event or Announcement by Year	FECCA Response
2015	
Release of federal budget 2015–16	FECCA says funding for multicultural affairs in the 2015–16 budget is difficult to assess as it is largely dispersed throughout the Families and Communities program of the Social Services portfolio.
Citizenship review	In its submission to the government's consultation on Australian citizenship, FECCA opposes the discriminatory and unnecessary proposed changes to the citizenship test, pledge, and eligibility criteria included in the government's citizenship discussion paper.
Proposed amendments to Australian citizenship	The Australian Citizenship Amendment (Allegiance to Australia) Bill 2015, introduced into Parliament last month, has been referred to the Parliamentary Joint Committee on Intelligence and Security. FECCA's submission opposing the passage of the bill in its current form raises concerns about the effect of automatic cessation or revocation of citizenship for dual nationals, including children, and about various procedural elements of the bill, which FECCA believes do not provide adherence to fundamental individual rights.
Asylum seeker policies	In response to the positions taken by both major parties on boat turnbacks, FECCA calls on both the Australian government and the Opposition to stand by Australia's international obligations and responsibilities.
Racism directed towards Adam Goodes	FECCA joins with a number of other organizations in a statement of support of Indigenous sportsperson Adam Goodes following the racism directed towards him.
Release of Productivity Commission's draft report on Australia's Workplace Relations Framework	FECCA's submission to the inquiry highlighted a number of issues involving employment conditions and the workplace relations framework as it relates to CALD Australians and migrant workers. The Commission's recommendations discourage workers' reporting of breaches of their employment and visa conditions. With compliance being the key focus, the draft report proposes little to support vulnerable migrant workers in situations of exploitation. The recommendations adopt a punitive approach towards already exploited workers, whereby the unpaid wages are paid by the employer to the government.

Proposed changes to citizenship law	FECCA appeared before the Joint Parliamentary Committee on Intelligence and Security to discuss the Citizenship Amendment (Allegiance to Australia) Bill, highlighting concerns raised by the community at consultations held by state and territory members, including that many feel the bill would create two classes of citizens.
Planned mosque protests	FECCA and its member organizations across Australia stand strongly in condemnation of planned mosque protests in October.
Australian Bureau of Statistics releases data on personal income of migrants in Australia	Data indicate that the average employee income of family visa holders was well below the national average of Australian taxpayers. Family stream migrants represented 22% of total migrant income in 2009–10, while 58% reported owning their own business.
Intelligence Committee recommendations on amendments to Australian citizenship	FECCA makes a submission to the inquiry and appears before the committee to discuss its concerns about the bill, including the effect that the legislation, if passed, will have on social cohesion, its impact on children, and its compliance with fundamental rights.
Government increases intake of Syrian refugees	FECCA welcomes the Australian government's commitment to offer permanent protection to 12,000 Syrian refugees, in response to the global refugee crisis, but calls for a longer-term vision with sustainable, equitable, and non-discriminatory humanitarian practices. With over 4 million people displaced by the crisis, it is important to have a humanitarian program responsive to the refugee situation and that meets growing global needs for resettlement.
Release of draft report on vulnerabilities of migrant workers	FECCA and the Salvation Army appear together before a public hearing to discuss the recently released Productivity Commission draft report on Australia's Workplace Relations Framework.
Senate Committee releases report on Department of Social Services tendering processes	FECCA raises concerns that ethno-specific and multicultural organizations, which no longer receive funding for their programs and projects, would need to scale back or discontinue services to their communities, with some organizations at risk of having to close.
Announcement of Women's Safety Package	FECCA welcomes the announcement of the government's Women's Safety Package, particularly the inclusion of measures targeting CALD women.
Watering down of vilification laws	Last year, thousands of community members and their organizations expressed fear that the proposed watering down of vilification laws would strip protection from the most marginalized members of our society and threaten social cohesion in Australia.

Table A.1. Responses of the Federation of Ethnic Communities Councils Australia (FECCA) to Events and Government Legislation and Policies relating to Multiculturalism and Immigration (Continued)

Event or Announcement by Year	FECCA Response
2015	
FECCA's 2020 Vision for Older CALD Australians	FECCA has been working to promote better outcomes and improve access to services for older CALD Australians as they age and enter the aged care system in Australia. This includes services in the home and residential aged care.
Mental health moves towards individualized care	FECCA welcomes the government's announcement on a complete mental health reform, following the National Mental Health Commission's Review of Mental Health Program and Services.
Release of Quality and Safeguarding Framework consultation report by the National Disability Insurance Scheme	FECCA makes a number of recommendations about the provision of information about the insurance scheme, rights of parties, and relevant laws and regulations, with emphasis on CALD communities.
Australian Citizenship Amendment (Allegiance to Australia) bill passes Parliament	FECCA made a submission to the Parliamentary Joint Committee on Intelligence and Security when it examined the bill, and also appeared before a public hearing of the committee. The committee made a number of recommendations, which were adopted by the government and incorporated into the bill. FECCA is encouraged by many of these recommendations, particularly those relating to children and addressing procedural concerns raised in the conduct of the inquiry.
Release of Mid-Year Economic and Fiscal Outlook 2015–16 measures	The government is proposing to save AU$225 million over four years by removing exemptions from the Newly Arrived Resident's Waiting Period for new migrants who are family members of Australian citizens or permanent residents from 1 January 2017. Under the current law, new migrants to Australia generally have to wait two years after the grant of their permanent visa before they can access most income support payments. However there are some exemptions from this two-year waiting period, which include an exemption for a person who is a family member of an Australian citizen or permanent resident (of at least two years). FECCA calls on the government not to proceed with this proposal.
FECCA submission on migrant intake	FECCA commends the Productivity Commission on its draft report, which is comprehensive and gives due regard to the social and cultural benefits of migration.

2016	
Proposed changes to humanitarian resettlement program, increased monitoring of migrants	FECCA is concerned by the proposals outlined in the leaked cabinet document signalling changes to the humanitarian resettlement program and the increased monitoring of migrants.
Australian Labor Party plan to tackle inequality and support early childhood	FECCA chair Caputo says: "We welcome Federal Labor's agenda outline targeted strategies for CALD families, to ensure children from CALD backgrounds are given the same opportunities as every other Australian child."
Parliamentary report recommends promoting benefits of cultural diversity to employers	FECCA makes a submission to the inquiry and appears before the committee to give evidence about issues specifically affecting CALD workers. Key barriers to employment include difficulty having overseas qualifications recognized, negative stereotypes and racism, absence of personal networks, and lack of Australian work experience. FECCA recommends that education for employers is necessary to promote the benefits of having a culturally diverse workforce to improve productivity, innovation, and growth.
Release of the report of the Victorian Royal Commission into Family Violence	FECCA chair Caputo says: "We applaud the Victorian Royal Commission for ensuring the breadth and scope of the report and recommendations extends to include women from CALD backgrounds, who are a vulnerable group."
Release of proposed child care reforms	In response to the release of the Senate Education and Employment Legislation Committee report on the Family Assistance Legislation Amendment (Jobs for Families Child Care Package) Bill 2015, which recommends that the bill be passed in its current form, FECCA chair Caputo says: "The Senate report failed to examine the particular impact of the proposed child care reforms on migrant and refugee children and families."
Calls for more diversified media	FECCA supports calls by industry, media, and other commentators for the media to better reflect Australia's cultural and linguistic diversity.
Calls for respectful, informed, and reasonable debate on refugee issues	FECCA chair Caputo says: "At FECCA we are calling for the discussion to be brought within the bounds of acceptable discourse. We are concerned that the current tone could incite division among communities in this very sensitive area." The appeal is particularly relevant in view of comments by Peter Dutton, Minister for Immigration and Border Protection, relating to an increase of the refugee intake resulting in "illiterate and innumerate" refugees taking Australians' jobs.

Table A.1. Responses of the Federation of Ethnic Communities Councils Australia (FECCA) to Events and Government Legislation and Policies relating to Multiculturalism and Immigration (Continued)

Event or Announcement by Year	FECCA Response
2016	
Questions about the major parties' commit to policies and actions to support Australia's multicultural communities in the coming federal election	FECCA asks the three major parties to answer the following ten questions: 1. Will you develop a national legislative framework on multiculturalism? 2. Will you develop an integrated national policy framework on languages? 3. Will you commit to policy action on harnessed productivity through diversity? 4. What steps will you take to ensure that government boards reflect our multicultural society, particularly addressing the extremely low level of representation of women from non-English-speaking background on decision-making public bodies? 5. Will you review the approach to setting targets for eligible partners in the family migration stream, with a view to implementing an entirely demand-driven system? 6. Will you guarantee 24 hours of subsidized child care per week as a minimum standard for every child, regardless of parents' ability to meet an activity test, in view of the benefits of early childhood education for children from CALD backgrounds? 7. Will you ensure that people seeking to escape family violence are entitled to crisis payments regardless of their visa status? 8. Will you adopt a comprehensive national communications policy that supports public broadcasting in languages other than English and ethnic and multicultural community broadcasters? 9. Will you take targeted and comprehensive measures to empower CALD consumers in consumer-directed care reforms, including aged care, the National Disability Insurance Scheme, and mental health, to ensure equitable access and experience? 10. Will you develop a National Community Relations Strategy with funding earmarked for national and community-based projects?
Australian Labor Party releases multiculturalism policy	FECCA welcomes the Australian Labor Party's multicultural policy, Community Cohesion Program-Investing in New Migrants.

Recognition and support of CALD women	FECCA welcomes the parties' policies and actions to support Australia's multiculturalism, but is disappointed by the lack of genuine commitment that would be underpinned by targeted policy and budget initiatives from the major parties to address the challenges faced by CALD women. With one week to go to the 2016 federal election, FECCA calls for all parties to adopt a policy platform that addresses the particular needs of Australia's CALD population.
CALD Aged Care Fund	FECCA welcomes the Australian Labor Party's commitment to establish a CALD Aged Care Fund.
Productivity and growth through diversity	FECCA calls for a real commitment by all parties to adopt policies that respond to Australia's cultural and linguistic diversity, where multicultural issues move from the margins of public policy to the core of all government policies and programs.
Proposed changes to family migration	FECCA chair Caputo says: "FECCA is fundamentally opposed to the imposition of a fee for immigration to Australia. Australia's migration intake should be balanced and merit-based, not based on the financial means of a potential migrant. A holistic approach should be adopted, looking at the skills and other contributions of migrants."
New temporary sponsored parent visa	FECCA is concerned that a shift away from permanent parent visas to flexible temporary parent visas will leave many individuals without a social safety net and no access to crucial services. This will put pressure on Australian families and individuals who hold temporary parent visas. It could also create a class of migrants who are not supported to settle in Australia, affecting social cohesion.
Need for balanced debate on temporary migrant workers	FECCA expresses concern that the decision to reduce the period that 457 visa-holders can remain in Australia after ceasing to work for their sponsors – from 90 days to 60 days – increases the vulnerability of these workers, and discourages them from leaving workplaces where they experience exploitation and mistreatment.
Inflammatory statements regarding immigration to Australia	FECCA expresses concerns over the recent comments by Peter Dutton, Minister for Immigration and Border Protection, criticizing former Liberal prime minister Malcolm Fraser's policy of welcoming refugees and migrants, referred to refugees as "delivering their troubles onto our shores," and linking specific communities to broader law and order challenges.
Responsibility of parliamentarians to protect Australia's CALD communities	FECCA chair Caputo says: "The re-opening of the debate about section 18C of the Racial Discrimination Act sends a message that racism is acceptable in the name of free speech. As it stands, the provisions of the Racial Discrimination Act strike a balance between the right to freedom of expression and the right to freedom from racial vilification."

Table A.2. Coding of Variables for Tables 7.6 and 7

Variable	Scoring
Income	12-point scale, low income = 1, high income = 12
Birthplace	
South Asia	Southern and Central Asia = 1, else = 0
Northeast Asia	Northeast Asia = 1, else = 0
Southeast Asia	Southeast Asia = 1, else = 0
Southern and eastern Europe	Southern and eastern Europe = 1, else = 0
Reference category: Northwest Europe	
Ancestry of parent 1	
Southern and Central Asia	Southern and Central Asia = 1, else = 0
Northeast Asia	Northeast Asia = 1, else = 0
Southeast Asia	Southeast Asia = 1, else = 0
Southern and eastern Europe	Southern and eastern Europe = 1, else = 0
Reference category: Northwest Europe	
Ancestry of parent 2	
Southern and Central Asia	Southern and Central Asia = 1, else = 0
Northeast Asia	Northeast Asia = 1, else = 0
Southeast Asia	Southeast Asia = 1, else = 0
Southern and eastern Europe	Southern and eastern Europe = 1, else = 0
Reference category: Northwest Europe	
Language Spoken at Home	
Southern Asian language	Southern Asian language = 1, else = 0
Eastern Asian language	Eastern Asian language = 1, else = 0
Southeast Asian language	Southeast Asian language = 1, else = 0
Southern European language	Southern European language = 1, else = 0
Northern European language	Northern European language, excl. English = 1, else = 0
Reference category: English	
English proficiency	
Very well or well	Very well, well = 1, not well, not at all = 0
Time of arrival	
2000 or before	2000 or before, else = 0
2001–05	2001–05, else = 0
Reference category: arrived 2006–11	
Age	1 = 18–24, 2 = 25–9, 3 = 30–4, 4 = 35–9, 5 = 40–4, 6 = 45–9, 7 = 50–4, 8 = 55–9, 9 = 60–4, 10 = 65–9, 11 = 70–4, 12 = 75–9, 13 = 80–4, 14 = 85 and over
Education	certificate = 1, diploma = 2, bachelor's degree = 3, graduate diploma = 4, postgraduate degree = 5
Gender	male = 1, female = 0
Citizenship	Australian citizen = 1, non-Australian citizen = 0

References

Alba, Richard, and Nancy Foner. 2009. "Entering the Precincts of Power: Do National Differences Matter for Immigrant Minority Political Representation?" In *Bringing Outsiders In: Transatlantic Perspectives on Immigrant Political Incorporation*, ed. Jennifer Hochschild and John H. Mollenkopf, 277–93. Ithaca, NY: Cornell University Press.

Aldrich, John, Jacob Montgomery, and Wendy Wood. 2011. "Turnout as Habit." *Political Behavior* 33 (4): 535–63. https://doi.org/10.1007/s11109-010-9148-3.

Aguilera, Michael Bernabé. 2002. "The Impact of Social Capital on Labor Force Participation: Evidence from the 2000 Social Capital Benchmark Survey." *Social Science Quarterly* 83 (3): 853–74. https://doi.org/10.1111/1540-6237.00118.

Anderson, Stephanie. 2016. "The History of the Racial Discrimination Act." *ABC News*, 30 August 2016. Available online at http://www.abc.net.au/news/2016-08-30/racial-discrimination-act-explainer/7798546, accessed 3 January 2017.

Andeweg, Ruby B., and Jacques J.A. Thomassen. 2005. "Modes of Political Representation: Toward a New Typology." *Legislative Studies Quarterly* 30 (4): 507–528. https://doi.org/10.3162/036298005X201653.

Andrew, Caroline, John Biles, Myer Siemiatycki, and Erin Tolley, eds. 2008a. *Electing a Diverse Canada: The Representation of Newcomers and Minorities in Canadian Cities*. Vancouver: UBC Press.

Ang, Ien. 1993. "Migrations of Chineseness: Ethnicity in a Postmodern World." In *Cultural Studies: Pluralism and Theory*, ed. D. Bennett, 32–44. Melbourne: University of Melbourne.

Ang, Ien. 2001. *On Not Speaking Chinese*. London: Routledge.

Ang, Ien, Lisa Law, Sharon Chalmers, and Mandy Thomas. 2000. *Alter/Asians: Asian-Australian Identities in Art, Media and Popular Culture*. Sydney: Pluto Press.

Ansolabehere, Stephen, and Shanto Iyengar. 1994. "Riding the Wave and Claiming Ownership Over Issues: The Joint Effects of Advertising and News Coverage in Campaigns." *Public Opinion Quarterly* 58 (3): 335–57. https://doi.org/10.1086/269431.

Appiah, K. Anthony. 1994. "Identity, Authenticity, Survival: Multicultural Societies and Social Reproduction." In *Multiculturalism*, ed. Amy Gutmann, 107–49. Princeton, NJ: Princeton University Press.

Arat-Koc, Sedef. 1999. "Neo-Liberalism, State Restructuring and Immigration: Changes in Canadian Policies in the 1990s." *Journal of Canadian Studies* 34 (2): 31–56. https://doi.org/10.3138/jcs.34.2.31.

Aspinall, Edward, and Mada Sukmajati, eds. 2016. *Electoral Dynamics in Indonesia: Money Politics, Patronage and Clientelism at the Grassroots*. Singapore: NUS Press.

Austin, Sharon D. Wright, Richard T. Middleton, and Rachel Yon. 2012. "The Effect of Racial Group Consciousness on the Political Participation of African Americans and Black Ethnics in Miami-Dade County, Florida." *Political Research Quarterly* 65 (3): 629–41. https://doi.org/10.1177/1065912911404563.

Australian Bureau of Statistics. n.d., 1991, 1996, 2001, 2006, 2011, and 2016. *Australian Censuses of Population and Housing*. Canberra.

Australian Bureau of Statistics. 2011. *Migration Australia*, Cat. no. 3412.0. Canberra: Australian Bureau of Statistics.

Australian Public Service Commission. 2013. "State of the Service Report: The APS in the Asia Century." Canberra. Available online at http://www.apsc.gov.au/__data/assets/pdf_file/0005/59387/SOSR-2012-13-chapter-8.pdf.

Azuma, Eiichiro. 1993. "A History of Oregon's Issei, 1880–1952." *Oregon Historical Quarterly. Oregon Historical Society* 97 (2): 315–67.

Banducci, Susan, Todd Donovan, and Jeffrey Karp. 2004. "Minority Representation, Empowerment, and Participation." *Journal of Politics* 66 (2): 534–56. https://doi.org/10.1111/j.1468-2508.2004.00163.x.

Barry, Brian. 2001. *Culture and Equality: An Egalitarian Critique of Multiculturalism*. Cambridge, UK: Polity Press.

Basavarajappa, K.G., and Ravi B.P. Verma. 1985. "Asian Immigrants in Canada: Some Findings from the 1981 Census." *International Migration (Geneva, Switzerland)* 23 (1): 97–121. https://doi.org/10.1111/j.1468-2435.1985.tb00568.x.

Bashi-Bobb, Vilna, and Averil Clarke. 2001. "Structuring the Perception of Opportunities for West Indians." In *Islands in the City: West Indian Migration to New York*, ed. Nancy Foner, 162–93. Berkeley: University of California Press.

Basran, Gurcharn S, and Li Zong. 1998. "Devaluation of Foreign Credentials as Perceived by Visible Minority Professional Immigrants." *Canadian Ethnic Studies* 30 (3): 6–22.

Bauder, Harold. 2003. "'Brain Abuse,' or Devaluation of Immigrant Labor in Canada." *Antipode* 35 (4): 699–717. https://doi.org/10.1046/j.1467-8330.2003.00346.x.

Bean, Clive, Rachel Gibson, Ian McAllister, and Juliet Pietsch. 2013. *Australian Election Study*. Canberra: Australian Data Archive.

Bean, Clive, David Gow, and Ian McAllister. 1998. *Australian Election Study*. Canberra: Australian Data Archive.

Bean, Clive, David Gow, and Ian McAllister. 2001. *Australian Election Study*. Canberra: Australian Data Archive.

Bean, Clive, Ian McAllister, Rachel Gibson, and David Gow. 2004. *Australian Election Study*. Canberra: Australian Data Archive.

Bean, Clive, Ian McAllister, David Gow, and Rachel Gibson. 2007. *Australian Election Study*. Canberra: Australian Data Archive.

Bebbington, Anthony, Samuel Hickey, and Diana Mitlin, eds. 2008. *Can NGOs Make a Difference?* New York: Zed Books.

Becker, Gary. 1971. *The Economics of Discrimination*. 2nd ed. Chicago: Chicago University Press. https://doi.org/10.7208/chicago/9780226041049.001.0001.

Berggren, Niclas, Henrik Jordahl, and Panu Poutvaara. 2006. "The Looks of a Winner: Beauty, Gender and Electoral Success." IZA Discussion Paper 2311. Bonn: Institute for the Study of Labor.

Bilodeau, Antoine. 2008. "Immigrants' Voice through Protest Politics in Canada and Australia: Assessing the Impact of Pre-Migration Political Repression." *Journal of Ethnic and Migration Studies* 34 (6): 975–1002. https://doi.org/10.1080/13691830802211281.

Bilodeau, Antoine, ed. 2016. *Just Ordinary Citizens? Towards a Comparative Portrait of the Political Immigrant*. Toronto: University of Toronto Press.

Bilodeau, Antoine, Ian McAllister, and Mebs Kanji. 2010. "Adaption to Democracy among Immigrants in Australia." *International Political Science Review* 31 (2): 141–65. https://doi.org/10.1177/0192512110364737.

Bird, Karen. 2005. "The Political Representation of Visible Minorities in Electoral Democracies: A Comparison of France, Denmark, and Canada." *Nationalism & Ethnic Politics* 11 (4): 425–65. https://doi.org/10.1080/13537110500379211.

Bird, Karen. 2016. "What Accounts for the Local Diversity Gap? Supply and Demand of Visible Minority Candidates in Ontario Municipal Politics." In *Just Ordinary Citizens? Towards a Comparative Portrait of the Political*

Immigrant, ed. Antoine Bilodeau, 180–201. Toronto: University of Toronto Press.

Bird, Karen, Thomas Saalfeld, and Andreas M. Wüst, eds. 2011. *The Political Representation of Immigrants and Minorities: Voters, Parties and Parliaments in Liberal Democracies*. New York: Routledge.

Black, Jerome H. 2008. "The 2006 Federal Election and Visible Minority Candidates." *Canadian Parliamentary Review* 31 (3): 30–6.

Black, Jerome H. 2011. "Visible Minority Candidates and MPs: An Update Based on the 2008 Federal Election." *Canadian Parliamentary Review* 34 (1): 30–4.

Black, Jerome H. 2013. "Racial Diversity in the 2011 Federal Election: Visible Minority Candidates and MPs." *Canadian Parliamentary Review* 36 (3): 21–36.

Black, Jerome. 2016. "Who Represents Minorities? Question Period, Minority MPs, and Constituency Influence in the Canadian Parliament." In *Just Ordinary Citizens? Towards a Comparative Portrait of the Political Immigrant*, ed. Antoine Bilodeau, 201–24. Toronto: University of Toronto Press.

Black, Jerome H. 2017. "The 2015 Federal Election: More Visible Minority Candidates and MPs." *Canadian Parliamentary Review* 40 (1): 16–23.

Black, Jerome H., and Lynda Erickson. 2006. "Ethno-Racial Origins of Candidates and Electoral Performance: Evidence from Canada." *Party Politics* 12 (4): 541–61. https://doi.org/10.1177/1354068806064733.

Black, Jerome H., and Bruce M. Hicks. 2006. "Visible Minority Candidates in the 2004 Federal Election." *Canadian Parliamentary Review* 29 (2): 26–31.

Blainey, Geoffrey. 1984. *All For Australia*. Melbourne: Methuen.

Bloemraad, Irene. 2005. "The Limits of de Tocqueville: How Government Facilitates Organizational Capacity in Newcomer Communities." *Journal of Ethnic and Migration Studies* 31 (5): 865–87. https://doi.org/10.1080/13691830500177578.

Bloemraad, Irene. 2006a. "Becoming a Citizen in the United States and Canada: Structured Mobilization and Immigrant Political Incorporation." *Social Forces* 85 (2): 667–95. https://doi.org/10.1353/sof.2007.0002.

Bloemraad, Irene. 2006b. *Becoming a Citizen: Incorporating Immigrants and Refugees in the United States and Canada*. Berkeley: University of California Press.

Bloemraad, Irene. 2013. "Accessing the Corridors of Power: Puzzles and Pathways to Understanding Minority Representation." *West European Politics* 36 (3): 652–70. https://doi.org/10.1080/01402382.2013.773733.

Bloemraad, Irene. 2015. "Theorizing and Analyzing Citizenship in Multicultural Societies." *Sociological Quarterly* 56 (4): 591–606. https://doi.org/10.1111/tsq.12095.

Bloemraad, Irene, and Karen Schönwälder. 2013. "Immigrant and Ethnic Minority Representation in Europe: Conceptual Challenges and Theoretical

Approaches." *West European Politics* 36 (3): 564–79. https://doi.org/10.1080/01402382.2013.773724.

Bonilla-Silva, Eduardo. 2003. *Racism without Racists: Color-Blind Racism and the Persistence of Racial Inequality*. Lanham, MD: Rowman and Littlefield.

Booth, Alison, Andrew Leigh, and Elena Varganova. 2012. "Does Ethnic Discrimination Vary Across Minority Groups? Evidence from a Field Experiment." *Oxford Bulletin of Economics and Statistics* 74 (4): 547–73. https://doi.org/10.1111/j.1468-0084.2011.00664.x.

Borchert, Jens. 2003. "Professional Politicians: Towards a Comparative Perspective." In *The Political Class in Advanced Democracies*, ed. Jens Borchert and Jürgen Zeiss, 1–25. New York: Oxford University Press. https://doi.org/10.1093/0199260362.003.0001.

Borchert, Jens, and Gary Copeland. 2003. "United States: A Political Class of Entrepreneurs." In *The Political Class in Advanced Democracies*, ed. Jens Borchert and Jürgen Zeiss, 393–415. New York: Oxford University Press. https://doi.org/10.1093/0199260362.003.0021.

Borjas, George. 1994. "The Economics of Integration." *Journal of Economic Literature* 32 (4): 1667–717.

Boucher, Anna. 2014. "Obstacles and Challenges to Migrant Organising in Global Economic Immigration Debates." Australian Political Science Association Conference, 28 September, Sydney. https://doi.org/10.2139/ssrn.2461091.

Boyd, Thomas, and Stephen Markman. 1983. "The 1982 Amendments to the Voting Rights Act: A Legislative History." *Washington and Lee Law Review* 40 (4): 1347–428.

Bratton, Kathleen. 2006. "The Behavior and Success of Latino Legislators: Evidence from the States." *Social Science Quarterly* 87 (5): 1136–57. https://doi.org/10.1111/j.1540-6237.2006.00420.x.

Brett, Judith. 2003. *Australian Liberals and the Moral Middle Class*. Melbourne: Cambridge University Press. https://doi.org/10.1017/CBO9780511481642.

Brett, Judith. 2005. "Relaxed and Comfortable: The Liberal Party's Australia." *Quarterly Essay* 19: 1–102.

Bryden, Joan. 2015. "Liberals' Senate advisory board to fill empty seats." *Huffington Post*, 12 March. Available online at http://www.huffingtonpost.ca/2015/12/03/liberals-senate-reform-advisory-board_n_8708152.html.

Budge, Ian, and Dennis Farlie. 1983. *Explaining and Predicting Elections: Issue Effects and Party Strategies in Twenty-Three Democracies*. London: Allen & Unwin.

Bueker, Catherine Simpson. 2005. "Political Incorporation among Immigrants from Ten Areas of Origin: The Persistence of Source Country Effects." *International Migration Review* 39 (1): 103–40. https://doi.org/10.1111/j.1747-7379.2005.tb00257.x.

Calliste, Agnes. 1993–94. "Race, Gender and Canadian Immigration Policy: Blacks from the Caribbean, 1900–1932." *Journal of Canadian Studies* 28 (4): 131–48. https://doi.org/10.3138/jcs.28.4.131.

Campbell, Angus, Philip Converse, Warren Miller, and Donald Stokes. 1960. *The American Voter*. New York: Wiley.

Campbell, Rosie, and Philip Cowley. 2014. "What Voters Want: Reactions to Candidate Characteristics in a Survey Experiment." *Political Studies* 62 (4): 745–65. https://doi.org/10.1111/1467-9248.12048.

Canadian Race Relations Foundation. 2014. Information Handout on Religion, Racism, Intergroup Relations and Integration Results. Toronto. April.

CEFA (Constitutional Education Fund Australia). 2017. "What Next? A Change of Government." Ultimo, NSW: Constitutional Education Fund Australia. Available online at http://www.cefa.org.au/ccf/what-next-changegovernment.

Chan, Gabrielle. 2014a. "Dio Wang, the diplomatic senator left to clean up PUP's mess." *Guardian*, 22 August. Available online at https://www.theguardian.com/world/2014/aug/22/dio-wang-the-diplomatic-senator-left-to-clean-up-pups-mess.

Chan, Gabrielle. 2014b. "Race law debate touched emotional chord – in parliament and out." *Guardian*, 28 March. Available online at https://www.theguardian.com/world/2014/mar/28/race-law-debate-touches-emotional-chord-in-parliament-and-out.

Chandra, Kanchan. 2011. "What Is an Ethnic Party?" *Party Politics* 17 (2): 151–69. https://doi.org/10.1177/1354068810391153.

Chang, Kornel. 2008. "Enforcing Transnational White Solidarity: Asian Migration and the Formation of the U.S.-Canadian Boundary." *American Quarterly* 60 (3): 671–96. https://doi.org/10.1353/aq.0.0027.

Chang, Kornel. 2009. "Circulating Race and Empire: Transnational Labor Activism and the Politics of Anti-Asian Agitation in the Anglo-American Pacific World, 1880–1910." *Journal of American History* 96 (3): 678–701. https://doi.org/10.1093/jahist/96.3.678.

Chaves, Mark, Laura Stephens, and Joseph Galaskiewicz. 2004. "Does Government Funding Suppress Nonprofits' Political Activity?" *American Sociological Review* 69 (2): 292–316. https://doi.org/10.1177/000312240406900207.

Colic-Peisker, V. 2005. "'At least you're the right colour': Identity and Social Inclusion of Bosnian Refugees in Australia." *Journal of Ethnic and Migration Studies* 31 (4): 615–38. https://doi.org/10.1080/13691830500109720.

Collet, Christian. 2005. "Bloc Voting, Polarization, and the Panethnic Hypothesis: The Case of Little Saigon." *Journal of Politics* 67 (3): 907–33. https://doi.org/10.1111/j.1468-2508.2005.00345.x.

Collet, Christian. 2008. "Minority Candidates, Alternative Media and Multiethnic America: Deracialization or Toggling?" *Perspectives on Politics* 6 (04): 707–28. https://doi.org/10.1017/S1537592708081875.

Creese, G., and E.N. Kambere. 2003. "What Colour Is Your English?" *Canadian Review of Sociology and Anthropology* 40 (5): 565–73. https://doi.org/10.1111/j.1755-618X.2003.tb00005.x.

Creswell, J.W. 2008. "Mixed Methods." In *The Sage Encyclopedia of Qualitative Research Methods*, ed. L.M. Given, 526–9. Los Angeles: Sage.

Crisp, Brian F., Betul Demirkaya, Leslie A. Schwindt-Bayer, and Courtney Millian. 2016. "The Role of Rules in Representation: Group Membership and Electoral Incentives." *British Journal of Political Science* (April): 1–21.

Curtice, John, and W. Phillips Shively. 2009. "Who Represents Us Best? One Member or Many?" In *The Comparative Study of Electoral Systems*, ed. Hans-Dieter Klingemann, 171–93. Oxford: Oxford University Press.

Dahlerup, Drude. 2007. "Introduction." In *Women, Quotas, and Politics*, ed. Drude Dahlerup, 3–31. New York: Routledge.

Dahlerup, Drude, and Lenita Freidenvall. 2003. "Quotas as a 'Fast Track' to Equal Political Representation for Women: Why Scandinavia Is No Longer the Model." 19th International Political Science Association World Congress, Durban, South Africa, 29 June–4 July.

Dalton, Russell. 2004. *Democratic Challenges, Democratic Choices*. Oxford: Oxford University. https://doi.org/10.1093/acprof:oso/9780199268436.001.0001.

Daniels, Roger. 2001. "Two Cheers for Immigration." In *Debating American Immigration, 1882–Present*, ed. Toger Daniels and Otis Graham, 5–73. Lanham, MD: Rowman & Littlefield.

Denver, David, and Gordon Hands. 1997. *Modern Constituency Electioneering*. London: Frank Cass.

Denver, David, Gordon Hands, Justin Fisher, and Iain MacAllister. 2002. "The Impact of Constituency Campaigning in the 2001 General Election." *British Elections & Parties Review* 12 (1): 80–94. https://doi.org/10.1080/13689880208413071.

DeSipio, Louis. 2002. *Immigrant Organizing, Civic Outcomes: Civic Engagement, Political Activity, National Attachment, and Identity in Latino Immigrant Communities*. Irvine: University of California, Center for the Study of Democracy.

Dharssi, Alia. 2015. "Canada federal election candidates include more visible minorities in 2015 than in the past four votes." *National Post*, 19 October. Available online at http://nationalpost.com/news/politics/study-says-canadas-three-major-parties-are-fielding-more-visible-minority-candidates, accessed 6 January 2017.

Duleep, Harriet, and Mark Regets. 1999. "Immigrants and Human Capital Investment." *American Economic Review* 89 (2): 186–91. https://doi.org/10.1257/aer.89.2.186.

Dunn, Kevin, and Jim Forrest. 2007. "Contemporary Manifestations of Racism in Australia." In *Racisms in the New World Order: Realities of Cultures, Colours and Identity*, ed. Narayan Gopalkrishnan and Babacan Hurriyet, 95–106. Newcastle, UK: Cambridge Scholars.

Dunn, Kevin, and Jacqueline Nelson. 2011. "Challenging the Public Denial of Racism for a Deeper Multiculturalism." *Journal of Intercultural Studies* 32 (6): 587–602. https://doi.org/10.1080/07256868.2011.618105.

Dunn, Kevin, Danielle Pelleri, and Karin Maeder-Han. 2011. "Attacks on Indian Students: The Commerce of Denial in Australia." *Race & Class* 52 (4): 71–88. https://doi.org/10.1177/0306396810396603.

Duverger, Maurice. 1995. *The Political Role of Women*. Paris: United Nations Educational, Scientific and Cultural Organization.

Eggert, Nina, and Marco Giugni. 2011. "The Impact of Religion on the Political Participation of Migrants." In *Social Capital, Political Participation and Migration in Europe: Making Multicultural Democracy Work?* ed. Laura Morales and Marco Giugni, 219–37. Basingstoke, UK: Palgrave Macmillan. https://doi.org/10.1057/9780230302464_10.

Escobar, Cristina. 2004. "Dual Citizenship and Political Participation: Migrants in the Interplay of United States and Columbian Politics." *Latino Studies* 2 (1): 45–69. https://doi.org/10.1057/palgrave.lst.8600060.

Espiritu, Yen Le. 1992. *Asian American Panethnicity: Bridging Institutions and Identities*. Philadelphia: Temple University Press.

Farrell, David, and Ian McAllister. 2006. "Voter Satisfaction and Electoral Systems: Does Preferential Voting in Candidate-Centred Systems Make a Difference?" *European Journal of Political Research* 45 (5): 723–49. https://doi.org/10.1111/j.1475-6765.2006.00633.x.

Faulks, Keith. 1998. *Citizenship in Modern Britain*. Edinburgh: Edinburgh University Press.

Favell, Adrian. 1998. *Philosophies of Integration: Immigration and the Idea of Citizenship in France and Britain*. Basingstoke, UK: Palgrave Macmillan.

Feagin, Joe R. 2001. *Racist America: Roots, Current Realities, & Future Reparations*. New York: Routledge.

FECCA (Federation of Ethnic Communities Council Australia). 2016. "Will You Develop a National Legislative Framework on Multiculturalism?" Canberra: Federation of Ethnic Communities Council.

Fennema, Meindert, and Jean Tillie. 2001. "Civic Community, Political Participation and Political Trust of Ethnic Groups." *Connections* 24 (1): 26–41.

Fieldhouse, Edward, and David Cutts. 2008a. "Diversity, Density and Turnout: The Effect of Neighbourhood Ethno-religious Composition on Voter Turnout in Britain." *Political Geography* 27 (5): 530–48. https://doi.org/10.1016/j.polgeo.2008.04.002.

Fieldhouse, Edward, and David Cutts. 2008b. "Mobilisation or Marginalisation? Neighbourhood Effects on Muslim Electoral Registration in Britain in 2001." *Political Studies* 56 (2): 333–54. https://doi.org/10.1111/j.1467-9248.2007.00690.x.

FitzGerald, David Scott, and David Cook-Martin. 2014. *Culling the Masses: The Democratic Origins of Racist Immigration Policy in the Americas*. Cambridge, MA: Harvard University Press. https://doi.org/10.4159/harvard.9780674369665.

Flap, Hendrik, and Beate Völker. 2004. *Creation and Returns of Social Capital*. London: Routledge.

Forrest, James, and Kevin Dunn. 2007. "Constructing Racism in Sydney, Australia's Largest EthniCity." *Urban Studies* 44 (4): 699–721. https://doi.org/10.1080/00420980601185676.

Fournier, Patrick, Fred Cutler, Stuart Soroka, and Dietlind Stolle. 2011. Canadian Election Study. Vancouver: University of British Columbia.

Frank, Kristyn. 2013. "Immigrant Employment Success in Canada: Examining the Rate of Obtaining a Job Match." *International Migration Review* 47 (1): 76–105. https://doi.org/10.1111/imre.12014.

Franzen, Axel, and Dominik Hangartner. 2006. "'Social Networks and Labor Market Outcomes: The Non-monetary Benefits of Social Capital." *European Sociological Review* 22 (4): 353–68. https://doi.org/10.1093/esr/jcl001.

Friedberg, Rachel. 2000. "You Can't Take It with You? Immigrant Assimilation and the Portability of Human Capital." *Journal of Labor Economics* 18 (2): 221–51. https://doi.org/10.1086/209957.

Galligan, Brian, and Winsome Roberts. 2004. *Australian Citizenship: See You in Australia*. Melbourne: Melbourne University Press.

Gatens, Moira. 2004. "Can Women's Rights Accommodate Women's Rights? Towards an Embodied Account of Social Norms, Social Meaning, and Cultural Change." *Contemporary Political Theory* 3 (3): 275–99. https://doi.org/10.1057/palgrave.cpt.9300178.

Gatens, Moira. 2012. "Collecting Imaginaries in Australian Multiculturalism: Women's Rights, Group Rights, and Aboriginal Customary Law." In *Political Theory and Australian Multiculturalism*, ed. Geoffrey Brahm Levey, 149–51. New York: Berghahn Books.

Gauja, Anika. 2013. *The Politics of Party Policy: From Members to Legislators*. Melbourne: Palgrave Macmillan. https://doi.org/10.1057/9781137318428.

Gimpel, James, and Wendy K. Tam Cho. 2004. "The Persistence of White Ethnicity in New England Politics." *Political Geography* 23 (8): 987–1008. https://doi.org/10.1016/j.polgeo.2004.05.008.

González-Ferrer, Amparo, and Laura Morales. 2013. "Do Citizenship Regimes Shape Political Incorporation? Evidence from Four European Cities." *European Political Science* 12 (4): 455–66. https://doi.org/10.1057/eps.2013.15.

Government of Canada. 2015. *Employment Equity Act: Annual Report 2015*. Ottawa: Employment and Social Development Canada.

Green, Antony. 2017. "The Senate." In *Double Disillusion: The 2016 Australian Federal Election*, ed. Anika Gauja, Peter Chen, Jennifer Curtin, and Juliet Pietsch, 185–211. Canberra: ANU Press.

Greene, Jennifer. 2007. *Mixed Methods in Social Inquiry*. San Francisco: Jossey-Bass.

Grönberg, Kirsten. 1993. *Understanding Nonprofit Funding: Managing Revenues in Social Services and Community Development Organizations*. San Francisco: Jossey-Bass.

Gutmann, Amy. 1993. "The Challenge of Multiculturalism in Political Ethics." *Philosophy & Public Affairs* 22 (3): 171–206.

Gutmann, Amy. 2003. *Identity in Democracy*. Princeton, NJ: Princeton University Press.

Hage, Ghassan. 1998. *White Nation: Fantasies of White Supremacy in Multicultural Australia*. Annandale, NSW: Pluto Press.

Hawthorne, Lesleyanne. 2007. "Foreign Credentials Recognition and Assessment: An Introduction." *Canadian Issues* (Spring): 3–13.

Heath, Anthony. 2007. "Crossnational Patterns and Processes of Ethnic Disadvantage." In *Unequal Chances: Ethnic Minorities in Western Labour Markets*, ed. Anthony Heath and Sin Yi Cheung, 639–95. Oxford: Oxford University Press. https://doi.org/10.5871/bacad/9780197263860.003.0015.

Heath, Anthony, and Sin Yi Cheung, eds. 2007. *Unequal Chances: Ethnic Minorities in Western Labour Markets*. Oxford: Oxford University Press. https://doi.org/10.5871/bacad/9780197263860.001.0001.

Heath, Anthony F., Stephen D. Fisher, Gemma Rosenblatt, David Sanders, and Maria Sobolewska. 2013. *The Political Integration of Ethnic Minorities in Britain*. Oxford: Oxford University Press. https://doi.org/10.1093/acprof:oso/9780199656639.001.0001.

Helbling, Marc, Tim Reeskens, Cameron Stark, Dietlind Stolle, and Matthew Wright. 2016. "Enabling Immigrant Participation: Do Integration Regimes Make a Difference?" In *Just Ordinary Citizens? Towards a Comparative Portrait of the Political Immigrant*, ed. Antoine Bilodeau, 130–49. Toronto: University of Toronto Press.

Hibbing, John, and Elizabeth Theiss-Morse. 2002. *Stealth Democracy: Americans' Beliefs about How Government Should Work*. Cambridge: Cambridge University Press. https://doi.org/10.1017/CBO9780511613722.

Hill, J.H. 2008. *The Everyday Language of White Racism*. Malden, MA: Wiley-Blackwell. https://doi.org/10.1002/9781444304732.

Hochschild, Jennifer L., and John H. Mollenkopf, eds. 2009. *Bringing Outsiders In: Transatlantic Perspectives on Immigrant Political Incorporation*. Ithaca, NY: Cornell University Press.

Horowitz, Donald. 1985. *Ethnic Groups in Conflict*. Berkeley: University of California Press.

Htun, Mala. 2004. "Is Gender Like Ethnicity? The Political Representation of Identity Groups." *Perspectives on Politics* 2 (3): 439–58. https://doi.org/10.1017/S1537592704040241.

Hughes, Melanie. 2011. "Intersectionality, Quotas, and Minority Women's Political Representation Worldwide." *American Political Science Review* 105 (3): 604–20. https://doi.org/10.1017/S0003055411000293.

Hutchings, Vincent, and Nicholas Valentino. 2004. "The Centrality of Race in American Politics." *Annual Review of Political Science* 15 (1): 63–77.

Inglehart, Ronald, and Christian Welzel. 2005. *Modernization, Cultural Change, and Democracy: The Human Development Sequence*. Cambridge: Cambridge University Press. https://doi.org/10.1017/CBO9780511790881.

Inglis, Christine, and Suzanne Model. 2007. "Diversity and Mobility in Australia." In *Unequal Chances: Ethnic Minorities in Western Labour Markets*, ed. Anthony Heath and Sin Yi Cheung, 45–101. Oxford: Oxford University Press. https://doi.org/10.5871/bacad/9780197263860.003.0002.

Ireland, Patrick. 2000. "Reaping What They Sow: Institutions and Immigrant Political Participation in Western Europe." In *Challenging Immigration and Ethnic Relations Politics*, ed. Ruud Koopmans and Paul Statham, 189–233. Oxford: Oxford University Press.

Isin, Engin, ed. 2008. *Recasting the Social in Citizenship*. Toronto: University of Toronto Press.

Ivison, Duncan. 2012. "Multiculturalism and Resentment." In *Political Theory and Australian Multiculturalism*, ed. Geoffrey Brahm Levey, 129–49. New York: Berghahn Books.

Jacobs, Dirk, Karen Phalet, and Marc Swyngedouw. 2004. "Associational Membership and Political Involvement among Ethnic Minority Groups in Brussels." *Journal of Ethnic and Migration Studies* 30 (3): 543–59. https://doi.org/10.1080/13691830410001682089.

Jacobs, Larry, and Robert Shapiro. 2000. *Politicians Don't Ponder: Political Manipulation and the Loss of Democratic Responsiveness*. Chicago: University of Chicago Press.

Johnson, Daniel P. 1996. "Anti-Japanese Legislation in Oregon, 1917–1923." *Oregon Historical Quarterly* 97 (2): 176–210.

Johnston, Ron, Kelvyn Jones, Rebecca Sarker, Carol Propper, Simon Burgess, and Anne Bolster. 2004. "Party Support and the Neighbourhood Effect: Spatial Polarisation of the British Electorate, 1991–2001." *Political Geography* 23 (4): 367–402. https://doi.org/10.1016/j.polgeo.2003.12.008.

Jones, Roger, Ian McAllister, David Denemark, and David Gow. 1993. *Australian Election Study*. Canberra: Australian Data Archive.

Jones, Roger, Ian McAllister, and David Gow. 1996. *Australian Election Study*. Canberra: Australian Data Archive.

Jones-Correa, Michael. 1998. *Between Two Nations: The Political Predicament of Latinos in New York City*. Ithaca, NY: Cornell University Press.

Jones-Correa, Michael. 2001. "Institutional and Contextual Factors in Immigrant Naturalization and Voting." *Citizenship Studies* 5 (1): 41–56. https://doi.org/10.1080/13621020020025187.

Jones-Correa, Michael. 2005. "Bringing Outsiders In: Questions of Immigrant Incorporation." In *The Politics of Democratic Inclusion*, ed. Christina Wolbrecht and Rodney Hero, 75–101. Philadelphia: Temple University Press.

Jones-Correa, Michael. 2016. "Does Prior Socialization Define Patterns of Integration? Mexican Immigrants and their Political Participation in the United States." In *Just Ordinary Citizens? Towards a Comparative Portrait of the Political Immigrant*, ed. Antoine Bilodeau, 83–98. Toronto: University of Toronto Press.

Joppke, Christian. 1996. "Multiculturalism and Immigration: A Comparison of the United States, Germany, and Great Britain." *Theory and Society* 25 (4): 449–500. https://doi.org/10.1007/BF00160674.

Juenke, Eric Gonzalez, and Robert R. Preuhs. 2012. "Irreplaceable Legislators? Rethinking Minority Representatives in the New Century." *American Journal of Political Science* 56 (3): 705–15. https://doi.org/10.1111/j.1540-5907.2012.00584.x.

Jupp, James. 1993. "The Ethnic Lobby and Immigration Policy." In *The Ethnic Lobby and Immigration Policy*, ed. James Jupp and Marie Kabala, 204–21. Canberra: Australian Govertnment Publishing Service.

Jupp, James. 1995. "From 'White Australia' to 'Part of Asia': Recent Shifts in Australian Immigration Policy towards the Region." *International Migration Review* 29 (1): 207–8. https://doi.org/10.2307/2547002.

Jupp, James. 1997. "New Politics and Social Movements: The Ethnic Dimension." *Journal of Australian Studies* 21 (54–5): 200–6. https://doi.org/10.1080/14443059709387351.

Jupp, James. 2003. *How Well Does Australian Democracy Serve Immigrant Australians?* Canberra: Democratic Audit of Australia, Australian National University.

Jupp, James. 2007. *From White Australia to Woomera: The Story of Australian Immigration*. 2nd ed. New York: Cambridge University Press. https://doi.org/10.1017/CBO9780511720222.

Jupp, James, and Juliet Pietsch. 2017. "A Different Dimension: Ethnic Politics and the 2016 Federal Election." In *Double Disillusion: The 2016 Australian Federal Election*, ed. Anika Gauja, Peter Chen, Jennifer Curtin, and Juliet Pietsch, 661–79. Canberra: ANU Press.

Kaiser, Cheryl, Benjamin Drury, Kerry Spalding, Sapna Cheryan, and Laurie O'Brien. 2009. "The Ironic Consequences of Obama's Election: Decreased Support for Social Justice." *Journal of Experimental Social Psychology* 45 (3): 556–9. https://doi.org/10.1016/j.jesp.2009.01.006.

Karlsen, Saffron, and James Nazroo. 2002. "Relation between Racial Discrimination, Social Class, and Health among Ethnic Minority Groups." *American Journal of Public Health* 92 (4): 624–31. https://doi.org/10.2105/AJPH.92.4.624.

Kee, Marilyn, and Henry Reynolds. 2008. *Drawing the Global Colour Line: White Men's Countries and the Question of Racial Equality*. Melbourne: Melbourne University Press.

Khalid, Asma. 2016. "The Shifting Allegiances of Asian-American Voters." *All Things Considered*, National Public Radio, 9 October.

Kim, Chon Kyun. 2005. "Asian American Employment in the Federal Civil Service." *Public Administration Quarterly* 28 (4): 430–59.

Kim, Thomas. 2007. *The Racial Logic of Politics: Asian Americans and Party Competition*. Philadelphia: Temple University Press.

King, Amy, and Andrew Leigh. 2009. "Beautiful Politicians." *Kyklos* 62 (4): 579–93. https://doi.org/10.1111/j.1467-6435.2009.00452.x.

King, Ronald F., and Cosmin Gabriel Marian. 2012. "Minority Representation and Reserved Legislative Seats in Romania." *Eastern European Politics and Societies* 26 (3): 561–88. https://doi.org/10.1177/0888325412441493.

Klein, Markus, and Ulrich Rosar. 2005. "Physische Attraktivität und Wahlerfolg: Eine empirische Analyse am Beispiel der Wahlkreiskandidaten bei der Bundestagswah" [Physical attractiveness and electoral success. An empirical investigation on candidates in constituencies at the German federal election 2002] *Politische Vierteljahresschrift* 46 (2): 263–90. https://doi.org/10.1007/s11615-005-0249-2.

Klüver, Heike, and Iñaki Sagarzazu. 2016. "Setting the Agenda or Responding to Voters? Political Parties, Voters and Issue Attention." *West European Politics* 39 (2): 380–98. https://doi.org/10.1080/01402382.2015.1101295.

Koopmans, Ruud, Paul Statham, Marco Giugni, and Florence Passy. 2005. *Contested Citizenship: Immigration and Cultural Diversity in Europe*. Minneapolis: University of Minnesota.

Koopmans, Ruud. 2004. "Migrant Mobilisation and Political Opportunities: Variation among German Cities and a Comparison with the United Kingdom and the Netherlands." *Journal of Ethnic and Migration Studies* 30 (3): 449–70. https://doi.org/10.1080/13691830410001682034.

Koopmans, Ruud, and Paul Statham. 2000. "Migration and Ethnic Relations as Field of Political Contention: An Opportunity Structure Approach." In *Challenging Immigration and Ethnic Relations Politics: Comparative European Perspectives*, ed. Ruud Koopmans and Paul Statham, 13–56. Oxford: Oxford University Press.

Koopmans, Ruud, and Paul Statham. 2003. "How National Citizenship Shapes Transnationalism: A Comparative Analysis of Migrant and Minority Claims-Making in Germany, Great Britain and the Netherlands." In *Toward Assimilation and Citizenship: Immigrants in Liberal Nation-States*, ed. Christian Joppke and Ewa Morawska, 195–238. Basingstoke, UK: Palgrave Macmillan.

Krieger, Nancy. 1999. "Embodying Inequality: A Review of Concepts, Measures, and Methods for Studying Health Consequences of Discrimination." *International Journal of Health Services* 29 (2): 295–352. https://doi.org/10.2190/M11W-VWXE-KQM9-G97Q.

Krogstad, Jens Manuel. 2015. "114th Congress Is Most Diverse Ever." Washington, DC: Pew Research Center.

Krook, Mona. 2009. *Quotas for Women in Politics: Gender and Candidate Selection Reform Worldwide*. Oxford: Oxford University Press. https://doi.org/10.1093/acprof:oso/9780195375671.001.0001.

Kukathas, Chandran. 2002. "The Life of Brian, or, Now for Something Completely Difference-Blind." In *Multiculturalism Re-considered: Culture and Equality and Its Critics*, ed. Paul Kelly, 184–203. Cambridge, UK: Polity Press.

Krook, Mona, and Diana O'Brien. 2010. "The Politics of Group Representation: Quotas for Women and Minorities Worldwide." *Comparative Politics* 42 (3): 253–72. https://doi.org/10.5129/00104151 0X12911363509639.

Kwok, Jen Tsen. 2013. "Australian Chinese Legislative Recruitment, Political Incorporation and Representation in the Global Moment (1973–2012)." PhD. University of Queensland.

Kwok, Jen Tsen, and Juliet Pietsch. 2017. "The Political Incorporation of Asian-Australian Populations since the End of White Australia." *AAPI Nexus Journal* 15 (1–2): 109–36.

Kymlicka, Will. 1989. *Liberalism, Community and Culture*. Oxford: Clarendon Press.

Kymlicka, Will. 1995. *Multicultural Citizenship: A Liberal Theory of Minority Rights*. New York: Oxford University Press.

Kymlicka, Will. 2010. "The Rise and Fall of Multiculturalism? New Debates on Inclusion and Accommodation in Diverse Societies." In *The Multiculturalism Backlash: European Discourses, Policies and Practices*, ed. Stephen Vertovec and Susanne Wessendorf, 97–112. New York: Routledge. https://doi.org/10.1111/j.1468-2451.2010.01750.x.

Kymlicka, Will, and Keith Banting. 2006. "Immigration, Multiculturalism, and the Welfare State." *Ethics & International Affairs* 20 (3): 281–304. https://doi.org/10.1111/j.1747-7093.2006.00027.x.

Lancee, Bram. 2012. *Immigrant Performance in the Labour Market: Bonding and Bridging Social Capital. IMISCOE Research*. Amsterdam: Amsterdam University Press. https://doi.org/10.26530/OAPEN_418150.

Leach, Michael. 2000. "Hansonism, Political Discourse and Australian Identity." In *The Rise and Fall of One Nation*, ed. Michael Leach, Geoffrey Stokes, and Ian Ward, 42–57. St Lucia: University of Queensland Press.

Leonard, Rosemary, and Jenny Onyx. 2003. "Networking through Loose and Strong Ties: An Australian Qualitative Study." *Voluntas* 14 (2): 189–203. https://doi.org/10.1023/A:1023900111271.

Levey, Geoffrey Brahm, and Tariq Modood, eds. 2009. *Secularism, Religion and Multicultural Citizenship*. Cambridge: Cambridge University Press.

Levitt, Justin. 2018. "Where Are the Lines Drawn?" *All about Redistricting*. Available online at http://redistricting.lls.edu/where.php.

Li, Peter. 1992. "The Economics of Brain Drain: The Recruitment of Skilled Labour to Canada, 1954–1986." In *Deconstructing a Nation: Immigration, Multiculturalism and Racism in '90s Canada*, ed. Vic Satzewich, 154–62. Halifax, NS: Fernwood Press.

Lien Pei-te. 1997. *The Political Participation of Asian Americans: Voting Behavior in Southern California*. New York: Garland.

Lien Pei-te. 2001. *The Making of Asian America through Political Participation*. Philadelphia: Temple University Press.

Lien Pei-te. 2004. "Asian Americans and Voting Participation: Comparing Racial and Ethnic Differences in Recent US Elections." *International Migration Review* 38 (2): 493–517. https://doi.org/10.1111/j.1747-7379.2004.tb00207.x.

Lien Pei-te, Margaret Conway, and Janelle Wong. 2004. *The Politics of Asian Americans: Diversity and Community*. New York: Routledge.

Lien Pei-te, and Jeanette Yih Harvie. 2012. "The Political Incorporation of Taiwanese Americans and Irish Americans Compared." *Taiwan in Comparative Perspective* 4: 128–53.

Lindbeck, Assar, and Dennis Snower. 1988. *The Insider-Outsider Theory of Employment and Unemployment*. Cambridge, MA: MIT Press.

Linz, Juan, and Alfred Stepan. 1996. *Problems of Democratic Transition and Consolidation: Southern Europe, South America, and Post-Communist Europe*. Baltimore: Johns Hopkins University Press.

Lopez, Mark. 2000. *The Origins of Multiculturalism in Australian Politics*. Melbourne: Melbourne University Press.

Manning, Jane. 2014. "Membership of the [113th] Congress: A Profile." Washington, DC: Congressional Research Service.

Mansbridge, Jane. 1999. "Should Blacks Represent Blacks and Women Represent Women? A Contingent 'Yes.'" *Journal of Politics* 61 (3): 628–57. https://doi.org/10.2307/2647821.

Mansbridge, Jane. 2011. "Clarifying the Concept of Representation." *American Political Science Review* 105 (3): 621–30. https://doi.org/10.1017/S0003055411000189.

Markus, Andrew. 2013. *Mapping Social Cohesion: The Scanlon Foundation Surveys National Report*. Melbourne: Monash University.

Marsh, Michael. 2000. "Candidate Centred but Party Wrapped: Campaigning in Ireland under STV." In *Elections in Australia, Ireland and Malta under the Single Transferrable Vote: Reflections on an Embedded Institution*, ed. Shaun Bowler and Bernie Grofman, 114–30. Ann Arbor: University of Michigan Press.

Marshallsea, Trevor. 2017. "How a dual citizenship crisis befell an immigrant nation." *BBC News*, 14 August. Available online at http://www.bbc.com/news/world-australia-40773930.

Martin, Jean. 1978. *The Migrant Presence: Australian Responses 1947–1977*. Boston: George Allen & Unwin.

Marwah, Inder, Triadafilos Triadafilopoulos, and Stephen White. 2013. "Immigration, Citizenship and Canada's New Conservative Party." In *Conservatism in Canada*, ed. David Rayside and James Farney, 95–119. Toronto: University of Toronto Press.

Matland, Richard, and Donley Studlar. 1996. "The Contagion of Women Candidates in Single-Member District and Proportional Representation Electoral Systems: Canada and Norway." *Journal of Politics* 58 (3): 707–33. https://doi.org/10.2307/2960439.

Maxey, Spencer. 2003. "Pragmatic Threads in Mixed Methods Research in the Social Sciences: The Search for Multiple Modes of Inquiry and the End of the Philosophy of Formalism." In *Handbook of Mixed Methods in Social & Behavioral Science*, ed. Abbas Tashakkori and Charles Teddlie, 51–90. Thousand Oaks, CA: Sage.

Maxwell, Rahsaan. 2013. "The Integration Trade-Offs of Political Representation." *European Political Science* 12 (4): 467–78. https://doi.org/10.1057/eps.2013.16.

McAllister, Ian. 2003. "Australia: Party Politicians as a Political Class." In *The Political Class in Advanced Democracies*, ed. Jens Borchert and Jörgen Zeiss, 26–44. Oxford: Oxford University Press. https://doi.org/10.1093/0199260362.003.0002.

McAllister, Ian. 2011. *The Australian Voter: 50 Years of Change*. Sydney: UNSW Press.

McAllister, Ian, Clive Bean, Rachel Gibson, Ian McAllister, and Juliet Pietsch. 2010. *Australian Election Study*. Canberra: Australian Data Archive.

McAllister, Ian, Roger Jones, and David Gow. 1990. *Australian Election Study*. Canberra: Australian Data Archive.

McAllister, Ian, and Toni Makkai. 1992. "Resource and Social Learning Theories of Political Participation: Ethnic Patterns in Australia." *Canadian Journal of Political Science* 25 (2): 269–93. https://doi.org/10.1017/S000842390000398X.

McAllister, Ian, and John Ravenhill. 1998. "Australian Attitudes towards Closer Engagement with Asia." *Pacific Review* 11 (1): 119–41. https://doi.org/10.1080/09512749808719247.

McCrone, David, and Frank Bechhofer. 2008. "National Identity and Social Inclusion." *Ethnic and Racial Studies* 31 (7): 1245–66. https://doi.org/10.1080/01419870701704677.

McKenzie, Robert. 1928. *Oriental Exclusion: The Effect of American Immigration Laws, Regulations, and Judicial Decisions upon the Chinese and Japanese on the American Pacific Coast*. Chicago: University of Chicago Press.

Minta, Michael D. 2009. "Legislative Oversight and the Substantive Representation of Black and Latino Interests in Congress." *Legislative Studies Quarterly* 34 (2): 193–218. https://doi.org/10.3162/036298009788314336.

Mitchell, Paul. 2000. "Voters and Their Representatives: Electoral Institutions and Delegation in Parliamentary Democracies." *European Journal of Political Research* 37 (3): 335–51. https://doi.org/10.1111/1475-6765.00516.

Morales, Laura. 2009. *Joining Political Organisations: Institutions, Mobilisation and Participation in Western Democracies*. Colchester, UK: ECPR Press.

Morales, Laura, and Marco Giugni, eds. 2011. *Social Capital, Political Participation and Migration in Europe*. Basingstoke, UK: Palgrave Macmillan. https://doi.org/10.1057/9780230302464.

Morales, Laura, and Miruna Morariu. 2011. "Is 'Home' a 'Distraction'? The Role of Migrants' Transnational Practices in Their Political Integration into Receiving-Country Politics." In *Social Capital, Political Participation and Migration in Europe: Making Multicultural Democracy Work?* ed. Laura Morales and Marco Giugni, 140–71. Basingstoke, UK: Palgrave Macmillan. https://doi.org/10.1057/9780230302464_7.

Morales, Laura, and Katia Pilati. 2011. "The Role of Social Capital in Migrants' Engagement in Local Politics in European Cities." In *Social Capital, Political Participation and Migration in Europe: Making Multicultural Democracy Work?* ed. Laura Morales and Marco Giugni, 87–114. Basingstoke, UK: Palgrave Macmillan. https://doi.org/10.1057/9780230302464_5.

Morawska, Ewa. 2003. "Immigrant Transnationalism and Assimilation: A Variety of Combinations and the Analytic Strategy It Suggests." In *Toward Assimilation and Citizenship: Immigrants in Liberal States*, ed. Christian Joppke and Ewa Morawska, 133–76. Basingstoke, UK: Palgrave Macmillan.

Moser, Robert. 2008. "Electoral Systems and the Representation of Ethnic Minorities." *Comparative Politics* 40 (3): 273–92. https://doi.org/10.5129/001041508X12911362382995.

Müller, Wolfgang C. 2000. "Political Parties in Parliamentary Democracies: Making Delegation and Accountability Work." *European Journal of Political Research* 37 (3): 309–33. https://doi.org/10.1111/1475-6765.00515.

Mutz, Diana. 2002. "The Consequences of Cross-Cutting Networks for Political Participation." *American Journal of Political Science* 46 (4): 838–55. https://doi.org/10.2307/3088437.

Myrberg, Gunnar. 2011. "Political Integration through Associational Affiliation." *Journal of Ethnic and Migration Studies* 37 (1): 99–115. https://doi.org/10.1080/1369183X.2011.521366.

Nergiz, Devrimsel Deniz. 2013. *I Long for Normality. A Study on German Parliamentarians with Migration Backgrounds*. Wiesbaden: Springer.

Newkirk, Vann. 2017. "The Supreme Court Finds North Carolina's Racial Gerrymandering Unconstitutional." *Atlantic*, 22 May 2017. Available online at https://www.theatlantic.com/politics/archive/2017/05/north-carolina-gerrymandering/527592/.

Norris, Pippa. 2011. *Democratic Deficit*. Cambridge: Cambridge University Press. https://doi.org/10.1017/CBO9780511973383.

Norris, Pippa, and Joni Lovenduski. 1995. *Political Recruitment: Gender, Race and Class in the British Parliament*. Cambridge: Cambridge University Press.

O'Malley, Nick, Philip Wen, and Michael Koziol. 2016. "Donations, Dastyari and Chinese soft power." *Sydney Morning Herald*, 10 September. Available online at http://www.smh.com.au/federal-politics/political-news/donations-dastyari-and-chinese-soft-power-20160909-grcfyk.html, accessed 17 December 2016.

Odgers, J.R. 2012. *Australian Senate Practice*. 13th ed. Canberra: Department of the Senate.

Østergaard-Nielsen, Eva. 2003. "The Politics of Migrants' Transnational Political Practices." *International Migration Review* 37 (3): 760–86. https://doi.org/10.1111/j.1747-7379.2003.tb00157.x.

Ozdowski, Sev. 2015. *Legislating Multiculturalism – A Case for a National Multicultural Act?* Canberra: Federation of Ethnic Communities Council Australia.

Pande, Rohini. 2003. "Can Mandated Political Representation Increase Policy Influence for Disadvantaged Minorities? Theory and Evidence from India." *American Economic Review* 93 (4): 1132–51. https://doi.org/10.1257/000282803769206232.

Pantoja, Adrian D., and Gary M. Segura. 2003. "Does Ethnicity Matter? Descriptive Representation in Legislatures and Political Alienation among Latinos." *Social Science Quarterly* 84 (2): 441–60. https://doi.org/10.1111/1540-6237.8402014.

Parliament of Australia. 2012. *House of Representatives Procedure*. 6th ed. Canberra: Department of House of Representatives.

Parliament of Australia. 2013a. *The Australian Community: The Australian Multicultural Council's Report on Multiculturalism and Social Cohesion in Australian Neighbourhoods*. Canberra: Australian Multicultural Council.

Parliament of Australia. 2013b. Parliament. Joint Standing Committee on Migration. *Inquiry into Migration and Multiculturalism in Australia*. Canberra.

Payton, Laura. 2012. "Ethnic riding targeting key to Conservatives' 2011 victory." *CBC News*, 23 October. Available online at http://www.cbc.ca/news/politics/ethnic-riding-targeting-key-to-conservatives-2011-victory-1.1142511, accessed 22 January 2015.

Peterson, Bill, Lauren Duncan, and Joyce Pang. 2002. "Authoritarianism and Political Impoverishment: Deficits in Knowledge and Civic Disinterest." *Political Psychology* 23 (1): 97–112. https://doi.org/10.1111/0162-895X.00272.

Petrocik, John, William Benoit, and Glenn Hansen. 2003. "Issue Ownership and Presidential Campaigning, 1952–2000." *Political Science Quarterly* 118 (4): 599–626. https://doi.org/10.1002/j.1538-165X.2003.tb00407.x.

Pharr, Susan J., Robert D. Putnam, and Russell J. Dalton. 2000. "A Quarter-Century of Declining Confidence." *Journal of Democracy* 11 (2): 5–25. https://doi.org/10.1353/jod.2000.0043.

Phillips, Anne. 1995. *The Politics of Presence*. Oxford: Oxford University Press.

Philpot, Tasha, and Hanes Walton, Jr. 2007. "One of Our Own: Black Female Candidates and the Voters Who Support Them." *American Journal of Political Science* 51 (1): 49–62. https://doi.org/10.1111/j.1540-5907.2007.00236.x.

Pietsch, Juliet. 2013. *National Survey of Asian Australians*. Canberra: Australian Data Archive.

Pietsch, Juliet. 2015. "Authoritarian Durability: Public Opinion towards Democracy in Southeast Asia." *Journal of Elections, Public Opinion, and Parties* 25 (1): 31–46. https://doi.org/10.1080/17457289.2014.933836.

Pietsch, Juliet. 2017. "Trends in Migrant and Ethnic Minority Voting in Australia: Findings from the Australian Election Study." *Ethnic and Racial Studies* 40 (14): 2463–80. https://doi.org/10.1080/01419870.2016.1250937.

Pietsch, Juliet, and Ian McAllister. 2016. "How Strong Is the Bond? First and Second-Generation Immigrants and Confidence in Australia Political Institutions." In *Just Ordinary Citizens? Towards a Comparative Portrait of the Political Immigrant*, ed. Antoine Bilodeau, 111–28. Toronto: University of Toronto Press.

Piller, Ingrid, and Kimie Takahashi. 2011. "Language, Migration and Human Rights." In *The SAGE Handbook of Sociolinguistics*, ed. Ruth Wodak, Barbara Johnstone, and Paul Kerswill, 583–97. London: Sage. https://doi.org/10.4135/9781446200957.n39.

Pitkin, Hannah. 1967. *The Concept of Representation*. Berkeley: University of California Press.

Portes, Alejandro, and Ruben G. Rumbaut. 2001. *Legacies: The Story of the Immigrant Second Generation*. Berkeley: University of California Press.

Portes, Alejandro, and Rubén G. Rumbaut. 2006. *Immigrant America: A Portrait*. Berkeley: University of California Press.

Putnam, Robert. 2000. *Bowling Alone: The Collapse and Revival of American Community*. New York: Simon & Schuster. https://doi.org/10.1145/358916.361990.

Quillian, Lincoln. 2006. "New Approaches to Understanding Racial Prejudice and Discrimination." *Annual Review of Sociology* 32 (1): 299–328. https://doi.org/10.1146/annurev.soc.32.061604.123132.

Ramakrishnan, Karthick. 2016. "How Asian Americans Became Democrats." *American Prospect* 27 (3). Available online at http://prospect.org/article/how-asian-americans-became-democrats-0.

Ramakrishnan, Karthick, and Irene Bloemraad, eds. 2008. *Civic Hopes and Political Realities*. New York: Russell Sage Foundation.

Ramakrishnan, Karthick, and Thomas Espenshade. 2001. "Immigrant Incorporation and Political Participation in the United States." *International Migration Review* 35 (3): 870–909. https://doi.org/10.1111/j.1747-7379.2001.tb00044.x.

Ramakrishnan, Karthick, Taeku Lee, Jane Junn, and Janelle Wong. 2012. *National Asian American Survey*. Ann Arbor, MI: Inter-university Consortium for Political and Social Research.

Rana, Abbas. 2016. "'We live in a globalized world,' House most ethnically diverse in Canadian history, but still has long way to go: research." *Hill Times*, 21 November. Available online at https://www.hilltimes.com/2016/11/21/mps-50-59-age-group-26-mps-four-children-politics-common-field-study-majority-mps-study/88112.

Ratcliff, Shaun. 2017. "Interest Aggregators, Not Office Chasers: Evidence for Party Convergence and Divergence in Australia."

Australian Journal of Political Science 52 (2): 236–56. https://doi.org/10.1080/10361146.2017.1301375.

Refugee Council of Australia. 2012. "History of Australia's Refugee Program." Available online at https://www.refugeecouncil.org.au/getfacts/seekingsafety/refugee-humanitarian-program/history-australias-refugee-program/, accessed 17 December 2016.

Rehfeld, Andrew. 2006. "Towards a General Theory of Political Representation." *Journal of Politics* 68 (1): 1–21. https://doi.org/10.1111/j.1468-2508.2006.00365.x.

Rehfeld, Andrew. 2009. "Representation Rethought: On Trustees, Delegates, and Gyroscopes in the Study of Political Representation and Democracy." *American Political Science Review* 103 (2): 214–30. https://doi.org/10.1017/S0003055409090261.

Rehfeld, Andrew. 2011. "The Concepts of Representation." *American Political Science Review* 105 (3): 631–41. https://doi.org/10.1017/S0003055411000190.

Rex, John. 2000. "Multiculturalism and Political Integration in Europe." In *Challenging Immigration and Ethnic Relations Politics: Comparative European Perspectives*, ed. Ruud Koopmans and Paul Statham, 57–74. Oxford: Oxford University Press.

Reynolds, Andrew. 2005. "Reserved Seats in National Legislatures: A Research Note." *Legislative Studies Quarterly* 30 (2): 301–10. https://doi.org/10.3162/036298005X201563.

Rubenstein, Kim. 2012. "Loyalty and Membership: Globalization and Its Impact on Citizenship, Multiculturalism, and the Australian Community." In *Political Theory and Australian Multiculturalism*, ed. Geoffrey Brahm Levey, 171–88. New York: Berghahn Books.

Russell, Andrew, David Cutts, Edward Fieldhouse, Justin Fisher, and David Denver. 2007. "Constituency Campaigning in 2005: Ever More Centralisation." In *Political Campaining*, ed. Dominic Wring, Jane Green, Roger Mortimore, and Simon Atkinson, 79–92. London: Palgrave Macmillan. https://doi.org/10.1057/9780230286306_9.

Saalfeld, Thomas, and Daniel Bischof. 2013. "Minority-Ethnic MPs and the Substantive Representation of Minority Interests in the House of Commons, 2005–2011." *Parliamentary Affairs* 66 (2): 305–28. https://doi.org/10.1093/pa/gss084.

Saalfeld, Thomas, and Wolfgang C. Müller. 1997. "Roles in Legislative Studies: A Theoretical Introduction." *Journal of Legislative Studies* 3 (1): 1–16. https://doi.org/10.1080/13572339708420496.

Saalfeld, Thomas, Andreas M. Wüst, and Karen Bird. 2011. "Epilogue: Towards a Strategic Model of Minority Participation and Representation." In *The Political Representation of Immigrants and Minorities: Voters, Parties and Parliaments in Liberal Democracies*, ed. Karen Bird, Thomas Saalfeld, and Andreas M. Wüst, 266–75. London: Routledge.

Saggar, Shamit, ed. 1998. *Race and British Electoral Politics*. London: UCL Press. https://doi.org/10.4324/9780203214053.

Saggar, Shamit. 2000. *Race and Representation: Electoral Politics and Ethnic Pluralism in Britain*. Manchester: Manchester University Press.

Saggar, Shamit. 2007. "Race and Political Behaviour." In *The Oxford Handbook of Political Behavior*, ed. Russell J. Dalton and Hans-Dieter Klingemann, 504–18. Oxford: Oxford University Press.

Saggar, Shamit. 2013. "Bending without Breaking the Mould: Race and Political Representation in the United Kingdom." *Patterns of Prejudice* 47 (1): 69–93. https://doi.org/10.1080/0031322X.2012.745991.

Saggar, Shamit. 2016. "British Citizens Like Any Others? Ethnic Minorities and Elections in the United Kingdom." In *Just Ordinary Citizens? Towards a Comparative Portrait of the Political Immigrant*, ed. Antoine Bilodeau, 63–83. Toronto: University of Toronto Press.

Saggar, Shamit, and Andrew Geddes. 2000. "Negative and Positive Racialisation: Re-examining Ethnic Minority Political Representation in the UK." *Journal of Ethnic and Migration Studies* 26 (1): 25–44. https://doi.org/10.1080/136918300115624.

Samson, Frank. 2014. "Segmented Political Assimilation: Perceptions of Racialized Opportunities and Latino Immigrants' Partisan Identification." *Ethnic and Racial Studies* 37 (3): 467–95. https://doi.org/10.1080/01419870.2013.783222.

Scarrow, Susan, and Burcu Gezgor. 2010. "Declining Memberships, Changing Members? European Political Party Members in a New Era." *Party Politics* 16 (6): 823–43. https://doi.org/10.1177/1354068809346078.

Schmidt, Ronald, Yvette M. Alex-Assensoh, Andrew L. Aoki, and Rodney E. Hero. 2013. *Newcomers, Outsiders, and Insiders: Immigrants and American Racial Politics in the Early Twenty-first Century*. Ann Arbor: University of Michigan Press.

Schuller, Tom. 2007. "Reflections on the Use of Social Capital." *Review of Social Economy* 65 (1): 11–28. https://doi.org/10.1080/00346760601132162.

Searing, Donald D. 1994. *Westminster's World: Understanding Political Roles*. Cambridge, MA: Harvard University Press.

Sellers, Robert, and J. Nicole Shelton. 2003. "The Role of Racial Identity in Perceived Racial Discrimination." *Journal of Personality and Social Psychology* 84 (5): 1079–92. https://doi.org/10.1037/0022-3514.84.5.1079.

Senate of Canada. 2010. Standing Committee on Human Rights. *Reflecting the Changing Face of Canada: Employment Equity in the Federal Public Service*. Ottawa. Available online at https://www.pdffiller.com/jsfillerdesk5/?projectId=162290875&expId=3102&expBranch=3#5be590b57e6942db8f613b45afb81e4c.

Shapiro, Ian. 2001. "Enough of Deliberation: Politics Is about Interests and Power." In *Deliberative Politics: Essays on Democracy and Disagreement*, ed. Stephen Macedo, 28–38. Oxford: Oxford University Press.

Smedley, Audrey, and Brian D. Smedley. 2011. *Race in North America: Origin and Evolution of a Worldview*. 4th ed. Boulder, CO: Westview Press.

Sobolewska, Maria. 2013. "Party Strategies and the Descriptive Representation of Ethnic Minorities: The 2010 British General Election." *West European Politics* 36 (3): 615–33. https://doi.org/10.1080/01402382.2013.773729.

Soininen, Maritta. 2011. "Ethnic Inclusion or Exclusion in Representation? Local Candidate Selection in Sweden." In *The Political Representation of Immigrants and Minorities: Voters, Parties and Parliaments in Liberal Democracies*, ed. Karen Bird, Thomas Saalfeld, and Andreas Wüst, 145–63. London: Routledge.

Song, Miri. 2004. "Introduction: Who's at the Bottom? Examining Claims about Racial Hierarchy." *Ethnic and Racial Studies* 27 (6): 859–77. https://doi.org/10.1080/0141987042000268503.

Soutphommasane, Tim. 2014. "Are Asian Australians trapped under a bamboo ceiling?" *Guardian*, 11 July. Available online at https://www.theguardian.com/commentisfree/2014/jul/11/are-asian-australians-trapped-under-a-bamboo-ceiling, accessed 20 September 2016.

Stasiulis, Daiva K., and Yasmeen Abu-Laban. 1991. "The House the Parties Built: (Re)Constructing Ethnic Representation in Canadian Politics." In *Ethno-Cultural Groups and Visible Minorities in Canadian Politics: The Question of Access*, ed. Kathy Megyery, 3–93. Toronto: Dundurn Press.

Statistics Canada. 2006. *Census of Population*. Ottawa, Ontario.

Statistics Canada. 2011. "Immigration and Ethnocultural Diversity in Canada." Cat. no. 99-010-X2011001. Ottawa: Statistics Canada. Available online at http://www12.statcan.gc.ca/nhs-enm/2011/as-sa/99-010-x/99-010-x2011001-eng.pdf.

Statistics Canada. 2011. *National Household Survey*. Ottawa, Ontario.

Stevens, Daniel, Benjamin Bishin, and Robert Barr. 2006. "Authoritarian Attitudes, Democracy, and Policy Preferences among Latin American Elites." *American Journal of Political Science* 50 (3): 606–20. https://doi.org/10.1111/j.1540-5907.2006.00204.x.

Stolle, Dietlind, Marc Hooghe, and Michele Micheletti. 2005. "Politics in the Supermarket: Political Consumerism as a Form of Political Participation."

International Political Science Review 26 (3): 245–69. https://doi.org/10.1177/0192512105053784.

Stratton, Jon, and Ien Ang. 1994. "Multicultural Imagined Communities: Cultural Difference and National Identity in Australia and the USA." *Continuum: The Australian Journal of Media & Culture* 8 (2): 124–58. https://doi.org/10.1080/10304319409365672.

Strøm, Kaare. 1997. "Rules, Reasons, and Routines: Legislative Roles in Parliamentary Democracies." *Journal of Legislative Studies* 3 (1): 155–74. https://doi.org/10.1080/13572339708420504.

Strömbäck, Jesper. 2009. "Selective Professionalisation of Political Campaigning: A Test of the Party-Centred Theory of Professionalised Campaigning in the Context of the 2006 Swedish Election." *Political Studies* 57 (1): 95–116. https://doi.org/10.1111/j.1467-9248.2008.00727.x.

Taylor, Charles. 1994. "Multiculturalism: Examining the Politics of Recognition." In *Multiculturalism*, ed. Amy Gutmann, 25–75. Princeton, NJ: Princeton University Press.

Tillie, Jean. 2004. "Social Capital of Organisations and Their Members: Explaining the Political Integration of Immigrants in Amsterdam." *Journal of Ethnic and Migration Studies* 30 (3): 529–41. https://doi.org/10.1080/13691830410001682070.

Todd, Douglas. 2014. "Most Chinese and South Asians in B.C. report discrimination." *Vancouver Sun*, 16 October. Available online at http://www.vancouversun.com/life/Most+Chinese+South+Asians+report+discrimination/10294503/story.html, accessed 20 September 2016.

Togeby, Lise. 2008. "The Political Representation of Ethnic Minorities: Denmark as a Deviant Case." *Party Politics* 14 (3): 325–43. https://doi.org/10.1177/1354068807088125.

Tolley, Erin. 2016. *Framed: Media and the Coverage of Race in Canadian Politics*. Vancouver: UBC Press.

United Nations Association in Canada. 2008. "Creating a Sense of Belonging: Report on the Survey Results of Canadians' Attitudes on Racism, Discrimination and Multiculturalism Issues in Canada." Ottawa: United Nations Association in Canada.

United States Census Bureau. 2011. *American Community Survey (ACS)*. Washington, DC.

United States Senate. 2016. *The Senate and the United States Constitution*. Washington, DC: Senate Historical Office.

Valtonen, Kathleen. 2001. "Cracking Monopoly: Immigrants and Employment in Finland." *Journal of Ethnic and Migration Studies* 27 (3): 421–38. https://doi.org/10.1080/136918301200266158.

Van Heelsum, Anja, Laure Michon, and Jean Tillie. 2016. "New Voters, Different Votes? A Look at the Political Participation of Immigrants in Amsterdam and Rotterdam." In *Just Ordinary Citizens? Towards a Comparative Portrait of the Political Immigrant*, ed. Antoine Bilodeau, 29–46. Toronto: University of Toronto Press.

Verba, Sidney, and Norman Nie. 1972. *Participation in America: Political Democracy and Social Equality*. New York: Harper & Row.

Verba, Sidney, Kay Lehman Schlozman, and Henry Brady. 1995. *Voice and Equality: Civic Voluntarism in American Politics*. Cambridge, MA: Harvard University Press.

Vertovec, Steven. 2009. *Transnationalism: Key Ideas*. London: Routledge.

Vertovec, Stephen, and Susanne Wessendorf. 2010. "Introduction: Assessing the Backlash against Multiculturalism." In *The Multiculturalism Backlash: European Discourses, Policies and Practices*, ed. Stephen Vertovec and Susanne Wessendorf, 1–32. London: Routledge.

Vickers, Jill, and Annette Isaac. 2012. *The Politics of Race: Canada, the United States, and Australia*. Toronto: University of Toronto Press.

Wahlke, John C., Heins Eulau, William Buchanan, and LeRoy C. Ferguson. 1962. *The Legislative System: Explorations in Legislative Behavior*. New York: Wiley.

Walker, David. 1999. *Anxious Nation: Australia and the Rise of Asia 1850–1939*. St Lucia: University of Queensland Press.

Waters, Mary. 2001. "Growing Up West Indian and American: Gender and Class Differences in the Second Generation." In *Islands in the City: West Indian Migration to New York*, ed. Nancy Foner, 237–56. Berkeley: University of California Press.

Weber, Max. 1965. *Politics as a Vocation*. Philadelphia: Fortress Press.

Weber, Max. 1978. *Economy and Society: An Outline of Interpretive Sociology*. Ed. Guenther Roth and Claus Wittich. Berkeley: University of California Press.

Weeden, Kim. 2002. "Why Do Some Occupations Pay More than Others? Social Closure and Earnings Inequality in the United States." *American Journal of Sociology* 108 (1): 55–101. https://doi.org/10.1086/344121.

Whitaker, Reg. 1991. *Canadian Immigration Policy since Confederation*. Ottawa: Canadian Historical Association.

Wilkins, Clara, and Cheryl Kaiser. 2013. "Racial Progress as Threat to the Status Hierarchy: Implications for Perceptions of Anti-White Bias." *Psychological Science* 25 (2): 439–46. https://doi.org/10.1177/0956797613508412.

Williams, Melissa. 1998. *Voice, Trust and Memory: Marginalized Groups and the Failings of Liberal Representation*. Princeton, NJ: Princeton University Press.

Winnick, Hannah. 2015. "Canadian Elections 2015: The Power of the 'Ethnic Vote.'" Washington, DC: Heinrich Böll Foundation.

Wolbrecht, Christina, and Rodney E. Hero, eds. 2005. *The Politics of Democratic Inclusion*. Philadelphia: Temple University.

Wong, Janelle, Lien Pei-Te, and Margaret Conway. 2005. "Group-Based Resources and Political Participation among Asian Americans." *American Politics Research* 33 (4): 545–76. https://doi.org/10.1177/1532673X04270521.

Wong, Janelle, Karthick Ramakrishnan, Taeku Lee, and Jane Junn. 2011. *Asian American Political Participation*. New York: Russell Sage.

Woolcock, Michael, and Deepa Narayan. 2000. "Social Capital: Implications for Development Theory, Research and Policy." *World Bank Research Observer* 15 (2): 225–49. https://doi.org/10.1093/wbro/15.2.225.

World Values Survey. n.d. *Wave 6 2010–2014 Official Aggregate*, v.20150418. Madrid: Asep/JDS for the World Values Survey Association.

Young, Iris Marion. 1990. *Justice and the Politics of Difference*. Princeton, NJ: Princeton University Press.

Yu, Ouyang. 2002. *The Eastern Slope Chronicle*. Blackheath, NSW: Brandl & Schlesinger.

Zappala, Gianni, and Stephen Castles. 2000. "Citizenship and Immigration in Australia." In *From Migrants to Citizens: Membership in a Changing World*, ed. Alexander Aleinihoff and Douglas Klusmeyer, 32–77. Washington, DC: Carnegie Endowment for International Peace.

Zeng Zhen, and Yu Xie. 2004. "Asian-Americans' Earnings Disadvantage Reexamined: The Role of Place of Education." *American Journal of Sociology* 109 (5): 1075–108. https://doi.org/10.1086/381914.

Zukin, Cliff, Scott Keeter, Molly Andolina, Krista Jenkins, and Michael X. Delli Carpini. 2006. *A New Engagement? Political Participation, Civic Life, and the Changing American Citizen*. Oxford: Oxford University Press. https://doi.org/10.1093/acprof:oso/9780195183177.001.0001.

Index

www.ingramcontent.com/pod-product-compliance
Lightning Source LLC
LaVergne TN
LVHW041113090826
844660LV00061B/864/J

* 9 7 8 1 4 8 7 5 0 4 1 5 1 *